Harm Not
The Earth

Megan McKenna

First published 2007 by
Veritas Publications
7/8 Lower Abbey Street
Dublin 1
Ireland
Email publications@veritas.ie
Website www.veritas.ie

10 9 8 7 6 5 4 3 2 1

ISBN 978 1 84730 024 9

Designed and typeset by Paula Ryan
Printed in the Republic of Ireland by Betaprint, Dublin

Cover image © Megan McKenna, 2007

Contents

Introduction   7

Chapter One   The Story Begins/Genesis 1:1-1:5   14

Chapter Two   Genesis 2–3:24   36

Chapter Three   Noah and the Ark   57

Chapter Four   Amos and Isaiah: The Prophets and the Land   77

Chapter Five   Trees   98

Chapter Six   Jesus' Geography as told by Water   120

Chapter Seven   New Heaven and New Earth   134

Chapter Eight   The Eighth Day – Job and Yahweh God in Conversation   156

The Last Words   They say: This is the Way the World Will End   180

Bibliography   184

In gratitude to the Indigenous Peoples of the World, their wisdom and enduring grace in their struggle to survive and to honour the earth, the skies, the waters and all creation. Especially to Victor Maqque and his family, Maybee, Diana and Megancita of the Quecha Nation, Puno, Peru, South America, who have made me part of their family with such hospitality and love, and for Jim Madden, MM, and Steve Judd, MM, and for Jean Marie Tognotti, OSB, of the Oglala Lakota Nation, Pine Ridge, South Dakota, who calls me sister and friend, and for Steve Sanford, SJ, Sacred Heart Parish, Pine Ridge, and for Joe Camacho, Alapaki Kim and Paul Neves of the Nation of Hawai'i, and for George De Costa, Hilo, Hawaii, good friends and brothers, and for Abigal Passman of the Bergen County Camera, Westwood, New Jersey, for her expertise and generosity of time in supervising the processing of so many of my photographs, including the cover of this book.

Introduction

We are and ever have been a people of covenant. The original covenant was the act of creation and God's sharing this floating ball we call earth with us for all time. But, though bearing the name *Homo sapiens* – meaning wise persons – we humans are not renowned for our faithfulness or for embodying wisdom. And so today, all around us, we witness God's cosmic covenant with us in shreds, and, along with it, the world and its inhabitants. Both human and non-human are stumbling and falling before the catastrophic sins of humanity. Our world and its inhabitants are suffering the lethal effects of our behaviours and choices – sins of injustice, greed, violence, pride, arrogance, envy, sloth, war, murder and rape, revenge, thievery, covetousness, and the invention and use of weapons that have half-lives of millions of years. We are no longer just destroying ourselves and the world we live in, but the world for generations to come. We are unravelling the threads of our covenant with God and with the world, and the strings of creation and existence, faster than the earth and the elements can refashion them and absorb the toxins we produce. Through our neglect of our peoples and our planet, we are experiencing the description of the earth and its peoples found in the book of Isaiah:

> Behold,
> The earth is withered, sear.
> The world languishes, it is sear.
> The most exalted people of the earth languish.
> For the earth was defiled
> Under its inhabitants;
> Because they transgressed teachings,
> Violated laws,
> Broke the ancient covenant.
>   (Isaiah 24:4-5)

This scenario is in stark contrast to the image of how we are asked to live. This image is found in John's gospel, as Jesus shares his last meal and speaks to those he loves before going to the death that awaits him. The image is rich in symbolism. It is the image of life shared and how we are to live with earth, air, water, fire and one another. This image is found in Jesus' words 'I am the true vine, and my Father is the vinegrower'. This is one of Jesus' 'I AM' statements – declaring his identity as God and human, enfleshed, and drawing all of us into that existence, rooted in the earth and yet equally rooted in the Spirit of God:

> I am the true vine, and my Father is the vinegrower. He removes every branch in me that bears no fruit. Every branch that bears fruit he prunes to make it bear more fruit. You have already been cleansed by the word that I have spoken to you. Abide in me as I abide in you. Just as the branch cannot bear fruit by itself unless it abides in the vine, neither can you unless you abide in me. I am the vine, you are the branches. Those who abide in me and I in them bear much fruit, because apart from me you can do nothing. Whoever does not abide in me is thrown away like a branch and withers; such branches are gathered, thrown into the fire, and burned. If you abide in me, and my words abide in you, ask for whatever you wish, and it will be done for you. My Father is glorified by this, that you bear much fruit and become my disciples. As the Father has loved me, so I have loved you; abide in my love. If you keep my commandments, you will abide in my love, just as I have kept my Father's commandments and abide in his love. I have said these things to you so that my joy may be in you, and that your joy may be complete.
>
> (John 15:1-11)

This reading is as densely packed as vines ready for the harvest. The verb 'abide' is used eleven times! It is a very religious and biblical word, and one that is not often used in familiar conversation. It means: to tolerate, endure, act in accordance with, remain faithful to (as in a promise). As an adjective, it connotes: lasting, constant, steadfast, everlasting, unchanging, fast, fixed, firm, immutable. It is indicative of being inside or intimate with another. One always abides 'in' – it isn't something one does alone. Even if we use the word to describe an enduring sense of well-being, such as 'abiding in peace', it has the association of abiding with all else and all others.

We are exhorted and reminded often that 'whatever we do to the least of our brothers and sisters, or whatever we refuse to do that is needed by our brothers and sisters', we do, or refuse to do, to God. It is time to start abiding, realising that whatever we do to the earth, to the air and the waters, the trees and all our resources, and all that God so lovingly created, we do to God. The earth is ours – but ours in covenant with God. Through our covenant with God, we have been entrusted 'to dress and keep' creation; to 'care and cultivate' the garden that is earth; to 'increase, have dominion over' (not dominate), in the image and likeness of God, all that God has called forth into existence and called 'good'.

We need to go back again and again to the creation stories, to learn them by heart and to take them to heart, and start making them come true. This book, *Harm Not the Earth*, is only a beginning, an attempt at new ways of exegesis, study and appropriation of the Word of God that abides in us, exploring what it demands we do in the world of creation, in obedience to the commandments of God from the beginning, and as they develop in the person and life of Jesus, the Word made flesh, abiding among us still. It is time for us to start bearing fruit, not for personal sanctification or salvation, but for the benefit of all the children of the world, beginning with the least of our kin and the most neglected of creation: the earth, seas, trees, air, resources and creatures of the world. If we are to be true followers of Jesus, who loved gardens and mountains and the sea, and prayed that we might all be one in God, then it is time for us to shift our attitudes towards who we think God is, what we think we are on this earth for, and what it means to live and be responsible for creation 'in the image and likeness of God'. We must learn what others have known long before us – the wisdom and power of a compassionate heart.

Where to begin? Begin with the Word!

This book is a beginning. It looks at a few portions of Scripture and seeks to dig into them from a number of very old and some new points of view, filtering them through the insistent demands of today's realities. So, I would ask that you read these chapters and the selected pieces of Scripture with a few things in mind. All the quotations from the earlier testament are from the Jewish translations, and much of the exegesis – the mining of the texts – is done from an ancient process of reading the Torah in levels.

Traditionally, there are four levels. In Hebrew they are: Pashat, Remez, Drosh and Sod. The four letters for these four levels are PRDS, which in Hebrew spells Pardes/Paradise. The Torah is believed and taught to be beyond the Torah, a text beyond the words. The letters fly off the page and into space – just as did the words of God, Blessed be God's Name, in speaking to Moses on Sinai. In the end, the whole world, inside and out, on earth and in the heavens, is Torah. And when all these levels, all these pieces of Torah and text and their meanings, are brought together – then it is Paradise. It is here, in the Scriptures, the Word of God abiding with us, that we will find our way clear to seeing the world and knowing what we must do together to save our world for all those who are to inherit it, along with our faith, after us.

These are the four traditional meanings to keep in mind when you read:

* The first is Pashat, the plain meaning. This is what the text is saying on the surface: the narrative, the facts, the people, the places, the plot. This is where it starts.

- The second is Remez, called the mystical meaning. This is when our heart, our experience of God and what is holy, is brought to bear on the text. It can start with the text, but drift far from it, extending into many other areas, so far that it might seem to contradict the text. An image of what it's like: look at a picture of yourself or someone else as a baby and then consider what they look like today! Same person, but so much has developed, changed, been lost, etc.
- The third is the Drosh, and this is where you begin to 'play', so to speak, with the text itself. All the resources of study are brought to bear on the text and its meanings: definitions, wordplay, etymology, references and allusions to other parts of the text, commentaries, legends, rabbinic teachings, apocryphal material and, more recently, poetry, stories and the biographies and histories of contemporary life.
- The last level is that of Sod, also referred to as a mystical interpretation but this one is more traditional – as found in the Kabbalah and other secret traditions that have new ways of looking at meaning. For those of us who borrow these levels from our elder Jewish brothers and sisters, it includes the writings of patristic fathers and mothers, the Orthodox traditions, the martyrs, and the lives of the poor who are the most in need of the Good News of God.

For Christians, there are more ways of reading the text, and we must get back to reading the text with others in study groups, as a means of furthering our knowledge and aiding our conversion, preparing us for worship and inspiring us to action. Here are some other ways that are used in this book:

- Reading with a spirit of appreciation and sheer delight: learn to observe, see and be brushed by the edge of mystery, questioned and confronted by the Spirit of God in the text and in those who study with you.
- Delving into the levels of meaning: there is always more than one true interpretation of the texts. In Judaism, there are forty-seven different levels of meaning for every phrase, word, space, punctuation mark and place in the text! The best image I have found of meaning in the Scripture is the dessert of baklava. In making this dish, a good Greek cook makes 122 layers of thin filo dough, mixed with chopped nuts, pure lard/butter and honey, with a touch of rosemary water. A scriptural text is like this, with many levels that can reveal and conceal at the same time – until its time is fulfilled. What is it saying for us today in the face of what we have done and are doing to the earth and what God has made?
- Entering dialogue with the text: it is told that God gave the law to Moses by day, but then told stories at night to elucidate and extend the text

almost endlessly into every situation imaginable. You too can adopt this approach. Dialogue with the text, with our times and the times before us, with those from earlier ages who have struggled to interpret it, to live its wisdom, gleaned from study and practice and prayer. Connect it to our place, geography, time, history, problems, issues, and always honour the interpretation of the poor first and foremost – what makes it good news, in reality, for them and for the earth?

- Becoming the text: stand on the text as on solid ground, praying and living it, believing in it and staking your life, money, time, resources and passion on it. Do not do this alone, but with others in community. We worship and pray: 'we believe; have mercy on us; peace be with you; our Father, etc.' This is what makes it religion: public communal demands made on one another to be faithful in covenant; to live out the values; to give witness by our work, by our choices; to seek alternatives to what is wrong in the world; and to strive to undo and repair harm already done.

- Making midrash with the text: write under, around, over and through it. The Spirit is in the text, in the community that reads it for conversion and transformation. The Spirit is in the world now. (The world is the sacrament of the Spirit of God, and everything in it reveals, tells, teaches, speaks, whispers and shouts. Take heed.)

- Beginning to honour the earth through making the Word a reality in art, music, poetry, dance, religious ritual and conversation: make sure all of this is translated into action, work for justice, transformation, conversion and politics, economics, science. It is time to re-member: to put back together the way it was created to be and to celebrate the healing, the making whole of creation again, bonding together usefulness and beauty (the architect Soleri), while keeping in mind all those who come after us. Become creators. We are the makers, the imitators and co-creators, the artisans and preservationists, the architects and cultivators, the caretakers and keepers. We must imitate God in creative boldness, in rest and life-giving, in risk-taking, proliferation and imagination. And we begin with the admonition not to harm, EVER, NEVER, or destroy or demean, to sever connections or cause extinction, to impair or manipulate for greed, avarice, violence, to disdain, or refuse to share. There is only one universe.

All interpretations of Scripture must be in the service of all life. Our interpretations must not primarily serve what has been or is the dominant view or what is in vogue for so long that only it is acceptable practice. There is no one single revered way to express the truth. No religious interpretation is truthful if it serves to continue the abuse, or to excuse human beings from their responsibilities. Scripture must be proclaimed in opposition to existing interpretations that serve those who dominate economically, politically or religiously. Like the universe and God's creation, truth expands always to reveal a larger reality not known, seen or understood before. Truth extends to awe and reverence at the wisdom of God.

'You cannot bear it now' are words Jesus mouthed to his friends before he died, but he has left his Spirit with us for the truth, to prove the world wrong about sin/violence, evil and injustice. Truth has its time for further revelation and demands. God always has more to tell us. Now is the time, and we must listen and obey, or there will be all too few days to come, and life will be so mangled and harmed as to be unrecognisable as the original, and certainly will be hard pressed to be described as 'good'.

Hope is built into the fabric of creation. And so I end this introduction and begin the book with a story of hope: hope in faithfulness; hope in miracles; hope in the continued intervention of God through the marvellous process of creation. It is a child's story from India, called 'The Tree and the Parrot':

Once upon a time there was a marvellous tree. It was taller than any other, its branches thick with leaves and wild with flowers, and it bore fruit in abundance, to the delight of the birds who nested within it. Its low-lying branches provided a thick cover of shade in the heat and warmth, and so it was the home and resting place of many small animals too. There was a parrot that had been born in the tree and had lived there all its life, happy and content.

Now some hunters spotted the tree and knew it would be a good place to hunt small game, so they came often with their poison-tipped arrows. They frequently missed their targets because the tree would warn the birds and creatures that they were in danger. Instead, the arrows would fly and embed themselves in the bark of the tree. But the tree could only take so much poison and, eventually, it weakened, grew sickly and slowly began to die. It took a long while for others to notice it, but the leaves fell and didn't come back as thick, the bark peeled off, the wood dried out and cracked, and more and more branches dropped to the ground. And as the tree began to die, the birds and the small animals left. Only the parrot remained. The other birds and animals cautioned the parrot and told it to leave or it too would sicken and die along with the tree, but the parrot refused to go. Over and over again, it kept saying, 'The tree is my friend. I was born here and the tree fed me and protected me and nurtured me and gave me so much. I can't leave now that the tree is alone and sick. I have to stay.'

So the parrot stayed. The tree was grateful, but it was so weak that it could barely talk anymore; there were no leaves or fruit on the remaining branches and the bark was scaley and smelled terrible. The parrot knew that the tree would soon be lifeless and soulless.

Now God, the Maker and Keeper of all things, was looking out over the earth one day and noticed a great blinding light coming from the vicinity of where the tree and the parrot dwelled. It was so strong and sure, so blindingly bright, like a star that had fallen to earth but had not burned out. God immediately sent some angels to go and see what was causing this unusual light. The angels returned baffled and said, 'All we found was a tree in terrible condition and a miserable-looking parrot sitting on one of its upper branches. The parrot explained that the tree was dying but that it had always been a good and faithful friend and so the parrot would be true and loving too and stay with it to the end.'

God, touched by the faithfulness of the parrot, bent down closer to see this thing of beauty, friendship and steadfast presence, even in the face of death. Seeing the terrible state of the tree and the sorrow of the parrot, God began to weep uncontrollably. The tears fell like rain and the rain fell on the tree and the parrot, drenching and soaking them through and through. Then something marvellous began to happen. The tree straightened up. The bark became supple and nutrients poured through the limbs. Leaves sprouted along with flowers the likes of which the parrot had never seen before, and berries and fruit. The tree began to smell luscious and sweet, fragrant and healthy. And the parrot's feathers turned brighter and more colourful. The parrot could feel life surging and coursing through every part of the tree and through its own flesh and feathers. Both the tree and the parrot began to rejoice, and they were soon joined by the other birds and animals. The surrounding trees and grasses and even the wind bent in their direction, wondering what in the world was happening. They had never seen or heard tell of anything like this before. Then God stopped weeping and the angels hovered in awe before God, whose tears formed a rainbow arched between heaven and earth. In answer to the angels' silent wonderings, God turned and shone like the light of the tree and the parrot, saying, 'It has been so long since anything loved like this that it became Light and brought life back to a piece of dying earth. If only there were more of that kind of friendship, that kind of love in the world.'

If only! If only there were more of that kind of friendship, that kind of love, that kind of rampant, wild, unbounded, pure, grateful love in the world, then the miracle of light and life that has been in all of creation since its beginnings, and since our arrival, would shine anew, and in no time at all our God would be saying with delight once again, 'Ah, it is good! It is very good! It is very, very good!' May it be so. May we bring such delight to our God once more.

Chapter One

The Story Begins/Genesis 1:1-1:5

The first chapters of the Book of Genesis tell our primeval story, of our roots, our beginnings. It is a story that falls into the category of 'How did things come to be?' or 'Why and how were we created?' Every culture, religion and people tell the same story in uncountable ways. This is the story of the peoples of the Book: Jews, Christians and Muslims together. It is how we interpret the story that determines its meaning for us and demands behaviour and ethics, binding us together as a people of God. In this chapter, we will concentrate on Jewish understandings, since it is their heritage first and they have been interpreting it for thousands of generations before us. In later chapters, we will look at it in light of the Incarnation and our Christian story in John's Gospel that begins the same way: 'In the beginning was the Word...' And with the addition of this story of the Word made flesh, and the further revelation of the Trinity and the mysteries of our religion, the story takes some decidedly different turns – some of them unbelievable and unimagined at the beginning, like the story of Incarnation and Resurrection and Eucharist, and some of them devastating and destructive, as Christianity interpreted older and newer stories to serve empires and dominant cultures rather than serve and extend the meaning of 'the good news of God, to the poor.

This Beginnings story is not about the past. It is the ongoing story of what was started billions of years ago and is still in the process of happening now. The telling is unlike many stories we are used to – as we wait for the 'happily ever after' part to come. It is more like a blueprint, a scientist's diagram, the sketch of an artist or sculptor, or a fingerprint of the Maker. In this story, more than many others, the importance is in the details, the verbs, and the patterns and pieces that divert from the carefully conceived structure. Genesis 1 is a late story in the tradition and theological history of Israel. The story that follows in chapter 2 of Genesis is the earlier one, and it sounds, for many of us, like a 'better' story because it uses more familiar terms and concepts. This first chapter and first story is usually referred to as the Priestly Creation narrative (or the P account). It was designed and written for the people of God long after the experiences recounted in the first five books of the Bible – the Torah – after David and the destruction of the Temple and Jerusalem, and the people sent into exile as slaves. The second story (the J account) is more primitive, a classic story of how we humans found ourselves on this earth/planet and what we are here for, though both stories are surprisingly theological and layered with sophisticated meanings. Many scholars believe that the two stories should be read in tandem, that together they form another story that fills in the gaps and so adds significantly to what must be cherished, studied and incorporated into belief and practice.

Bere'shit[1]

When God began to create heaven and earth – the earth being unformed and void, with darkness over the surface of the deep and a wind from God sweeping over the water – God said, 'Let there be light'; and there was light. God saw that the light was good, and God separated the light from the darkness. God called the light Day, and the darkness He called Night. And there was evening and there was morning, a first day.
(Genesis 1:1-3)

It seems that we don't begin at the very beginning but before things are created and put in order. It is a time and place of nothingness, of emptiness, of chaos and meaninglessness, a vacuum, a black hole, in the sense of horror and a formless wasteland, an abyss, sterile and desolate. The words in Hebrew have a sound of hollowness and terror, of reiterating this sense and deepening and extending it out endlessly (*tohu wabohu*). Earth is unformed and void, with darkness over the surface of the deep – this is the 'stuff' of creation – an undifferentiated mass of water. Then God steps into the story, intervenes and begins to bring order and harmony, place and time, heaven and earth, encompassing everything that exists and has been made by the Word of God. There is 'stuff' to begin with, but the Creator brings order out of a pit of chaos and destruction. There are basic ingredients of creation: the darkness, the deep (waters), chaos and the spirit of God (wind). This 'spirit' has been seen as God's glory, as the creative element of air and/or fire, even as divine intelligence, which gives form to matter.

'And a wind from God sweeping over the water': into 'this' comes God, comes life, comes hope, comes meaning and harmony, wholeness. It is the *ruah elohim*, the breath of God. The word has evocative meanings: breath, wind, air, soul, spirit, even whisper, and it comes forth from divinity, from the 'mouth' of God, so to speak. Sometimes it is translated 'And God's spirit hovered over on the face of the waters'. The word 'hover' (*merachefet*) has various associations, such as a mother eagle high in its nest, protecting, shielding and feeding her young until they can survive on their own and are strong enough to learn to fly (by being dumped out of the nest!). But for now, she lives devoted to them, hunting for them, and chewing up the raw pieces of meat if necessary so that they can swallow them (the image of Deuteronomy 32). Thomas Berry calls it 'a flaring forth'; in 1945, a Russian geologist, George Gamow, called it a 'primordial fireball'; others called it 'a big bang'. Mystics say that God started whispering into the stuff and breathing upon it, summoning it forth.

The story's power and depth is found in the verbs: hovers/sweeping over; said, saw; separated and called/named. This is the process and pattern that continues through the rest of the story. Now there will be six days of symmetry, and the last day, the seventh, culminates in the Creator resting, seeing, contemplating and observing the Sabbath. This seven-day cycle is the ancient circle of fullness, of completeness and wholeness or holiness. As one of the native peoples of the Brazilian western Amazon basin, Chea Hetaka, says, 'Every shape has its own power. Every form makes energy patterns. A circle bends the energies from its area inside and out, back onto itself, round and round, and creates a spiral' (Jones, 1999, p. 19). Many of the indigenous peoples have known this from observation and time's passage, imitating the Creator's penchant for patterns, circles and returns. Hehaka Sapa, an Oglala Sioux from North Dakota in the Americas, writes:

> You have noticed that everything an Indian does is in a circle, and that is because the Power of the World always works in circles, and everything tries to be round…The Sky is round and I have heard that the earth is round like a ball and so are all the stars. The Wind, in its greater power, whirls. Birds make their nests in circles, for theirs is the same religion as ours. The sun comes forth and goes down again in a circle. The moon does the same, and both are round. Even the seasons form a great circle in their changing, and always come back again to where they were. The life of man is a circle from childhood to childhood, and so it is in everything where power moves. (Jones, 1999, p. 19)

Light

And so in the first four days, God says, God sees, God separates, God calls and names, and the universe (the heavens and the earth and all that is) emerges and is birthed. But as we have recognised, this is not linear: it is circular, continual, developing, evolving and becoming, 'as it was in the beginning'. The first to be summoned and ordered into existence is light. This is the first event in a long string of events. These are the first words and they will continue until the end of the seven days, the week, the end of time. The story is starting, and there is so much that is happening, and it will grow increasingly in complexity. But what is this light? The lights, greater and lesser, of sun, moon and stars, have not yet been created.

Of course, there are numerous ways of looking at this light – traditionally, theologically (from the Jewish mystical teachings), scientifically, spiritually. Perhaps the simplest and clearest explanation is to quote a footnote from the Torah itself:

> 3-5: Since the sun is not created until the fourth day (1:14-19), the light of the first three days is of a different order from what we know. A midrash teaches that when God saw the corruption of the generations of the flood and of the tower of Babel, He hid that primordial light away for the benefit of the righteous in the world-to-come (b. Hag. 12a). Other ancient Near Eastern myths similarly assume the existence of light before creation of the luminaries. (p.13)

Other midrash teach that this is pure energy, or the light of the soul. They say that this light was so strong, so extensive and pure that it illuminated everything and revealed every minute and microcosmic bit of energy and matter, so that you could see across and through the whole universe. Ellen Bernstein (2005) says it this way:

> Light is luminous and radiant: it dazzles, emanates, flows, waves and jumps. It defies definition and constraint; it cannot be captured or contained. Because of its elusive nature, the rabbis said that the phrase 'it was so,' which they interpreted as 'it was established,' is curiously absent from the first day (it appears on every other). 'Established' implies a sense of a concrete reality, but light is not concrete; it is pure energy.
>
> A midrash teaches that all souls were created on day one. 'The soul of man is the lamp of God' sang Solomon. Our souls are like vessels for God, designed to receive God's light and shine it forth. Through the light of our souls we are bound to God, to each other, and to the soul of the world. (p. 7)

The Jewish Prayerbook opens up another possibility. The order of service begins every morning with the words: 'You illumine the world...and in your goodness day after day you continually renew the order of creation.' God is at work, keeping the world like that eagle, that hen, that force of energy pulsing through the universe and matter throughout all time/space. There is a repeating cycle of water, light, earth, night and day, hovering/sustaining us. It is as the old Gaelic hymn that often begins morning prayer reminds us:

Morning has broken, like the first morning.
Blackbird has spoken, like the first bird.
Praise for the singing, praise for the morning.
Praise for the springing fresh from the world.[2]

There is light, in obedience to God's wish 'Let there be', and the work of creation begins with the separating out of one element from another: light from darkness. Each is named: Day and Night. Time enters into the story as evening and morning, a first day. With the making of light, time becomes possible. We can now begin to 'mark time' and count the days. As is the Jewish tradition, the marking of the days begins with the evening and goes through the night, into the coming of daylight, until the light wanes – the opposite of how most days/nights are calculated worldwide since the industrial revolution. The demarcations are evening and morning – not dark and light, but the word *erev* (eveningtide), which means dusk, the blurring of boundaries, the disappearing, and *voker* (morning), which means awakening, clarity, perception of distinctions, becoming clearer, or as some of the rabbis explain: the reappearance of chaos and the coming once more of order. The pattern of the original creation is repeated daily.

What is remarkable is that between the making, calling forth and naming, there is the delight and the pleasure of God that is declared as 'good', an extension of the reality of God. Each and every thing that is set in place, put in motion, begun, is good, and God takes pleasure in it all. It can remind us of Meister Eckhart's words: 'What does God do all day long? God gives birth. From eternity, God lies on a maternity bed giving birth.' This is the work and the joy of creating that has begun.

Days Two, Three and Four

God said, 'Let there be an expanse in the midst of the water, that it may separate water from water.' God made the expanse, and it separated the water which was below the expanse from the water which was above the expanse. And it was so. God called the expanse Sky. And there was evening and there was morning, a second day.

God said, 'Let the water below the sky be gathered into one area, that the dry land may appear.' And it was so. God called the dry land Earth, and the gathering waters He called Seas. And God saw that this was good. And God said, 'Let the earth sprout vegetation: seed fruit with the seed in it.' And it was so. The earth brought forth vegetation: seed-bearing plants of every kind, and trees of every kind bearing fruit with the seed in it. And God saw that this was good. And there was evening and there was morning, a third day.

God said, 'Let there be lights in the expanse of the sky to separate day from night; they shall serve as signs for the set times – the days and the years; and they serve earth.' And it was so. God made the two great lights, the greater light to dominate the day and the lesser light to dominate the night, and the stars. And God set them in the expanse of the sky to shine upon the earth, to dominate the day and the night, and to separate light

from darkness. And God saw that this was good. And there was evening and there was morning, a fourth day.
(Genesis 1:6-19)

God the maker, the sculptor, the painter, begins to separate out, to divide, to peel away, to chip away, to laser, to hold in balance and sway using all the basic ingredients. First God separates the elements of light, water (waters above and waters below, sometimes called salt waters and sweet waters), earth and living plants, and then light again (sun, moon and stars), all that dwell in the waters and the air (birds, fish and swimming creatures) and all that live on land (animals and human beings). And this separating out, this distillation, doesn't come easily – it is work. It is work that affects what is separated and, the rabbis say, it affects God the Creator too. This is one of the ways in which it is described:

> From a midrashic perspective it seems that havdalah – separation, specialisation, the formation of difference and opposition – is generally achieved at some great sacrifice. When, for instance, the lower waters are separated from the higher waters on the second day of creation, the lower waters are described in midrashic sources as weeping: 'We want to be in the presence of the King.' The essential act of this second day is this act of division: 'He divided His works into different groups and reigned over them.' From now on, the notion of the sovereignty of God will depend on the differences and the many-ness of His subjects. But the idea of separation and difference has a tragic resonance: gone is the primal unity of 'God alone in His world'. New possibilities, new hazards, open up. The primary image of such separation, the division of the waters and their weeping expresses the yearning of the split off parts of the cosmos for a primordial condition of unity being.
>
> With division begins alienation, conflict, and yet, paradoxically, a new notion of divine sovereignty. In this new perspective, God is recognised as King only by that being who is most radically separated from Him. Man, created on the sixth day, is foreshadowed by the splittings and differentiations of matter that begin on the second day; his freedom to perceive and to act is founded on those primal disintegrations. (Zornberg, 1996, pp. 5–6)

The continual use of the phrase 'Let there be...' implies a deepening or strengthening of the separations and divisions. The heavens and earth are now created, but 'the expanse' is made that separates out the waters, above and below, so that the firmament, earth, can come forth on the third day, and they will be named Sky and Earth and Seas. This second making is called *rakia* among Hebrew scholars, and the same word is used by the prophet Ezekiel to describe the throne of God that was made by the outstretched wings of the cherubim. It is the waters (matter) hammered flat, and pressed down to become invisible, hence thought to be air. It is what makes this planet earth liveable for humans – we can breathe here. Around 85 per cent of the human body is composed of water, but we need oxygen. God sets about 'disturbing' the waters, creating what was visualised as a dome above the waters – the atmosphere. God calls it Sky. For us, it is an invisible blanket that protects all life on earth and in the oceans. It is layered, and today we are destroying the ozone layer, putting all life in danger of extinction.

Air and water interact, move, change, dissolve and take on different forms. Air/moisture freezes, melts, rises, mists, becomes rain, snow, sleet, hail, frost, dew. It evaporates, moves as wind, stirs above and below, in currents and storms, and is essential for the continuation of all life. Like air, water moves, vaporises, crystallises. Scientists say that for about the last three and a half billion years, this envelope of air has managed to hold a balance in tension – enough to protect us from the ultraviolet rays of the sun and enough to nurture and sustain all plant life on earth and in the oceans. These elements are often used to describe the movements and the action of the Spirit of God…they breathe, they vibrate, they transform and mutate. Minute changes cause massive responses, from butterflies to tsunamis to hurricanes, to avalanches and earthquakes. Creation is starting to take on form. From here on out, things/species will come forth from each other, be born from and reproduce from each other – co-creation is the order of the day! Everything is interconnected and interdependent. It is all one.

Earth

Next comes ground, Earth, a place to stand on, and the Seas, a place to swim in. God then invites vegetation, everything held in seed form, to come forth. One of the old names for God in Hebrew is Makom, meaning 'place', and we refer to God as the Rock we cling to. Through Moses, we are told early on that the ground whereon we stand is holy ground.

In the creation story, the earth itself has an inner force that drives it to produce, to see and to bring forth seeds, vegetation, trees and grasses. The seed within has massive ramifications for those who would tamper with and violate the process of seed-bearing plants (rice, corn, wheat, the staples of survival) and manipulate food so that when it is grown, it is a one-time thing, and will not reproduce of itself. There are over a hundred varieties of potato in Peru and Bolivia, which form the basis of the food chain for the indigenous peoples and are the highest sources of protein and energy. In contrast, fast-food chains pose a threat to these species by introducing an artificially produced 'thing' called a potato, engineered to 'fry up fast – fast food', the nutritional content of which is hardly comparable to the original. Its taste comes from sugar and other 'things' that are not revealed. Just fifty years ago in India and Japan, there were more than thirty thousand varieties of rice; now about ten varieties provide some 75 per cent of the rice crop (Rhoades, 1991). Earth was originally designed to replenish itself.

Waters to drink and food to eat arrive on the scene. There is wet and dry, solid and liquid. Boundaries and limits begin. We can swim but we can't breathe under water. What swims in the sea has trouble on earth and often dies in the air. There are places for everything, and everything will be put in its proper place so that it can bring forth new life, and life will continue through time. Air is given to all, the seas are for all, the earth is for all. The waters of the earth, about 80 per cent of the planet, have been referred to as the circulatory system, like those of our own bodies. Anything that affects these essential elements will impinge on all. A story from the Koran underlines how many of our actions belie humanity's culpable ignorance:

God takes Moses to the Red Sea and tells him to watch what happens. Moses sees a tiny bird, a little sparrow, dive down into the Sea and swallow a mouthful of water. He returns again and again. God speaks: 'Do you see how much water is in the sea? That is how much knowledge and mystery there is. And the water the sparrow drinks? That's how much humans know.'

Another rich perspective on the interdependence of all created things comes from the Maori people of New Zealand, in 'The Story of Earth and Sky':

In the beginning, the Sky loved Earth and hugged her so tightly that there was no space between them and no light could pass through. Together they had six children: the oldest was the Father of the Oceans, then the Father of Foods that are grown in the soil of Earth, the Father of the Forests, the Father of the People, the Father of the Wind and Storms, and the youngest, the Father of Wild Food. All the children grew up in the dark and they talked among themselves of how to separate their parents so that they'd have some breathing space and light could enter into their lives and home. All of them, except the Father of the Wind and Storms, agreed they had to part their parents, but they disagreed over how to do it. Father of the People was aggressive and wanted things done quickly and wanted to use force to kill the parents, eliminate them. But his brother, the Father of the Forests, the protector of all that lived in his domain, said, 'No, let's just pull them apart so that they both live, the Sky above, high above us, and the Earth below, so that we can stand here and live close to our mother.' The other brothers all agreed, but the Father of the Wind and Storms decided by himself that he would not let them do it.

All of them tried to tear Sky and Earth apart, but they didn't have the strength to do so. It was the Father of the Forests who decided to seed plants and trees that would root on Earth and grow tall, slowly pushing Sky away from Earth. This was progressing so slowly that, once there was an opening, they all pushed and shoved and managed to get the two away from each other. Sky and Earth were brokenhearted and they cried and wailed as they were torn from each other. Father of the Wind and Storms could not bear their cries and tears, and in anger, he began to lash out with rain, lightning, storms and fierce winds. Waters came and flooded Earth. All the fish fled to the bottom of the sea and all the snakes and reptiles escaped to the forest to hide (and they've all lived there ever since). After a long, long time, Sky and Earth stopped crying and Father of the Wind and Storms stopped too. The waters dried up and Earth was still again.

The other brothers had now learned to fight and quarrel among themselves. Earth, their mother, listened and watched them and worried where it would all end. She looked at her children. Some of them would always have something: the Forest would have its trees; the Ocean would have its fish; the Father of Foods would have its seeds/plants and roots; and Father of the Winds and Storms would have his anger at his other brothers. But what would the Father of the People have? If he had nothing, then he would keep the fight going. She decided she had to hide that brother's food in the ground so that he'd have to spend a lot of time looking for what he needed in order to survive. And so, even now to this day, the People work hard to find their food, to survive and store for hard times, both in the ground and in the ocean.

Sometimes when the brothers remember what they did to Sky and Earth, they grieve and they fight again. The Wind and Storms pick up in strength and the Ocean produces hurricanes and tsunamis or rips the trees and floods the land, tearing houses and canoes away from their homes, as once they did Sky and Earth. The other brothers, though, have learned to give gifts: reeds to make nets for fishing and instruments to make music.

Sky and Earth still love each other. If you listen, you can hear their sighs and see their tears in the mist and fog. If you stand still, you can hear the cries that make you lonely, and early in the morning you can see Sky's tears for his Earth so far away – they are called dew. Sky still loves Earth.

Starry Night

Once upon a time, on a starry, starry night, the Master decided to take his disciples outside and give them a lesson in astronomy. They were all commanded to lie down on the ground, in the dark, get comfortable and look up at the heavens, the night sky. 'Observe the stars,' he commanded them. (Don't fall asleep yet!) Long minutes later, he began: 'That is the Spiral Galaxy of Andromeda. It is as large as our Milky Way. It sends out rays of light that, at a speed of 186,000 miles a second, take 2.5 million years to get to us. It consists of 100,000 million suns, many larger than our own sun.' There was a long, heavy silence, with a few gasps and intakes of air, surprise! 'Ok, the lesson is over, you can get up now. Hopefully you now have your life in perspective. Go to bed and sleep in humility and peace.' (Attributed to the Islamic tradition.)

We now have more detailed cycles of time. The moon controls the tides of the seas and gives us the twenty-eight-day cycle of months that is revealed in seasons. Lunar calendars are still studied and used, and they are just as accurate as solar calendars. Rituals that draw Sky and Earth together follow the pattern of time decreed by the heavens, especially the lesser lights of the night. And humans study the planets' alignments and movements for information regarding births, dates, auspicious times for decisions, weddings, endeavours and omens of catastrophic and monumentous events that are portended in the skies – just as the wise men watched the rise of the star of the newborn king of the Jews.

This description of the making and the placement of the lights in the heavens is important because the sun dominates the day and the moon dominates the night, and they 'serve' the earth, and illuminate it, and separate day from night. The verb 'to dominate' is repeated in the creation description of human beings, and sheds light on how we are to relate to the rest of creation, imitating the Creator and what was created before our appearance.

The vastness, the power and the mystery of the lights of the heavens add to the complexity of the universe, as all its forces and energies work together. Scientists today know that more than 97.9 per cent of the universe is invisible. Carl Sagan was an American astronomer, astrobiologist and highly successful populariser of science. He reputedly responded to this wondrous knowledge, and to our vast ignorance of what is, with the words: 'What do we know about anything?'

Days Five and Six

God said, 'Let the waters bring forth swarms of living creatures, and birds that fly above the earth across the expanse of sky.' God created the great sea monsters, and all the living creatures of every kind that creep, which the waters brought forth in swarms, and all the winged birds of every kind. And God saw that this was good. God blessed them, saying, 'Be fertile and increase on the earth.' And there was evening and there was morning, a fifth day.

God said, 'Let the earth bring forth every kind of living creature: cattle, creeping things, and wild beasts of every kind.' And it was so. God made wild beasts of every kind and cattle of every kind, and all kinds of creeping things of the earth. And God saw that this was good.

(Genesis 1:20-25)

With days five and six comes the work of filling the air, the seas and the earth with living creatures, including humanity, men and women, and blessing them all, exhorting them to be fertile and multiply and replenish the earth for all future generations.

The structures and order of this creation narrative give to everything its place. There is a plethora of species in the waters, skies and on land. Life teems and is abundant. Every habitat is filled, and before the humans appear, all the creatures swarm, move in crowds, flocks, packs, hordes. The multitudes proliferate. In fact, they are blessed and commanded to fill the earth for all generations to come.

In his 'Cosmic Walk', Diarmuid O'Murchu explains a timeline of creation that is interactive with the creation story of Genesis. Referring to the emergence of life forms, he states:

> **3.5 billion years ago:** The rich array of cosmic liquids and chemicals formed a new alliance, birthing forth the earliest life-forms: tiny bacteria that thrive even to our time. And from these simple organisms emerges the canopy of life-forms that adorns creation today.
>
> **350 million years ago:** With flowers adorning the landscape, and trees towering above the earth itself, plants on earth and fishes abounding in the waters, the sea mammals move on to land, and the complexity of embodied life reaches a new apex of elegance and beauty.
>
> **7 million years ago:** Africa gives birth to the Human Species. Evolving out of Africa humans inhabit the entire planet, bringing forth new mental and spiritual powers through which matter becomes conscious of itself. Evolution moves to a new spiritual threshold with humans, as a young species, still struggling to make sense of their awesome existence.[3]

These days bring the first occurrence of blessing from God: be fruitful, fertile; be many; extend out into the earth and fill the seas. A beautiful Maori creation chant captures the promise of fecundity and abundance:

> From the conception, the increase; from the increase, the swelling; from the swelling, the thought; from the thought, the remembrance; from the remembrance, the consciousness, the desire.

Human beings are bestowed with the power to continue, to extend into the future through their own living and relating, to sustain themselves. The blessing is to provide excess, beyond what is needed just to survive. There was always meant to be more than just what was needed. The blessing provides an added energy, to boost progeny in the face of terrible odds, predators and climatic conditions. The blessing was built into the system so that no species was ever to become extinct! And yet, statistics say that some thirty species are lost every day and the number keeps rising. That is more than ten thousand in a year.

The blessing is given to those that dwell in the air and the seas and crawl on the ground, but not to the wild beasts, cattle and creeping things. The difference between those that crawl on the fifth day and those that creep on the sixth day has been thought to be size/height and the distinction of those creatures that are not given to humans to tame, domesticate and use. The blessing is given to the humans to procreate, to give and share life, but with a further injunction, which is the core of this book: to rule and to master the earth. This is the crux of the matter – the connection or opposition of ruling/mastering to harming the earth, the sea and the trees, which is the very command given to the angels in the Book of Revelation: 'Harm not the earth, nor the seas, nor the trees' (7:3a).

Human Beings

> And God said, 'Let us make man in our image, after our likeness. They shall rule the fish of the sea, the birds of the sky, the cattle, the whole earth, and all the creeping things that creep on the earth. And God created man in His image, in the image of God he created him; male and female He created them. God blessed them and God said to them, 'Be fertile and increase, fill the earth and master it; and rule the fish of the sea, the birds of the sky, and all the living things that creep on the earth.'
>
> (Genesis 1:26-28)

The most problematic phrase for many is 'Let us make...' Suddenly the Creator is either talking aloud, though alone, or consulting with others. Some rabbis say that God consulted creation – all the work that had already been finished, knowing that human beings would have radical effects on everything already made. Many stories in the Hebrew tradition posit that all the different 'species' of angels were created on the second day and that the Creator decided to tell all of them about the plan to create human beings in God's own image, asking them what they thought about it! Here is one account I learned from a rabbi. It's just called 'The Making of Men and Women' (the word 'man' is used to mean all human beings).

'And God said: Let us make man' (Genesis 1:26).

Rabbi Simon said:
When the Holy One, blessed be he, came to create the first man, the ministering angels divided into parties and factions, one saying: Let him not be created, and another saying: Let him be created.
Mercy saying: Let him be created, for he will be merciful, and

Truth saying: Let him not be created, for he will be all lies.
Righteousness saying: Let him be created, for he will do righteous deeds.
Peace saying: Let him not be created, for he is all contention.
What did the Holy One, blessed be he, do?
He took Truth and flung him to the earth.
The ministering angels said to the Holy One, blessed be he:
Master of the universe, do you disgrace your seal?
Raise Truth from the earth
Rav Huna said:
While the ministering angels were still arguing and disputing, the
Holy One, blessed be he, created man.
Then he said to them:
Why do you argue? Man is already made. (Gen. Rab 8:4,5)[4]

The consensus of the rabbinic/midrashic tradition is that God knew what human beings would/could do with the universe that was created so lovingly and that gave the Creator such delight, every step of the way. There would be righteous human beings and there would be wicked human beings. And yet the Creator decided to create human beings for the sake of the ones who would be righteous, who would follow the path and pattern modelled for them in the Torah and the Law. The midrash teaches that God partnered Godself with the quality of Mercy to create all human beings, in spite of the kind of evil/wickedness we are capable of doing. We are made with massive potential: the possibility of attaining and practising truth and making peace, living with loving kindness and righteousness, imitating the merciful Creator, and we are equally capable of lies, contention, discord, war, brutality and acting mindlessly, as the swarms of insects and animals created before us, without consciousness and without the image of the Holy One. Righteousness, holiness, justice and truth, mercy and loving kindness must come into the world, and come through us. That, in the rabbis' teaching, justifies the creation of human beings. Psalm 85:12 reads, 'Truth will grow up from the earth', and it will grow up in us! Simi Peters, in her exegesis of the midrash quoted above, says:

...R. Simon [in the midrash] is not only asserting that *Adam* is valuable because of his potential for qualities which angels cannot manifest, but he is also addressing the vexed question of what to do with the human's potential for evil and its effects upon the supreme value of Truth...If Truth has been dethroned by the ascension of *Adam*, it will have to be restored by growing up from the earth. Truth will no longer be a static, absolute, divine quality, but an evolving, organic component of the created world – something for which human beings will have to strive. The ending of R. Simon's story is highly significant because it is ultimately so optimistic about humankind. If people are flawed, on R. Simon's reading, they are nonetheless also capable of at least striving for – if not totally attaining – divine qualities. (Elper and Handleman, 2006, p. 304.)

God knew that giving us a share in the Creator's power and making us in the Creator's own image and likeness was entrusting a great responsibility into the care of the human community, and that we would more often than not constantly betray that trust and use the gift of power shared for our own ends, scarring the earth and manipulating it for our goals, in our greed, rather than imitating the Creator by delegating power, sharing it with others and tending to life in all the universe. By making us in the image and likeness of God, even making us co-creators, God's desire was that humankind would be 'very good'.

The rabbis play on the name of Adam (representing human beings)...the name 'Adam' and the word 'very' have the same letters, just arranged differently. Adam is very good – playing with the fact that we are capable of giving great delight to the One who made us. The teachers end with the reminder that God is God, and it is and was God's will and good pleasure to make us, and, whether we ever understand what sourced that desire, God's making of us reveals something essential about God, that we must strive to understand and imitate.

In the sense that we image God, human beings can be said to be superior to what had been created previously. Oddly enough, we are not given our own day of creation, for we share the sixth day with many other creatures – 'every kind of living creatures: cattle, creeping things, and wild beasts of every kind'. We are still intimately connected with all else in creation, interdependent and interrelated. This quote from Rabindranath Tagore puts it well:

The same stream of life that runs through my veins night and day runs through the world and dances in rhythmic measures. It is the same life that shoots in joy through the dust of the earth in numberless blades of grass and breaks into tumultuous waves of leaves and flowers. It is the same life that is rocked in the ocean-cradle of birth and of death, in ebb and in flow. I feel my limbs are made glorious by the touch of this world of life. And my pride is from the life-throb of ages dancing in my blood this moment. (Reagan, 2002, p. 54)

The exhortation given expressly to humans begins with the command to 'be fertile and increase, fill the earth and master it; and then...to rule the fish of the sea, the birds of the sky, and all the living things that creep on the earth'. It begins with the same need and blessing of all else that dwells on earth, sea and sky. This is not so much to do with a high birth rate but, in light of being male and female, a hope and a blessing to be sexually active, bear children, and know earth and all that has been created as 'very good' and given to us to share.[5] Humankind is like God – profligate with life, all made in the image of God's own life and goodness.

The command to have dominion over, or master, or rule the creatures that live in the sea, the air and on the ground, and the whole earth, must be seen in light of a returning people, long enslaved, with no power, no land, no possessions, no identity as exiles, refugees, indentured servants and slaves in a foreign country. They are being told that their owners/conquerors are not the only ones given rights (and responsibilities) over the land and its possessions. The earth and all its creatures belong to everyone, not only or primarily to the strong, the dominant, the ones who win in war/conquest and destruction, taking to themselves what others possess, even taking their lives in bondage. This 'dominion', this rule and mastering is not over and above earth and all the creatures of earth, but in relationship to earth and all that has been made. They are not to act as did those who conquered them and destroyed their lives, their land and their Temple. They are to imitate God, not Babylon and the other nations/rulers/kings. Or as it is succinctly put in David Cotter's commentary on Genesis:

> Humanity is given the one blessing that pertains to the earth: 'Be fruitful and multiply, and fill the earth and subdue it; and have dominion over the fish of the sea and over the birds of the air and over every living thing that moves upon the earth' (Genesis 1:28). Like the other living creatures, humanity is given the power to procreate and so possesses at least a reflection of the divine power to give life. To that is added the blessing of subduing and having dominion over the world. This might well mean, especially given the context of blessing, to lead, to guide, or to tend (as a flock; note 1 Kings 3:7-9; 5:4). To be in God's image means to be blessed with the responsibility of ruling the world in such a way that it is the ordered, good, life-giving place that God intends it to be. Perhaps an analogy will make the point better. God: Universe: Humanity: World. As God is to the entire universe – the One who creates a good, blessed, non violent place where life is possible and order reigns – so Humanity is to be to the world. We live up to this responsibility when we make the world good, live in just nonviolence, and render the blessed life possible here. (2003, p. 18)

The blessing spoken of in this quote refers to the words that Solomon responds with when he is instructed to ask something of God in a dream. He answers:

> You dealt most graciously with Your servant my father David, because he walked before You in faithfulness and righteousness and in integrity of heart. You have continued this great kindness to him by giving him a son to occupy his throne, as is now the case. And now, O Lord my God, You have made Your servant king in place of my father David; but I am a young lad, with no experience in leadership. Your servant finds himself in the midst of a people You have chosen, a people too numerous to be numbered or counted. Grant, then, Your servant an understanding mind to judge Your people, to distinguish between good and bad; for who can judge this vast people of Yours?
>
> (1 Kings 3:6-9)

This is the way to rule (though Solomon and others often failed by exploiting and impoverishing the people while sating themselves). It is ruling with a listening heart to all. The blessing itself is found in the book of Wisdom. It is worth quoting because it reveals how we, in imitation of God, are to image the rule, the mastering and the dominion of the earth and all creatures in the world.

> God of my fathers, Lord of mercy, you who have made all things by your word
> And in your wisdom have established man to rule the creatures produced by you,
> To govern the world in holiness and justice, and to render judgement in integrity of heart:
> Give me Wisdom, the attendant at your throne, and reject me not from among your children;
> For I am your servant, the son of your handmaid, a man weak and short-lived and lacking in comprehension of judgement and laws.
> Indeed, though one be perfect among the sons of men, if Wisdom, who comes from you, be not with him, he shall be held in no esteem.
> …Now with you is Wisdom, who knows your works and was present when you made the world;
> Who understands what is pleasing in your eyes and what is conformable with your commands.
> Send her forth from your holy heavens and from your glorious throne dispatch her
> That she may be with me and work with me, that I may know what is your pleasure.
>
> (Wisdom 9:1-6, 9-10)

This is a far cry from any notion of dominion, rule or mastering that has been attributed to this reading on many occasions. You cannot find in these words, if read in the context of imaging God the Creator of the Universe, anything that could be construed as a licence to be irresponsible, to decimate the land and natural resources, let alone to kill, to conquer, to seize disproportionately the goods/lands of the earth, or to harm or enslave or rape the earth or any of its inhabitants. In fact, it is the exact opposite – an exhortation to imitate God the Creator, to take pleasure in propagating life, protecting it and setting in motion what is necessary for its continuation, its increase and its wild diversity and variety. This God is the God of life, and we are not given ownership of the land or its resources and inhabitants, but we are blessed so that we can do for the earth and all that has been made, what God has done for us, as human beings.

This blessing is continued in the book of Leviticus when the people are reminded: 'But the land must not be sold beyond reclaim, for the land is Mine; you are but strangers, resident with Me. Throughout the land that you hold, you must provide for the redemption of the land' (25:23-24). The entire chapter 25 of Leviticus, referred to as the Jubilee, demands in great detail how the land and all creatures, plants, resources, even people are to remember and respond to God the Creator.

In the Book of Exodus, it is not just the jubilee year, but it is the Sabbath every seven years that is ritually introduced into the religious life, the economy and the practice of the Israelites to remind them of how they are to treat the land/creation and all that dwells/resides on the land.

Six years you shall sow your land and gather in its yield; but in the seventh you shall let it rest, and lie fallow. Let the needy among your people eat of it, and what they leave let the wild beasts eat. You shall do the same with your vineyards and your olive groves (Exodus 23:10-11).

The monstrous excess of greed that has led to the abuse of the land and natural resources to accommodate capitalism and individual rapaciousness means that future generations will have to cope with the destruction we are leaving them as their inheritance. Life itself, the air, the waters, the resources and the land are tenuously clinging to survive with any of the grace and power, majesty and promise that was seeded in them during creation. We have reversed the life forces hidden in the patterns of creation and are not taking the blessing that was given to human beings to heart. Instead of regenerating the earth and all living creatures, we are decimating it, and our children are suffering from the effects: weather extremes, pollution of our water and food, the ultimate destruction caused by war, with the accompanying horror of chemical/biological and nuclear weapons. How far we have come from the Creator's original design, intent and hope.

Concerning Food

God said, 'See, I give you every seed-bearing plant that is upon the earth, and every tree that has seed-bearing fruit; they shall be yours for food. And to all the animals on the land, to all the birds of the sky, and to everything that creeps on earth, in which there is the breath of life, [I give] all the green plants for food.' And it was so. And God saw all that he had made, and found it very good. And there was evening and there was morning, the sixth day.

(Genesis 1:29-31)

In the beginning, we all eat the same food and survive physically on the same plane as those created with us on the sixth day. We do not eat the birds, cattle or other animals that we have domesticated. In the beginning, we are frugivores (eating the seeds of plants and trees). We are not even vegetarians, *per se*. We are not meant to eat any species too close to us. This original food chain is altered just chapters later in Genesis, when Cain kills his brother, Abel, and violence and murder proliferate in the land. Changes to the covenant between Noah and God attempt to salvage the relationship between God and human beings (the Noah story). Over the generations in the Jewish community, there have been many jokes about humans being created on the same day as many of the other animals, as God's not-too-subtle way of reminding us that we share many characteristics and behaviour patterns with other creatures – the more negative and inhuman ones when we are not acting in imitation of our Maker.

Chapter 1 of Genesis ends on this sixth day with everything being very good and all the work done, but there is a bridge into the second story of Genesis that is also a creation story – it is the seventh day, and there is a description of God the Creator and of how one is to live in the image of God, after the hard work of creating and sustaining life is set in motion. It is important to see this seventh day as the pinnacle of creation (not just as the time of creation of human beings). This is how God is. This is how we are supposed to be on earth. This is the culmination of creation, and yet at the same time it is the beginning of the next story, the next week, and all that comes after creation.

Genesis 2: The Seventh Day

The heaven and the earth were finished, and all their array. On the seventh day God finished the work that He had been doing, and He ceased on the seventh day from all the work that He had done. And God blessed the seventh day and declared it holy, because on it God ceased from all the work of the creation that He had done. Such is the story of heaven and earth when they were created.

(Genesis 2:1-4a)

God rested and ceased from work on this day. (Is it our turn now?) Then God blessed the seventh day and declared it holy, just as God had once blessed the creatures of air/sea and land and human beings. These words are also used in the Friday evening service that begins the celebration of the Sabbath today and again before the first meal of the Sabbath. Now God is in time, with all peoples and all of creation. In light of this being a text written by the priestly community after the exile, the people are being told that they can still worship God and find God everywhere, in time and place, even if they do not have a temple or a city in which to worship as a community. Worship is found in life, as surely as it is found in a place, a temple or a tabernacle. This is the exhortation in Exodus for the people who are made in the image and likeness of God, reminding them to imitate this God, their creator, every week, and especially on this day.

> God spoke these words, saying…
> Remember the Sabbath day and keep it holy. Six days you shall labour and do all your work, but the seventh day is a Sabbath of the Lord your God: you shall not do any work – you, your son or daughter, your male or female slave, or your cattle, or the stranger who is within your settlements. For in six days the Lord made heaven and earth and the sea, and all that is in them, and He rested on the seventh day; therefore the Lord blessed the Sabbath day and hallowed it.
> (Exodus 20:10-12)

The last day marks the end of the formal work of creation, and the processes for the continuation of life are set in motion. The last day also marks the last separation – this day is separated out from all the others to be hallowed, to be blessed and different from the other six that have gone before. The creation story tells us of the way God dreamed the world. There are two sides to being and living in the likeness of the Creator – the work and the ceasing of work, the resting and hallowing, and the blessing upon all that has been done. Just because there are six days of work doesn't mean that the emphasis is on those days; in fact, the day that is separated out, the Sabbath, takes precedence over all other things. It makes and fulfils creation so that it reeks of God's presence. The Sabbath is the pivot point for all time, place, space and creatures, especially for human beings made in the Creator's image.

On the Sabbath, we are to practise making holy, sanctifying everything, everyone, even time and place. In fact, we are to learn how to bless, how to transfer power and how to separate out as God does. We are to take time to be alone, as God was once alone, and we are to dwell in community, since all of creation reveals a God who shares even the power and intense pleasure of creating life with the myriad creatures of creation, including human beings, in a way that consciously reveals who God is. Though God has no gender, we are made in God's likeness, male and female – in relationship, in attraction, in procreating and in protecting all of creation together.

This God shares dominion with us and knowingly gives us the power to master and rule and have dominion over all creation, or to choose to dominate and reverse the processes of life and creation that have been set in motion and keep moving throughout all time. This world and all that is in it has been given to us, but it does not belong to us. It belongs to its Maker and Keeper, the Lord, Dominus. When we greet one another (in the old Latin) with the words '*Dominus vobiscum*' – the Lord be with you – this is the model and the blessing of dominion that we share with God over the whole world and creation. If we subdue the earth, we do so as servants, and we make sure, as God does, that everything has its place and is given its due – its justice and its fullness of life. Our becoming the likeness of God begins with the Sabbath, the seventh day, which is to be the pattern and depth of our lives throughout all the other days of the week and through all time. This God is not about power, domination and force. This God is not about exclusion of others, or hierarchy, but about equality and universality and communion with all peoples, men and women alike. We are to be a blessing on all of earth, as God has blessed us. We are to image this Creator God in our way of being together on the earth, with all else that has been created, including the earth itself and the universe.

Like God, we are to recognise that all is 'good'. This is essential to sustaining and continuing the work of creation and allowing creation and created things to be profligate in their ways of living. We, like God, need a whole day just to see, name and pronounce a blessing – to appreciate the goodness that is inherent in everything that is. We need a day in which to stop, a day to take great pleasure in life, in our relationships with one another and with God, to celebrate our interdependence with all creation and to declare it all holy. In a sense, it is a day to contemplate.

My definition of 'contemplation' is taking a long, loving look at reality, especially reality that is hard/painful to look at, alone and with others. This is the 'work' of Sabbath, which makes the blessing of the days of the week effective and active, releasing the power of the blessing into our lives, our relationships, our procreating[6] and into the world. It is what activates our power to image God in the way we work, in the way we relate to all that has been created with the intent and the pleasure, the delight and the deeply embedded life with which God sourced every molecule of the universe. Without this contemplation and this day of ceasing and seeing and making holy, we far too quickly come to have only contempt in our hearts and behaviour for all that has been made, for one another and for the Creator. And we make creation contemptible rather than appreciating its wonders, its diversity, its power. This contempt leads us to compete with one another, fighting over creation and its resources, aggressively taking what is not ours, destroying creation, taking it for granted and dominating the world in a way that does not image the God of our beginnings. On the Sabbath, we are drawn to praise and to pray:

> Praise the Lord for he is good; sing to our God for he is loving;
> To him our praise is due.
> The Lord builds up Jerusalem and brings back Israel's exiles,
> He heals the broken-hearted, he binds up all their wounds.
> He fixes the number of the stars; he calls each one by its name.
> Our Lord is great and almighty; his wisdom can never be measured.
> The Lord raises the lowly; he humbles the wicked to dust...
> He covers the heavens with clouds; he prepares rain for the earth,
> Making mountains sprout with grass and with plants to serve our needs.
> He provides the beasts with their food and young ravens that call upon him.
> His delight is not in horses nor his pleasure in warrior's strength.
> The Lord delights in those who revere him, in those who wait for his love.
>   (Psalm (146) 147)

Late afternoon
the air is charged with energy and serenity,
the red hills ridge and Sopris near shorn of old snow
reveal green swards under blue wings of sky.
This is a landscape of grace.
Here I remember easily where I come from, expanse of vision.
The valley cradles body and soul lightly.
Soon the mystery of dusk will appear.
I hear the beating of wings, butterflies, moths, insects,
angels against the silence.
And I know that creation happened on the first late afternoon
when the Holy in loneliness and love split, separated into two
and lay together in a field, quiet, waiting for their first night
together.
And ever since God has been in love with us. This is true.
It is why loneliness always reveals God close by, watching,
waiting for us to turn and reach back for them (Him).
I oblige.[7]

Notes

1. The word 'Bere'shit' is the Jewish name for the first chapter, meaning 'Beginnings', literally, 'in the beginning'.

2. As a hymn-tune, it is usually called 'Bunessan', to be found in hymnbooks to the words of a carol, 'Child in the Manger'. The 'Gaelic Melody' is arranged by David Evans, 1874-1948. The words are a translation by Lachlan MacBean (1853–1931) of a Gaelic hymn by Mary MacDonald (1817–1890 or so), to be found in MacBean's *Songs and Hymns of the Scottish Highlands* (1888).

3. Diarmuid O'Murchu, *Cosmic Walk*, www.diarmuid13.com

4. The entire midrash is quoted in 'Na'aseh Adam' – 'Should We Make Adam?' A Midrashic Reading of Genesis 1:26, Simi Peters in *Torah of the Mothers: Contemporary Jewish Women Read Classical Jewish Texts*, Ora Wiskind Elper and Susan Handelman (eds), Urim Publications, Jerusalem/NY, 2006, pp. 291–306.

5. This is the Priestly account of creation and it was written after the destruction of Jerusalem, the Temple and the slaughter of many of the Israelites. Those who lived went into exile as slaves, and they were now returning. The emphasis in this tradition is on the fact that human beings are good, in spite of their sinfulness. There is a further emphasis on beginning anew in the land of their ancestors, the land of promise, of fecundity and of life so abundant that they would live on milk and honey. It was essential that they repopulate the land and become a people again, after their return from Babylon.

6. Making love on the Sabbath is a law in the Jewish Practice of Sabbath.

7. *Dancing with Angels: Selected Poems*, Megan McKenna, Continuum, NY, 1998, p. 31; written by the author after reading again that God created us because there was no one to tell the stories to and God was lonely.

Chapter Two

Genesis 2–3:24

There are as many stories of creation as there are peoples. In fact, many indigenous people worldwide have a number of creation stories, or stories about how things came to be the way they are, how to live in the world and why things are done in a particular way. The following story, 'Creator and Dog', was told to me by Ken Feit, an itinerant preacher and storyteller.

In the beginning, Creator made earth and plants and fish and seas and air, and all the animals. And Creator went for a walk. Dog trotted alongside Creator. They walked and walked, up the mountains, along the riverbanks and shorelines, through the forests, the fields and the high grasses. Creator looked at everything – the animals, the birds, the fish, the trees, the flowers, the insects, the clouds – and sighed. 'Ah,' Creator said, 'my work is finished. Time for me to go.'

But Dog said, 'Don't go. Stay! Please, Grandfather. You are my friend, my only friend. I will be lonely.'

Creator said to Dog, 'Turn around and don't look. I will make you something, something new, a surprise!'

But Dog was curious and didn't want to wait and he started peeking at what Creator was up to. Creator yelled at Dog, 'Turn around!' After a while, Creator said, 'Ok, you can look now.' Dog ran to look. 'What do you think?' asked Creator. 'Oh, Grandfather,' Dog answered, 'it's wonderful. But what can it do?' Creator said, 'Walk!' – and it walked and walked and walked. 'Run!' – and it ran and ran and ran. 'Stop!' – and it stopped. 'Talk!' – and it talked and talked and talked! 'Stop!' said Creator. 'It is good to talk, but it is also good to be quiet and look around and listen too.' Then he said, 'Laugh!' – and it laughed and laughed and laughed. And Creator and Dog laughed too. 'Ok, now, I'm finished with my work,' said Creator. 'Time to go.'

But Dog said to Creator, 'Grandfather. It laughs, but does it know how to cry? Can you teach it to cry?' 'Cry!' said Creator – and it cried and cried and cried. And Creator and Dog cried too. Then Creator looked and said, 'Make a bow with your lips.' And when it did, Creator touched the bow and placed it in the sky, where it grew and expanded and became all the colours of the world. Then Creator walked away, up the bow. Creator turned and said, 'Goodbye Dog. Now you won't be lonely.' And Dog barked and Creator laughed.

You see, human beings were created so that dog would have a friend!

The two creation stories in the first two chapters of Genesis are radically different from each other. Yet each reveals truths that are necessary for our understanding of who we are and our relation to God, to the earth and to one another.

The Traditional Story: In the Garden

The story told in Genesis Chapter 2 is often alluded to as the second creation story. But it isn't really a creation story: the world is already made when we begin this chapter. The story is essentially about the garden, about Paradise or Eden and the choices human beings make on whether to live in Paradise by obeying the God of life or lose Paradise and live in a world that is torn and shredded by choices that defy the God of life or destroy life. The story ends in Genesis 3:24, when human beings are driven from the garden into the world. It seeks to deal with some of the hard realities that all human beings experience in living and dying, surviving and longing, knowing yet wanting to know more, and resorting to disobedience in the process.

The bridge that connects the original creation story in Genesis 1 (written most probably after the exile and return of the Israelites) and this story, which has much earlier origins, is the story of the seventh day, the Sabbath. God's likeness is reflected and revealed in the way human beings, especially the Israelites and Christians, hold the vision of the original creation of the world and their place in it.

This second story is more 'homey', sounds more like a story and is more primitive, seeking to explain huge and terrifying theological questions and the mysteries of life and death, knowledge and disobedience, and the pain that is associated with work, childbirth and surviving in community. Like all the other stories of the Scriptures, especially the earlier testament of the Jewish people, it has been used to give credence to those who are in power and who dominate parts of the world and parts of life, economics, politics and religion, put forward as a 'divine' reason for what they do, often in direct opposition to what the text and the stories actually espouse. This second story tells how things got to be the way they are, NOT the way they are supposed to be or could be if we would learn to obey the basic tenets of being human. The rest of the Scriptures are the stories that seek to prepare a people, and then all peoples, for imaging a God of justice and mercy, of peace and truth, of integrity and communion, of community and respect for every individual and for the earth. And that is a long and ongoing story.

This is commonly called the Yahwist tradition, and the name for God in this section of Genesis is Yahweh Elohim. Creation is a reality, but now it is in a specific locality, a garden, where God interacts with all that has been created and continues to be created, delineating work for Adam (the human being who is still genderless but lonely). Now the story is about how humans live, work, marry, have children, suffer, try to survive, experience loneliness and die. It speaks of culture / agriculture as the foundation of the society where the story originates, and of the relationship of humans to animals, both wild and domesticated – all very practical things. It examines and explains cultural details: why do men and women marry? Why do they wear clothes? Why are humans ashamed of being naked? Why is there pain in childbirth? Why is it so hard to find food and live off the land? Why are human beings lonely and why are men and women drawn to each other – so strongly that they will leave the bond of mother / child and cling to one another in an altogether different intensity of relationship? The story tackles philosophical questions, positing very primitive responses to issues such as: What is good and what is evil? Why do all things die? Why do men and women suffer? Why do we not live in Paradise and why do humans long for security, for knowledge, for something other than what is? Why do we feel so far from God, the Creator? Why do we do things that destroy the fabric of creation and change what has been the given reality? Why do we hide from one another? Why do we lie to one another? Why do we not stay in communication with God?

Genesis 2

Such is the story of heaven and earth when they were created.

When the Lord God made earth and heaven – when no shrub of the field was yet on earth and no grasses of the field had yet sprouted, because the Lord God had not sent rain upon the earth and there was no man to till the soil, but a flow would well up from the ground and water the whole surface of the earth – the Lord God formed man from the dust of the earth. He blew into his nostrils the breath of life, and man became a living being.

The Lord God planted a garden in Eden, in the east, and placed there the man whom He had formed. And from the ground the Lord God caused to grow every tree that was pleasing to the sight and good for food, with the tree of life in the middle of the garden, and the tree of the knowledge of good and bad.

(Genesis 2:4-9)

We begin with two very different and significant details. First, the name of God, which is the Tetragrammaton (YHVH), which believers are forbidden from speaking aloud, translated by Christians as Lord, and in Hebrew as Adonai, and in other groups of Jews as ha-Shem. Second, there is a reverse order of creation – now it is earth and heaven (the previous story was heaven and earth). And in contrast to the first story of creation in Genesis chapter 1, where there is a surplus of water, so excessive that it must be separated out and given boundaries, here there is too little water (an actual experience of life in Israel and many Middle Eastern countries to this day). Here, Adam is not made theoretically or verbally in the image of God, but out of the dust of the earth. The human being is born of water, dust, and made human, made whole and holy by the very breath of God that once hovered and blew over the chaos and the face of the deep. God draws near to the human being and breathes life, soul and humanity into the creature. In some traditions and stories, it is said that God kissed the newly created creatures.

Here God is a gardener, a farmer, a botanist, who keeps and tends trees, setting out and planting. It is here that God 'plants', places, puts the human being into the garden – this is our place. But it is still God that causes every tree and bush and blade of grass to grow, and human beings are to till the soil. The garden is gorgeous and plentiful, gracious in appearance and lush with fruit. In it, there are two specific trees: the Tree of Life in the heart of the garden and the Tree of the Knowledge of Good and Bad. The intimate detailed setting has been laid out.

Next comes the placing of the garden in a larger geographical setting – a biosphere, an ecological habitat. The description is very detailed, concentrating on rivers (the necessity of water for the garden), and now the places are named, an oral mapping of the terrain. As an aside, mention is made of ores/gold and jewels – resources very separate from anything that grows in a garden:

> A river issues from Eden to water the garden, and it then divides and becomes four branches. The name of the first is Pishon, the one that winds through the whole land of Havilah, where the gold is. (The gold of that land is good; bdellium is there, and lapis lazuli.) The name of the second river is Gihon, the one that winds through the whole land of Cush. The name of the third river is Tigris, the one that flows east of Asshur. And the fourth river is the Euphrates.
>
> (Genesis 2:10-14)

Where was Eden if there ever was an actual garden? The two major rivers mentioned – the Tigris and the Euphrates – are today found in Iraq, a country now polluted by war and the detritus of war, where raw sewage replaces clean water and the entire infrastructure has been deliberately and systematically destroyed by bombing.

Eden is described as lush, fertile, capable of growing food that is both nutritious to eat and delightful to see – it is a true garden, not just a farm. Adam is given the task of tilling the soil and caring for it; this is humankind's main work – to cultivate food and beauty of place where life produces more abundant life. This is the human being's home and place in the world. And now a relationship begins, a dialogue between Yahweh God and humankind:

> The Lord God took the man and placed him in the garden of Eden, to till it and tend it. And the Lord God commanded the man, saying, 'Of every tree of the garden you are free to eat; but as the tree of knowledge of good and bad, you must not eat of it, for as soon as you eat of it, you shall die.'
>
> The Lord God said, 'It is not good for man to be alone; I will make him a fitting helper for him.' And the Lord God formed out of the earth all the wild beasts and all the birds of the sky, and brought them all to the man to see what he would call them; and whatever the man called each living creature, that would be its name. And the man gave names to all the cattle and to the birds of the sky and to all the wild beasts; but for Adam no fitting helper was found.
> (Genesis 2:15-20)

Adam, the human being, has been created from the ground, formed of both earth and God's own spirit/breath. He shares an affinity with earth that is intimate and knowing. Adam lives in the biosphere and is its caretaker, entrusted with the work of ensuring its continued fertility and variety, as well as its physical beauty and wholeness. Here is the work that Adam was entrusted to do:

Till: v. tr. cultivate (land), plow, farm, work, dig, hoe, harrow.
Tend: v. 1. take care of; look after. 2. give attention to. 3. watch over, mind, minister to, protect. 4. attend to, see to, deal with, handle.

The verbs and definitions not only refer to actual physical labour but they describe attitudes and intentions that reveal a relationship to the land, to the produce, to the plants, trees and all that is involved in this work. Our understanding of our function in this world, on this earth, is now ever more crucial when we have so polluted the air and ground and water, to the point that much of the food we eat is poisoned and dangerous. Members of Presbyterian Churches USA interpreted this biblical charge through an ecological lens:

> ...'tilling' symbolises everything we humans do to draw sustenance from nature. It requires individuals to form communities of cooperation and to establish systematic arrangements (economies) for satisfying their needs. Tilling includes not only agriculture but mining and manufacturing and

exchanging, all of which depend necessarily on taking and using the stuff of God's creation.

'Keeping' the creation means tilling with care – maintaining the capacity of the creation to provide sustenance, for which tilling is done. This, we have come to understand, means making sure that the world of nature may flourish, with all its intricate, interacting systems upon which life depends.[1]

Yahweh God sees and observes that the human being is alone and that this situation is not good. And so, Yahweh God goes into creation mode again, making and bringing forth all kinds of wild beasts and birds, all formed, like Adam, out of the dust of the earth, in the hope of finding a fitting helper for the human – someone equal to him, like him, as human beings are like God. And Yahweh God also deigns to share the power of naming, and so taking responsibility for what you have named, with Adam.

They are working together in the garden, but Adam needs another to relate to – not as he relates to Yahweh God, but as human beings relate, both born of the dust/water of the ground and with the breath/spirit of God within them. Adam will name this one, who is given to him by God, created by God to be with him. In the ancient world, naming had no connotations of superiority or control or belonging – only of relationship and responsibility or of belonging with, such as a tribe or a clan or kin. The naming serves to assign a distinguishing characteristic or to single one out as separate from another. This is the reason for the need to find Adam a fitting helper that is the heart of the story.

Adam cannot live fully alone. The nature of how God has created human beings, like God, is to be in relation, to be in dialogue, to be with, to be in communion and to be one, while at the same time being separate and unique. It is part of the wonder and the diversity, the terror and the delight of being a human being. Yahweh God knows this and so creates a fitting helper who, like Adam, is formed out of the dust and water but also out of Adam's bones, specifically the ribs, bones that protect the heart. Out of Adam's rib, Yahweh God fashions a woman, created 'in the image and likeness of God':

> So the Lord God cast a deep sleep upon the man; and while he slept, He took one of his ribs and closed up the flesh at that spot. And the Lord God fashioned the rib that He had taken from the man into a woman; and He brought her to the man. Then the man said,
>
> 'This one at last
> Is bone of my bones

And flesh of my flesh.
This one shall be called Woman,
For from man was she taken.'

Hence a man leaves his father and mother and clings to his wife, so that they become one flesh.
(Genesis 2:21-24)

The process of life begetting life, and life evolving from life, ever expanding and at the same time diversifying and being more deeply interconnected with all else, continues. But this story makes the process and the pattern more intimate. Yahweh God is the initiator of all life, male and female, and is intimately involved in giving them to each other, to share and to live life more abundantly. Adam, once the word for all human beings, is now named as the first human. The name assigned to him is a reminder of what he is at his heart – of the earth itself. And the second human being, the first woman, is now named Issa (meaning woman), Adam's equal, who can fill up his void, his emptiness, his lack of a friend, an aide, a companion and helper. In English, the word 'human' is derived from the word *humus*, meaning ground or, more specifically, topsoil – reminding all human beings of our intimate connection with earth. What happens to earth, happens to us, children of the earth, formed from the flesh of the earth and the breath of Yahweh God.

The Iroquois Nation (from the northern New York state and the borders of Canada) describes man and woman this way:

For his bones, I take the birches; for his flesh, the salmon and the stag; the black bear's hide shall be his hair, and the good red clay his skin. The dark of deep waters shall shine in the shadow of his eyes. His private spirit shall be strong magic and great medicine. His nature shall be noble, fiery, heaven-bent, and proud. And in the book of the world, his name shall be written: Man.

For her bones I take the slim white clouds; for her flesh, the dove and the doe; the blackbird's gloss shall glitter in her hair, and sweet fruit ripen in her skin. The black tears of the pine tree shall be melted in her eyes. Her private spirit shall be great medicine and strong magic. Her nature will be yielding, unpredictable, resilient and bright. And in the book of the world, her name shall be written: Woman. (Jones, 1999, pp. 15–16)

The rabbis see Adam (all humans) as a creature alone and in need, and that aloneness is not good. They say that when Yahweh God brought all the species of animals before Adam, they were brought in pairs, thus making Adam aware of his disconnection to anything on earth and of his need and lack. He alone had no partner, no mate, no one like himself. With that realisation, they say, he immediately fell asleep! But God moved to intervene and create again. The rabbis' description of what God had in mind is arresting:

> In view of all this, man's aloneness is 'not good'; it lends itself to a misconception about the nature of man. What he requires is a 'fitting helper.' This arresting description (lit. a help against him) draws an equally arresting comment from Ramban: it was important to realise man as two matched creatures, rather than one androgynous being (even if he were capable of procreation), because 'God saw that it was good that his helpmate should stand in front of him [kenegdo, translated here as 'fitting,' has confrontational implications], so that he may see her, and separate from her, and unite with her, according to his will' (Ramban, 2:18). For Ramban, man as alone and autonomous is 'not good,' because he would live a static, unchanging, and unwilled life. Man needs to live face-to-face with the Other, dancing to the choreography of his own freedom. (Zornberg, 1995, p. 15)

Just as God the Creator is somehow 'diminished' in the process of calling forth creation, Adam is diminished (loses a rib) in the process of becoming aware of what it means to be a human being. In the process of creating with God, as co-creators with God, we are diminished. We always lose something of ourselves as we seek to create and share power, energy, life and imagination with others, with earth and with the universe. Somehow this losing, this diminishment, opens up the possibility of a more complex form of unity and inter-relatedness. In some mysterious fashion, we are created, fashioned bodily and spiritually, to save one another from death by loneliness. All human beings are given to one another for this work, and men and women are strengths for each other; when woman (Issa) is created, Adam now becomes man (Is).

In this story, Adam and Woman are created, not by word or the mouth of God, but by the hands of God touching and moulding, forming and fashioning them, and then breathing life into their nostrils (or kissing them). We are the 'work of the hands of God'. And there is no one made by the hands of God that is the same as any other – each is singularly alone in the image and likeness of God. This is the basis for respecting and honouring each individual, every man and woman of the world. God is partial to every creature, especially to those formed with God's own hands and held while God's own spirit and force of life was blown into them.

After the creation of Adam as now both Adam (Is) and Issa, man and woman, human beings together, the story ends as do many 'thus so' stories around the world: 'Hence, a man leaves his father and mother and clings to his wife, so that they become one flesh.' This is why there is marriage and startlingly different and more intense relationships than the enduring and necessary one between parents and child. The relationship that the human race, procreation and life continuing in the world is dependent upon is that of man and woman, of sexuality, pleasure and sustainability, and procreation. This, in this story, is part of the order of things, as they were experienced and as it should be at this point in time and creation. Many primitive cultures would describe why and how marriage is practised in much the same way:

> We love our daughters and sons the same. We bear the burden of both nine months, and there is no difference in the birth pangs. Sadly, our daughters must leave us to become part of another family. But then, our sons bring home someone else's daughters to carry on our lineage...[2]

In a sense, human beings need a place to stand, a place to be put, a place to belong on the earth, but just as importantly, perhaps more importantly, every person needs someone to fill the lack, the emptiness inside them. Humans are created to long for, to yearn for, to reach for, to know consciously that they are not completely alone, and this need for the other is not only or necessarily filled in marriage. It can be found there, but underneath and through it all, human beings long for the Other, Yahweh God, or whatever name we call the Holy that has made us and keeps us in existence. The following story reminds us of that in a forceful yet gentle way. A version of it, from Uganda, is found in *African Folktales*, edited by Charlotte and Wolf Leslau. I call it 'Mutima' (1963). This is the way I have heard it told.

In the beginning Kabezya-Mpungu (God) had created the heavens and the earth and just two human beings, a man and a woman. They had been given reason, thought and mind, but as of yet, they had no heart, Mutima. Kabezya-Mpungu had four children: the Sun, the Moon, the Dark and the Rain. He gathered his children together and told them that he was leaving. They wanted to know why. 'It is better,' he said, 'that man and woman no longer see me. It is hard to explain, but one day, they will know why I go. Meanwhile, I want you four to know that I'm leaving and I want to know what you plan on doing when I'm gone!'

And so each of the children answered their father in turn. The first to speak up was the elder brother, Rain. 'Oh, I can't wait. I will rain down waters, pouring them down upon the earth, wetting and soaking everything, until the watercourses run and there is water everywhere!' 'No! No! No! You can't do that,' Kabezya-Mpungu interjected. 'Look over there at those two, man and woman. Look at how small and fragile they are. They wouldn't know what to do if you rained all the time. They don't know how to breathe under water. They'd drown, or curse the mud and the earth they live on. No, you must learn restraint…try alternating with your sister, the Sun.'

Then Kabezya-Mpungu asked the elder sister, Sun, what she would do when he left. 'Oh,' she said, brightly and powerfully, 'I'm going to burn and warm and shine and bake everything, the ground, the plants, the trees, dry up the water and sometimes set fires with the heat.' 'Why would you do that, child?' Kabezya-Mpungu asked. 'Is that what you were created for? Haven't you learned yet to dance with the Rain and your other sister and brother? You must partner and take turns. Look at those two, so poor and weak. They need your warmth and your presence for light and food, but they will burn easily and die of thirst.'

Next was the Dark, the younger sister. Kabezya-Mpungu was almost afraid to put the question to her. 'What are you going to do when I'm gone?' 'I'm going to rule always and cover everything all the time.' Kabeyza-Mpungu was appalled. 'What? Have you not looked around at my earth and all that I've created – the fish, the birds, the tigers, the pumas, the big cats, the giraffes, the elephants and the lions, even the serpents and the snakes and small creatures that run? Have you even looked at the mountains and the valleys, the rivers and plains of grasses and herds? Even if you haven't looked at them and admired them, they all need to be able to see in order to live. You too have to learn the dance. Try dancing with your younger brother, the Moon. See how he waxes and wanes, disappears and reappears – take turns with each other. All that I have made need to see and live in the world, as well as rest and sleep and close their eyes.'

Kabezya-Mpungu then announced that it was time for him to go, adding, 'I may have stayed too long already'. And with that, he was gone. Soon after, Kabezya-Mpungu sent Mutima – heart – in his place, to earth. Mutima, the youngest of all the children, finally found his brothers and sisters, and was crying and sobbing. 'Where is Father?' he kept asking. They told him, 'Oh, he's gone. He has left already. He is coming back, but he didn't say when.' Mutima stopped crying, though he ached and longed for his father. Finally, he noticed man and woman. They looked so forlorn and lost, so alone and wretched. He pitied them and thought, 'They look like I feel. Perhaps I should go and stay in them until Father comes back. I'll be safe there while I wait.' He was small and he soon disappeared deep inside man and woman.

And so, until this day, man and woman feel they have heart. Mutima dwells within us all. Mutima has been with us for generations untold, seeking and longing for the face of the Father. Human beings, every man and woman, have this ache, this longing to see God. Mutima beats strong in them, like the drum amidst the dancing.

This story touches deeply upon the incompleteness and the depth of our relationship to the Creator. The story of Genesis 2 may add a tag on that, seeking to explain the ritual of marriage, of keeping the tribe together and recreating the world by procreation (which is never mentioned). The relationship of man and woman is one flesh, unity, harmony and equality that holds the other strong and fills up some of what we sense to be lacking in us. But our longings go so much deeper than any individual relationship, of marriage or friendship or companionship, even community. Integral to being made in the image and likeness of God is this longing for expression, for creating, for caring for and tending to what is created, for seeking to know this God ever more closely. It is part of our spiritual and biological gene structure.

So human beings dwell in Eden, or this was the dream, the hope and the promise of what could be: equality, work, bound to everything in creation, sharing custody of the earth and everything in the garden, mutuality, monogamy, a measure of completion. So the story goes. And then the images shatter and the dream fades and reality changes everything.

The Serpent and the Question

Adam and Eve dwell in the garden. It is only Adam who has received the prohibition against eating from the two trees in the centre of the garden – the Tree of Life and the Tree of the Knowledge of Good and Bad. Adam, it seems, has relayed the commandment to Eve, though there is an added phrase in the command: 'You shall not even touch it, lest you die.' This was not in the original. Who added it? Adam or Eve? Whoever did it, it is what gives the serpent an opening to debate with Eve and shatter her reasoning and make her doubt Yahweh God's words to Adam, and vicariously to her. This portion of the story is weighted with interpretations that are not in the text at all. Medieval theology and philosophy devised an entire theological system around sin and evil, women and men, sexuality, dominance and punishment, so much in fact that it is hard to read the account of the serpent and the tree and the woman and Adam with any balance.

We all know the story, at least the basic outline. The serpent is crafty and uses the words the woman gives him, after his question to her, to make her question and doubt God's word that she has heard through her husband. (They are in this together.) He baits her with three things: 1. that she won't die, but be like God, living eternally with no end; 2. that she will be like God and have knowledge of good and bad; and 3. now that she is really looking at the tree, that she might have access to it with impunity, that it is pleasant, good for eating and a delight to the eyes.

This story seeks to explain why many things happen in the world. It is important to remember that it is not an account of an actual event, and the characters in the story are not real people, but represent all people since the beginning of time making the type of choices that people make. So we should not get fixated on the individuals or, as in the story, seek to point the blame. Adam blames his wife, and the woman blames the serpent (which is closer to the reality at least). (Note: Whenever the serpent speaks to the woman it speaks in the plural form, thus to the man as well.) This is not the way life is supposed to be, or even why it is the way it is – it is but one telling from one tradition of how things got to be this way. While it has elements of the truth in it, it must be seen in light of the rest of the story, the Torah, the Scriptures and, for Christians, the Newer Testament and the person of Jesus Christ revealing God as Trinity – an intimate community, intimate and loving, of Father, Child and Spirit, that seeks unity and communion with all human beings.

The woman and Adam overstep a boundary, move beyond the limit placed upon them in the garden by Yahweh God. It has been referred to as a transgression (like trespassing) and as sin (which means missing the mark). Religious teachers have said that this is how chaos was reintroduced back into the world. On the other hand, religious teachers have also said that without the breaching of the boundaries and the taking of the fruit of the tree, there would be no world, no history, no humanity and life as we know it, as it has developed over the last tens of thousands of years. Humans, just as they long for another, also reach beyond, risk, break boundaries and push limits. The effect is exile from the garden (a fictitious place to describe life that is 'perfect'), which seeks to explain why there is pain, suffering and bad in the world now. Every time a boundary is crossed, there are consequences, and the story posits that this is why bad things happen in the world. Disobedience, not listening to the Creator, sets in motion change, awareness and knowledge of what is good or bad. But in all the stories of the world that deal with this reality, it is something that had to be done. Humans are made with freedom seeded deep inside them, and one must use that freedom for good or bad. One learns how to be more and more human by making choices through experiences, both good ones and bad ones. The first one that is labelled sin is murder/fratricide/violent killing of another. From that initial killing, violence escalates. The first human to commit sin – in the sense of a deliberate evil act that is in its essence destructive – is Cain, not the woman and the man. They just decide not to listen to the words of the Creator God and make a bad choice…and both learn the knowledge of the tree that they have eaten from freely.

Note the words of the Lord God after the choice has been made, the action taken:

Then the Lord God said to the serpent,
'Because you did this,
More cursed shall you be
Than all the cattle
And all the wild beasts:
On your belly shall you crawl
And dirt shall you eat
All the days of your life.
I will put enmity between you and the woman,
And between your offspring and hers;
They shall strike at your head,
And you shall strike at their heel.'
And to the woman He said,
'I will make most severe
Your pangs in childbearing;
In pain shall you bear children.
Yet your urge shall be for your husband,
And he shall rule over you.'
To Adam He said, 'Because you did as your wife said
And ate of the tree about which I commanded you, "You
Shall not eat of it,"
Cursed be the ground because of you;
By toil shall you eat of it
All the days of your life;
Thorns and thistles shall it sprout for you.
But your food shall be the grasses of the field;
By the sweat of your brow
Shall you get bread to eat,
Until you return to the ground –
For from it you were taken.
For dust you are,
And to dust you shall return.'

The man named his wife Eve, because she was the mother of all the living. And the Lord God made garments of skins for Adam and his wife, and clothed them.
    (Genesis 2:14-21)

It sounds brutal, harsh, vengeful, punishing. This is how Yahweh God deals with the first bad choice, when neither would have known that their actions would have consequences. Yahweh God knew they would take the fruit – that's why the two trees were planted in the centre of the garden! The man and the woman now know fear, shame, nakedness and a sense of disorientation, blame, lack of responsibility and a break in their own relationship, as well as a fracturing of their relationship with the Creator. The Creator speaks to them both for the first time and it is devastating. A corner has been turned in human consciousness and development and there is no going back – to unawareness, to ignorance, to innocence.

This story is trying to come up with a way to explain why things are the way they are, and it lays the blame on 'first man and first woman' and on a very demanding, angry and punishing God – the opposite of the God that has appeared and been revealed in the previous stories. This God tests and observes, and there are always consequences; in this case, terrible ones that are experienced by every human being in all time. It is important to remember that this story is not about the way things should be, but, rather sadly, about the way they are.

Both serpent and ground are cursed, but the humans, however heavy their punishment, are not cursed. It seems the snake had told only part of the truth: that they would know bad but not that acts have consequences. The interest in vv. 14-121 is etiological: why snakes do not have legs, why people fear snakes, why childbirth hurts, why there is sexual desire, why men dominate women, why work is burdensome, why people die.

It should be noted that these, especially male dominance, are the undesired realities of a sinfully disordered world. Our author is attempting to explain the mysterious realities of the world in which he (or she) lived. Why are there such improbable and undesirable realities as one gender dominating the other? For the author, it was evidence that the world is not the way it ought to be. And, one might add, it remains evidence that the world is not the way it ought to be. A sign of this dominance is the Man giving a name to the Woman, as he had earlier to the animals. Yet this act of domination is softened by the name given, hawwa, a feminine form of the word 'life'.

Having shown them the consequences of their choice, God acts to save them by making them clothes. The garment given them is special, however. A kuttonet is always worn by the one in authority, showing that, however diminished their standing, they still act with divine authority. (Cotter, 2003, pp. 35–6)

Simply put, the story answers some questions. Why is the world the way it is? It's the way it is because we choose to make it that way and we live in this world that we choose. Where does bad come from (and it will develop into evil with the murder of Abel)? It comes from our choices, our freedom, and every choice each of us makes, alone and with others, has consequences that we sometimes cannot know until we have made the choice.

One of the disastrous aspects of this story is that instead of looking at the situation and seeking to correct what is going on in the world (for at least the last three thousand years that the story has been around), human beings, especially men, have sought to keep the story as it is, continuing the evil and the consequences of the bad choices. What Adam did continues today – Eve (all women) is still blamed and dominated and forced to suffer the consequences of bad choices, such as murder, war, aggression and slavery.

Yet there have always been voices that have sought to correct this distortion. They have been clear in saying that it is Adam who is more culpable in the first choice for disobedience. Why? He lies. It is Adam who has heard the command from Yahweh God, and yet when he passes it on to The woman, he changes what was said – from, 'Of every tree of the garden you are free to eat, but as for the Tree of the Knowledge of Good and Bad, you must not eat of it; for as soon as you eat of it, you shall die' (Genesis 2:16), to, 'God said: "You shall not eat of it or touch it, lest you die."' The addition of 'touch it' makes it easier for the serpent just to touch it, and prove that piece of the statement wrong, and so put into question the rest of the statement as well – about dying. It was in that moment that the woman began to distrust the man. If what he had said to her about the tree was a lie, what else was not true? Why didn't he tell her the truth? (A long reflection on this is found in Natan's chapter in *Traditions*, Kugel, 1998, pp. 102–3.)

But there are many other ways to look at it. This is from Dorothee Solle (1993).

> In the biblical text, the words 'sin' and 'fall' do not appear, but 'expel' does occur. Expulsion is one phase of giving birth: the foetus is expelled from the mother's body where all that is necessary for life has been provided. It is after the expulsion that life begins – work, exertion, and sexuality. (Moyers, 1996, p. 43)

After the consequences have been stated, the reversal of what was in the beginning of the story begins with their expulsion from the garden.[3] This is the passage from what was or could have been (fictionalised/fantasy/hope) and what living in the world is actually like:

And the Lord God said, 'Now that the man has become like one of us, knowing good and bad, what if he should stretch out his hand and take also from the tree of life and eat, and live forever!' So the Lord God banished him from the garden of Eden, to till the soil from which he was taken. He drove the man out, and stationed east of the garden of Eden the cherubim and the fiery ever-turning sword, to guard the way to the tree of life.
(Genesis 3:22-24)

Human beings are in the world now, and they are mortal, and if you look around this is how it is…and this is as good a way to tell how it got this way as any other. The rabbis are quick to add that the story begins with an act of kindness – Yahweh God clothing the naked. (The Torah ends with God burying Moses.) The story doesn't say that we would be immortal, but it does set up the later teachings that the Torah is the Tree of Life, that Wisdom (personified as a woman, Proverbs 3:18) is the Tree of Life, and that all who reach for it and grasp it can know life in a way that is like the knowledge of God; 'the Torah gives life to those who practise it, in this world and in the world-to-come' (m.'Avot 6.7) This study of the Word of God, and listening to it (meaning to obey it), is the primary way to push back the chaos of the world, to renew creation and know once again the intimacy with God as it was in the beginning.

The texts are always open to interpretation and must always be bent towards life, towards hope, towards possibility and ever more humanness for people. One very creative way of looking at this story, and specifically at Eve and the fruit (traditionally a pomegranate), is found in Bill Moyers (1996). It's fascinating and opens a more positive take on human life in the world than the ones that still lag with us from the Middle Ages (which weren't called the Dark Ages for nothing!)

When Eve bit into the apple, she gave us the world as we know the world – beautiful, flawed, dangerous, full of being…Even the alienation from God we feel as a direct consequence of her Fall makes us beholden to her: the intense desire for God, never satisfied, arises from our separation from him. In our desire – this desire that makes us perfectly human – is contained our celebration and rejoicing. The mingling, melding, braiding of good and mischief in every human soul – the fusion of good and bad in intent and art – is what makes us recognisable (and delicious) to one another; without it – without the genetically transmitted knowledge of good and evil that Eve's act of radical curiosity sowed in our marrow – we should have no need of one another…of a one and perfect Other…Eve's legacy to us is the imperative to desire. (1996, p. 43)

The man named her Eve, usually translated as the 'mother of all the living', or a variant on the word 'life' itself. Perhaps her naming had more power than what we have hitherto known or appreciated. Eve gave birth to the world as we know it, the world that the poet Elizabeth Barrett Browning described as 'Earth is crammed with heaven. And every common bush afire with God. But only he who sees takes off his shoes...' Yahweh God expelled them from the garden, and since then every woman that gives birth expels the child she bears and has carried for nine months in her womb out into the world, so that they can learn how to be human, to mature as adults, and to know desire, longing, love and ecstasy, as well as suffering, labour, lies, hard choices, responsibility and eventually death. Perhaps the woman images the likeness of God giving birth to humans, expelling them from the garden. God made the world, the universe, not the garden, as the place for humans to stand and to belong and to plunge into, and to learn how to keep the chaos at bay, to create, to imagine and to take great pleasure in. And there can be no real pleasure for humans without pain and loss.

We need to stop going back to the garden and bemoaning and blaming others, especially women, for the evil and harm that is done in the world by all human beings, personally, in institutions, groups, communities, nations and religions, and in collusion with others. It's a story – not reality – and one of the marvels of stories that teach and pass on values and traditions is that you can change the endings, you can imagine new ways to become, you can dig into the stories (especially if you believe that they are inspired by the Spirit of God) to find answers of life, of hope, of blessing, of wild possibilities that God has been waiting for us to find. It is the belief among storytellers and religions that revelation both reveals and conceals – it conceals truth and meaning, insight and power, until its time has come. Indeed, the time has come to change some of this story radically, fundamentally, and make it creative and communal, and not so individualistic; to make it easier, for example, to give birth to children (as men have sought to make work easier), to rectify the imbalance of domination in the world of men and women, rich and poor, slave and free, among nations and races and religions. We must keep in mind and remember (re-member, put back together the way it could be, reassemble the pieces) that we are made in the image and likeness of the Creator God, and there are endless, wondrous, wild, imaginative and deliriously graceful, freeing ways to order the universe, and live in balance, harmony, with one world, one song, one psalm and so many verses, so many singers, dancers, drummers, scientists, believers, artisans, gardeners, peace-makers. It is time to learn to conjure mystery and seize matter and energy for wholeness and holiness. Our God is the God of life, everlasting life, freedom and risk (look at creation as the biggest risk of all!), and boundless, unfathomable love.

Cain/Abel and the Generations until Noah

The story of the murder of Abel by his brother again seeks to explain why there are such terrible things in the world as fratricide and why it is so hard and so painful for parents to raise their children. In fact, it is thought that the 'pain in childbirth' is better translated as the pain of bearing and bringing up children by both parents. And it brushes the question of why God chooses the youngest (or does not choose the firstborn, as many parents seem to favour their eldest son or daughter over the others). It also deals with the preference in all the Scriptures for shepherds over those who labour in the fields or mine ore.

The story contains some ethical imperatives as well. God is to be worshipped and acknowledged regularly with the first fruits of one's labour, no matter what it entails as its end product. The first of everything we work for belongs to God, not to us – this is the notion of sacrifice (offering), and it bears the first mention of the word 'sin'. It is God who utters the word first. Listen:

> And the Lord said to Cain,
> 'Why are you distressed,
> And why is your face fallen?
> Surely, if you do right,
> There is uplift.
> But if you do not do right
> Sin couches at the door;
> Its urge is toward you,
> Yet you can be its master.'
> (Genesis 4:6-7)

God now speaks in poem form! It is Cain himself who is addressed, not Abel, who is still alive, or his parents. Cain is being given another chance. He didn't choose wisely when he picked his offering to God, and now he can choose again. But he doesn't respond to God. He systematically sets up the murder of his brother by inviting him into a field. The first sin, the primeval evil, is fratricide, and all sin is somehow connected to fratricide (connecting us to each other and affecting each other horribly). Meaning and insight are always couched and hidden in the details that are repeated in story after story in the Scriptures; here, the small details of Cain luring Abel into a field will be echoed and repeated throughout all of the Scriptures – as so many are butchered, murdered and killed in fields. Cain kills his brother, and the word 'brother' is mentioned over and over again (seven times). Cain refuses to be in relationship with his own family, kin and another human being. He isolates himself – the ultimate individualism – not wanting, needing or connecting to another, so eliminating and putting the other, his perceived problem, out of existence. This is sin.

The story also gives the first response of God to sin, to murder, to those who would put others out of existence: they are not to be killed in revenge. One does not do to another what they have done, no matter how horrible and unbelievably inhuman. One is to act like God, who marks Cain out so that no one is to harm him. This is the first moral and ethical injuction: HARM NOT ONE ANOTHER, and this will grow into HARM NOT THE EARTH, for the two are intricately entwined and braided together. What we do to one another and to the earth reverberates and comes back to the other. Cain's punishment is in wandering: he has no place to stand, no place to belong. Cain leaves the presence of God, but God does not leave Cain. The option is always open to repent and to turn towards being human once again. What Cain does to Abel is countered by God with an act of mercy and the protection of life, even the lives of murderers. This is the original glimpse of Yahweh God in relation to all human beings. It is thought in many traditions of Judaism that this story was the original account of the first, primal sin and the cause for the expulsion from paradises (see Jewish Study Bible, p. 19).

What follows in the story is the accounting of Cain's marriage and long sets of genealogies, the listing of ancestors, where they lived and what they did for work and survival, and who gave birth to whom, from Adam and Eve's children down through the generations of their children and wives (it seems the practice of having many wives starts early) and how long they lived. Titbits are included. From Cain's line comes those who are skilled in metalwork and music; his name means 'smith'. Abel's name meant 'breath' – and he lived but a short breath of time. We hear of Lamech, about whom we know nothing except that he tells his wives that he has killed a young man in vengeance, just for annoying him. The intimation that violence, murder and brutality are spreading and escalating as the population of human beings in the world increases is inserted into the genealogies. Then Seth, meaning 'God has provided me with another offspring', is born, and Seth's son is called 'Enosh'. Enosh means 'man', and he is the grandchild of Adam and Eve. There are ten generations from Adam to Noah. The story continues, repeating that God created human beings in God's image and likeness and that the children who are born are also made in God's image and likeness.

From the beginning, procreation has huge implications theologically for the history of the Jewish people (and those from whom they are descended – not from Cain, whose lineage dies out after the flood, but from the child that was given after Abel's death, Seth). The story comes to Noah, who will be another Adam, this one righteous and obedient, and, through Noah, there will be another/newer covenant between Yahweh God and all human beings and all things that are created, and even earth itself, all bound as one.

Let's draw this chapter to a close with a story called 'Back to the Garden', which returns us to the garden and to Yahweh God's words to Adam – to all human beings:

> When God created Adam, he led him around the Garden of Eden and said to him: 'Behold my works! See how beautiful they are, how excellent! All that I have created, for your sake did I create it. See to it that you do not spoil and destroy MY world: for if you do, there will be no one to repair it after you.' (Ecclesiastes Rabbah 7:13)

These two creation stories and chapters of Genesis reveal that everything that God has created expresses something of God. Creation is the first book that God wrote for us. All things reveal God, even things we find distasteful or threatening in creation – even snakes! So to remind us of how, in the image of God, God makes all things 'good', we end this chapter with a poem that might help to restore and redeem all things, even snakes! I wrote this poem when I first moved to the desert and had to learn the wisdom of all things that frighten and yet speak of holiness and meaning as deeply as they may cause fear in us.

And to Restore and Redeem all things – even Snakes

I stumble upon Spirit's trace…a side-winder's* trail, spied in sand,
fills me with awe and down-right fear. I wonder how recent
that track is and what that sentence says…
It is a language unknown to me – snaketalk tho I've heard it spoken
a number of times before, always when I was alone, isolated
and hungry for sun's blessings and the ways of going apart
and silence, like sand, makes the tongue clearer, the sound
more intimate.
I crouch close, reading like one with poor eyesight,
thinking nearness will aid in my interpretation.
The pattern captures me and drags me in.
Such calligraphy, such warning, such sheer exquisite
dancing language.
For one leaping second I sense what it means and it sings
its way through me,
sending me deep down inside, to that place where only I
stand, or crouch
before the Great Spirit's glance – sideways usually but
for this instance

straight on, wrapping itself around my heart.
The Holy is a side-winder!*

Now we dwell outside the garden and all earth is ours.[4]

* A 'side-winder' is a rattler.

Notes

1. 'Restoring Creation for Ecology and Justice', a Report Adopted by the 202nd General Assembly (1990), Presbyterian Churh (USA), p. 7.
2. Keotiwali, villager in Nimkhera, India.
3. Stories from all over the world are based on how to get back what was lost, usually using three tests to get gifts that will allow the hero/heroine to do what is humanly impossible.
4. Published in *Marrow of Mystery: Selected Poems*, Megan McKenna, Rowman and Littlefield (also known as Sheed and Ward), 2003.

Chapter Three

Noah and the Ark

Three Crows – A Native American Tale

Once upon a time, there were three crows. They'd been together since they were born. They'd played together, grown up together, flew around the world together, found food together. They were inseparable. But as they got older, they tired more quickly, and surviving wasn't as easy as it had been before. They talked things over and decided that it was time for them to find a band of crows that they could live with – it was always easier to survive in a larger group. So off they went. They scouted around and found the group they thought was good – these crows always had food, they stuck together and their nesting places were high, away from predators and in great old trees. So the three of them presented themselves one morning to the crows when they were still all gathered together before leaving for their day's work and journeys.

'We want to join you,' they said. When the larger group of crows heard that, they lined up in the branches, with an old crow (the leader obviously) standing on a separate branch. 'Well,' he said, 'that depends.' 'On what?' the three asked. 'Well, you have to pass a test,' the old crow said. The three crows were stunned. A test! It had never occurred to them that they'd be given a test – they just thought they could go and slip into the group and that would be it. 'Yes,' said the old crow. 'We don't have a lot of time, so let's start right now. I will ask each of you the same question and you must each give a different answer.' He looked at the one who had asked if they could join the group and he put the question to him: 'For a crow, what is the most dangerous thing in the world?' The first crow was grateful – he'd have the simplest and best answer. He replied almost without thinking, 'The most dangerous thing for a crow is a human with a bow and arrow.' There were a number of caws. He was in.

The old crow turned to the next crow, the skinny one of the three, and asked him the same question: 'For a crow, what is the most dangerous thing?' The crow had been thinking of what his answer would be from the moment he'd heard the question the first time and he was a bit panicky – the other crow had given his answer! He breathed deeply and he found he had an answer. He said that the most dangerous thing for a crow is a human with a bow and arrow who has skill. There were a few caws but quiet too. 'What do you mean?' some asked, but the old crow smiled and said, 'Good answer.' Turning to the others, he said, 'What good is a bow and arrow if you don't have any skill with it? You're in.'

The old crow turned to the last crow, who was becoming increasingly pale, afraid he wouldn't get in. What in the world was he supposed to answer? The others had said the most obvious and he was left to fend for himself. He hopped from foot to foot on the branch and hadn't a clue what to say. All the other crows were quiet. The old crow asked the question for the third time: 'For a crow, what is the most dangerous thing in the world?' And there was silence. The crow was desperate, his mind running everywhere, and then, he couldn't believe it – he had his answer. He spoke with assurance, 'For a crow, the most dangerous thing in the world is a human with a bow and arrow with little or no skill.' Silence again. Not one caw in the bunch. The old crow looked at him curiously and after a moment said, 'What do you mean?' The crow answered, 'It's one thing for a human with a bow and arrow to have skill, but if you know he does, then he's pretty good at hitting his target, his prey, us! And so, if you watch him carefully, you can dodge his arrows, knowing they will aim for where you are standing. However, if a human has a bow and arrow and little or no skill, you're dead – you don't know where to fly to, or whether to stay put or drop off your branch. His arrow could go anywhere, and you could get hit even if you're good at evasion.' 'Hmmmm,' said the old crow. 'That's the best answer I've heard in a long, long time. You are very observant and wise for your age. You're in too!' And all the crows cawed and cawed.

But before they dispersed for the day, the old crow told them he had something to say. 'I've been your leader for a long time and I'm getting old. I came up with these tests not just to see what kind of crows would be joining our band, but to see if I could find someone to replace me. I've found him! You, my last young crow, you're our new leader. Now, I'm just an old crow!' And he went off crowing and cawing at the top of his lungs. (As told to me by Joe Bruchec, Abenaki, New York)

When I tell this story, people love it. Especially when I get to the third crow and ask them what they'd answer – putting everyone on the spot to see if they can name what is the most dangerous thing for the crows. Most people never expect the answer. After the story is told in the discussions, people love to play with the idea of which crow they are – one of the three, the old crow looking for another leader, or one of the bunch in the trees. They are especially interested in the way leadership is passed on in the group, and whether or not they'd actually let go of a position, and how they'd do it. I find it utterly amazing that it rarely if ever dawns on people that they're not crows, but they are in fact the most dangerous thing in the world for crows and for most of the creatures of earth and for the earth itself – human beings with weapons, but little or no skill, plus greed, the urge often to kill just for the sport and feel of it, or for the sense of power that it gives them. After this statement there is always silence, hopefully signalling reflection and mindfulness of the truth it contains and acknowledgement of how it applies in their lives, personally and among the groups and nations they belong to.

Now we come to Noah. It takes only six chapters, one of them a genealogy, to get to the end of the rope, so to speak. Men and women live long lives and it seems that those long lives are spent doing evil and learning every form of violence, killing, murder, sexual perversity and abomination – everything that makes human beings inhuman. God is witness to all that is done on the earth, to what those who were made in God's image are doing – and it is time to stop the evil and the killing.

Genesis 6

The Lord saw how great was man's wickedness on earth, and how every plan devised by his mind was nothing but evil all the time. And the Lord regretted that he had made man on earth, and His heart was saddened. The Lord said, 'I will blot out from the earth the men whom I created – men together with beasts, creeping things, and birds of the sky; for I regret that I made them.'

(Genesis 6:5-7)

To read it silently or aloud instils terror. God, saddened by the wickedness of humankind, decides to blot out from the earth all that was made on that sixth day of creation. (We are bound to the animals, birds and sea creatures so closely that our behaviour is linked to their destruction as well.) God is behaving very much like a human being, with feelings propelling him to action. God's emotions are strong, overpowering. God's heart regrets our existence and what we have come to. God goes into mourning: the image of God has died in humankind. What traces remain are slight. Those who do good or look upon creation as good are few. The evil that humankind does seeps into the earth and other creatures, like osmosis, affecting everything, infecting everything. The remedy is to blot out the evil, erase it and its effects. God regrets. Humankind was commanded to 'make the world' as God did, and all that God did was good. Now humankind does only what is evil.

Then the whole endeavour is averted with the next sentence: 'But Noah found favour with the Lord.' Noah's name is 'favour' spelled backwards! His name can also mean comfort/relief and rest. So it seems that one human being who is good, who is righteous, can remake the world, save the world from destruction. A Jewish saying puts it this way: 'When a righteous person comes into the world, goodness comes into the world.'

Maybe the story of Noah and the ark teaches us how to be righteous, revealing how God wants us to act on earth, in relation to all species and the earth itself, to be creators once again, doing good and making all things good. Noah is described as 'walking with God', unlike Cain, who leaves the presence of God and wanders on the earth, finding no place to stand, no place to be or to make good.

God talks to Noah, telling him the plan, but altering it because of Noah. God is very precise on what Noah is to do to preserve the creatures of the earth, and Noah is also told precisely what God intends to do to the earth to purify it, rid it of the filth and evil that has been its experience for so long.

Genesis 6:11-22

The earth became corrupt before God; the earth was filled with lawlessness. When God saw how corrupt the earth was, for all flesh had corrupted its ways on earth, God said to Noah, 'I have decided to put an end to all flesh, for the earth is filled with lawlessness because of them: I am about to destroy them with the earth. Make yourself an ark of gopher wood; make it an ark with compartments, and cover it inside and out with pitch. This is how you shall make it: the length of the ark shall be three cubits. Make an opening for daylight in the ark, and terminate it within a cubit of the top. Put the entrance to the ark in its side; make it with bottom, second and third decks.

For my part, I am about to bring the Flood – waters upon the earth – to destroy all flesh under the sky in which there is breath of life; everything on earth shall perish. But I will establish My covenant with you, and you shall enter the ark, with your sons, your wife, and your sons' wives. And of all that lives, of all flesh, you shall take two of each into the ark to keep alive with you; they shall be male and female. From birds of every kind, cattle of every kind, every kind of creeping thing on the earth, two of each shall come to you to stay alive. For your part, take of everything that is eaten and store it away, to serve as food for you and for them.'

Noah did so; just as God commanded him, so he did.

Noah obeys the command of God, as Adam had disobeyed. He obeys down to every single detail of what God orders. God, now, is a boat designer, with

Noah and his sons as the builders. The original creation and abundance of life has been lost through human choices. As humankind grows and increases, and moves throughout the earth, it leaves a heavy footprint, beginning with the blood it has shed that drains into the earth. With Cain, human beings begin to be isolated and out of touch with the earth, and instead of creating what is good, there is only thought for destruction, rapacity, greed, selfishness and violence. Agriculture, metalworking, 'smithing', the taking of ore/stones from the earth, leads to cities and the domination of the earth and of other human beings. Humans, as they proliferate on the earth, descend into destruction quickly. On a global scale, human beings are degrading the earth and one another. This is contrasted with the original creation process, which was rife with life. This was part of the goodness of everything.

The Ark

God's bias for life will be contained in an ark, to save the basic components for new generations. Instead of the world being ever created anew and life being profligate, humans are reversing the order of creation, turning it back towards chaos. In the present, all that the Creator set in motion is collapsing around us. Evil is swelling and is given birth to on earth – this is the knowledge of good and evil, but evil is in the ascendancy because of humans' choices. The rabbis say that the verb God uses to destroy the earth – *emheh*, meaning 'to blot out' – also means 'he is dust and I will bring water upon him to dissolve him!' The elements of the earth that we share will be used to undo us.

The boat that is constructed to save everything on earth, including Noah's family, is no ordinary boat, but an ark. The word is used only one other time in the Torah, to describe the basket that Moses' sister Myriam constructed to float Moses down the river so that he would be found by the Egyptian woman, who would take him in and raise him in Pharaoh's court. The ark has three floors and four sides. It is a prison in a sense, with the world that is corrupted and will be destroyed remaining outside and the world that will be saved and restored inside. So much of earth will be destroyed, but God's mercy will be part of the outcome, with a new covenant (the first time the word is used in Genesis) that will define God's new and ever-developing relationship with humankind. And so, with the completion of the ark, the command comes for Noah and all the animals to enter. There are many sevens in the description...in seven days' time the rain will come. Noah is to take seven pairs of clean animals and birds and two pairs of unclean birds and animals...and then it will rain for forty days.

'All the fountains of the great deep burst apart. And the floodgates of the sky broke open.' The waters are loosed from above and below – the undoing of creation in the original story. And Noah and his wife and sons and their wives are 'shut in' by God. For forty days and forty nights, the waters rise and everything perishes. The waters cover the mountains and the ark drifts on the waters. We are told, soberly and solemnly, that 'only Noah was left and those with him in the ark'. It is done.

The ark is a microcosm of the world, with all that is needed sealed inside it so that creation survives with the possibility of a future. God remains outside, to be present to and witness the end of all that has been made. The Flood is calculated with very precise time frames, 364 days, one year to the date of Noah's birthday and when they all enter the ark. Then the waters start to recede and, just as in the first creation, God 'caused a wind to blow across the earth, and the waters subsided. The fountains of the deep and the floodgates of the sky were stopped up, and the rain from the sky was held back; the waters then receded steadily from the earth'. The ark comes to rest on the mountains of Ararat. Then the other mountains appear as the waters keep going down. This turning point begins with the simple words: 'And God remembered Noah' and all that was in the ark with him (Genesis 8:1b). This God is both a God of justice and judgement and a God of mercy and remembering – of putting back together as it was in the beginning.

Creation will start to become again, cleansed, washed out, emptied of the evil that it had been accumulating for so many generations. Recreation is now part of the reconstruction and sustainability of the world. After forty days, Noah sends out the raven, which keeps flying back and forth until the waters have dried up. Then he sends out the dove, and it returns. He waits seven days and then sends out the dove, and again the dove returns. He waits yet another seven days, sends out the dove once more, and this time the dove does not come back. The waters no longer cover the earth. God summons Noah out of the ark and all is released, freed into the world again. Then God repeats the command, 'Be fertile and increase on earth.' (There is no repetition of the exhortation to rule or master.)

Noah's first act is to offer sacrifice, taking of every clean animal and clean bird and giving them as burnt offerings. The smell is pleasant to God – a pun on Noah's name – and the offerings are accepted. Then we are invited into the mind/heart of God to overhear and know something of how God thinks.

Genesis 8:21-22

The Lord smelled the pleasing odour, and the Lord said to Himself: 'Never again will I doom the earth because of man, since the devisings of man's mind are evil from his youth; nor will I ever again destroy every living being, as I have done.

So long as the earth endures,

Seedtime and harvest,

Cold and heat,
Summer and winter,
Day and night
Shall not cease.'

But God continues his wording of the covenant with warnings and blessings:

Genesis 9:1-11

God blessed Noah and his sons, and said to them, 'Be fertile and increase, and fill the earth. The fear and the dread of you shall be upon all beasts of the earth and upon all the birds of the sky – everything with which the earth is astir – and upon all the fish of the sea; they are given into your hand. Every creature that lives shall be yours to eat; as with the green grasses. I give you all these. You must not, however, eat flesh with its life-blood in it. But for your own life-blood I will require a reckoning: I will require it of every beast; of man, too, will I require a reckoning for human life, of every man for that of his fellow man!
Whoever sheds the blood of man,
By man shall his blood be shed;
For in His image
Did God make man.
Be fertile, then, and increase; abound on the earth and increase on it.'

And God said to Noah and to his sons with him, 'I now establish My covenant with you and your offspring to come, and with every living thing that is with you – birds, cattle, and every beast as well – all that have come out of the ark, every living thing on earth. I will maintain My covenant with you: never again shall all flesh be cut off by the waters of a flood, and never again shall there be a flood to destroy the earth.'

The covenant has two parts, the first regarding human beings, but it is very different to the way things were in the beginning. Now everything on the earth that was created with us on the sixth day lives in dread and fear of us, and of what we can and will do to them, beginning with eating them. There is one stipulation: not to eat flesh with its life-blood still in it. Humans may eat meat in the hope that they will not eat one another alive and that eating the flesh of animals, birds and fish will stem the violence and stop them from killing one another. The fact that humans are made in the image of God must be ingrained and honoured – and humans must respect one another because of this image of God at the heart of every person. There will be a reckoning for everything on earth, human beings and all created things, but especially for human beings and what they do to one another. The evil that began with Cain killing Abel, brother shedding the blood of brother, must be stopped, reckoned with – the image of God is not to be killed by human beings. This act is expressly forbidden by God. So the first moral and ethical imperative is the commandment: thou shalt not kill, for any reason, any other human being. If one offers sacrifice to God, then one must obey these commandments.

The second part of the covenant is God's side. This is the first of the four covenants: the others being with Abraham, Sinai and David. The covenant is made with human beings and every living creature on the earth and with the earth itself – it will be sustained and will never be destroyed by God, by water, again. Then a sign is given to Noah and his kin, but it is given to all human beings for all time.

Genesis 9:12-17

God further said, 'This is the sign that I set for the covenant between Me and you, and every living creature with you, for all ages to come. I have set My bow in the clouds, and it shall serve as a sign of the covenant between Me and the earth. When I bring clouds over the earth, and the bow appears in the clouds, I will remember My covenant between Me and you and every living creature among all flesh, so that the waters shall never again become a flood to destroy all flesh. When the bow is in the clouds, I will see it and remember the everlasting covenant between God and all living creatures, all flesh that is on earth. That,' God said to Noah, 'shall be the sign of the covenant that I have established between Me and all flesh that is on earth.'

It is new, different than before, but God is moving closer, in spite of the fact that humans move farther away. It is God's choice, God's decree and God's faithfulness that is put forth. The unspoken piece is that if there is destruction of the earth and all living creatures, it is humankind that will do it, and there will be a reckoning for all that we do. The sign is a bow – such as was fashioned by human beings, for destruction and killing. But the bow is bent backwards, away from the earth, linking heaven and earth, and it is made of light and energy and the colours of the earth, a 'rain-bow', made of water and air. Seeing the rainbow depends on where one stands. God will see and remember (from every point of view). Humans will see, depending on where they are standing, and they are to remember and take to heart God's word of faithfulness and life, and also to remember and take to heart the prohibitions against killing. This, now, is the God of life and the God of peace and the God that will not do violence or harm earth and all living flesh. Hopefully, the new covenant will help earth and all living creatures to rebound and once again begin the process of ever-more abundant life, and the choosing of goodness and violence will be curtailed and restrained. Now it is decreed: it is the first ruling in a court of law.

The Ark and Noah's Work

Noah does not say anything in the whole story! Noah just works, like God works in making creation, in planting a garden and putting Adam in it, and in ruling over all that has been made. The story is once again trying to image what it is that we are supposed to be doing in the world. It says that Noah was a righteous man. And it prompts the question: in what way was he righteous? Did Noah learn righteousness through obedience to God's commands to build the ark and to care for the animals, fish and birds, keeping them alive for the whole year? Is it this that God sees in Noah (seeing the past/present and future all at once)? Norman Wirzba (2000) writes about Noah becoming appreciative of creation once again by 'hands on' work – perhaps the pattern we must all relearn:

> According to Rabbinic tradition, the ark was a laboratory experience in which the lessons of attention and care for creation were to be learned. The miracle isn't simply that Noah built the ark when there were no signs of rain, but that he spent an entire year taking care of the animals. Some rabbis note that during the twelve months in the ark Noah was so busy with the animals that he did not even have time to sleep! Can we conceive, let alone appreciate, the wisdom of attention, sympathy, and nurture such care-taking would involve. *Noah emerged from the ark bearing all the concrete marks of a righteous one, as a sustainer of life, for as the midrash Tanhuma has it, the 'Righteous One' knows the needs of others, even the needs of animals.* (Original emphasis) (2000, pp. 28/29)

We must, like Noah, work at learning to appreciate, care for and sustain all species, and learn how their existence and presence is bound with our own on earth. In fact, they sustain and enrich our lives. The following Hawaiian creation story, 'Once the Birds were Invisible!', startles us with its insight – that even the birds know us and serve us and that their very existence is interwoven with us.

> Once upon a time the birds were invisible! People could hear them – their songs and twittering, their loud cries and caws, their shrieks and melodies – but they couldn't see them! And so they would often be afraid when they would hear them. Early in the morning, they would awake to the sounds of the birds singing, and they would think, 'the spirits are talking; the spirits are all around us', and they would be afraid. Whenever they were in the forests and on the edges of the volcanoes and standing on the shore or sitting in their canoes, they would hear them and shudder and look around, wondering what the spirits wanted. Sometimes a wing

would brush their head or the air would move as one darted swiftly by them, as though something were caressing their cheek, touching their skin, and they would shudder and look all around. This is the way it used to be.

Now Maui was the people's greatest warrior and leader and he knew the birds – he'd seen them! But it was their secret. He kept the knowledge of the birds hidden in order to protect them and to let them live in their wild freedom as it was meant from the beginning. Then one day the people were startled to see others coming across the waters toward the island in great long canoes. They were strong, pulling together in the waters. Where had they come from? What did they want? All the people stood on the beach and waited for the strangers to arrive. They met them with flowers, with food and with gourds for drinking.

But the newcomers did not want to be welcomed. They came to take the land and the people and all that the islands held as their own. They were there to do battle. Then Maui stepped forward and said, 'We will fight in the ancient ways. You choose your best warrior and we will choose ours, then we will have a debate.' It was agreed that whoever won the debate would take the islands and people and all its creatures for themselves. And so it was Maui that was chosen and he stood against their challenger and they began the debate.

The other was the guest, so he began first, saying, 'Our people are stronger than yours. We have come from afar across the waters to this place in our great canoes. We deserve to take your land and waters as our own.'

Maui stood his ground and spoke back, 'We are stronger because we do not seek out other islands and waters. We know our own and they know us. We have waters teeming with sharks and fish and great whales and pods of dolphins and great supplies of oysters and shrimp.'

The challenger said, 'On our home islands we have beauty that is unsurpassed, great tall palm trees laden with heavy coconuts and figs, dates and trees of breadfruit, more than enough for us to eat.'

And Maui said, 'Here on these islands our beauty is breathtaking. The flowers bloom all year round, high on the tops of the trees, hanging in great leis and garlands and vines, wet with morning dew and the tears of the night, every colour of the rainbow.'

Again the other challenged him, 'On our islands, we have deep, clear rivers of fresh water that run to the sea and lakes high up in the hills and that are as blue as the waters above.'

Maui smiled and said, 'We too have rivers of sweet water, but we have cascading waterfalls – look – running down the sides of the hills and volcanoes and hidden in the forests, throwing water and light into deep pools, casting rainbows even when there is no rain.'

Again the challenger spoke, 'On our islands we have great game, creatures to eat that run on the ground and make their homes inside the earth, meat that is tender and juicy. When we cook it, the smells are strong and they make us strong. That is how we could come here to your lands.'

Maui was quiet. This was something the people did not have. They had chickens and ducks and pigs, but nothing like what this man was talking about, if it was indeed so. The people were quiet and fearful, watching Maui to see what he would say next. If he didn't come up with something, they would lose everything, including their freedom, and the lands and waters that they so cherished and loved. Then Maui knew what he would say, but it was not his say alone. He must consult the others. He asked for some time to speak with the others, explaining that it was necessary for his next point in the debate. The people of both islands wondered what he meant. Whom would he speak with? But it was allowed.

So Maui summoned the birds, all of them, from the far reaches of the islands and across the waters, crying out to them. They came – hundreds, thousands, hundreds of thousands of them from every direction. The sound of their wings and their cries terrified all the people. They could hear them but they couldn't see them! They landed on the sand, on every bush and tree and on the tips of the grasses all around the people. And Maui explained to them that he had a great and awful request of them. He told them why the other people were here and that they had come to conquer them and take all the fish and flowers and land from them. They would live as slaves on their own islands. He needed to be able to boast of the birds to these people so that he could win the debate and save his own people. Would the birds be willing to show themselves and prove that this land was richer by far than others because of their presence? It was very, very silent for a moment and then the air was filled with cacophony, noises the people had heard in bits and pieces before, but never like this. They were terrified and clutched one another. And then there was silence again. Then one of the birds spoke and said, 'Yes, you may tell them about us and we will become visible. But do you know what it is that you are asking of us, Maui? In the beginning, when they see us and know that we exist, they will be amazed and wait for a glimpse of us. They will thrill to hear our songs and they will be delighted at our presence in their lives. But it will not be long before they will want us for themselves. They will not be content to find a feather or catch a glimpse of us as we brush near their faces. They will want all our feathers and they will want our songs and we will lose our freedom, for they will cage us. And then they will wonder if we are good to eat and our lives will be in the balance. This is a hard thing you ask of us. But we will do it to save the people. We have agreed together.'

Maui expressed his great thanks to them, bowing to them all, and then he turned to the people. 'There is nothing to be afraid of, but we have something that I know your people do not have, since you have not spoken of them. We have birds. They fly great distances; they live in the air. They are made of bones and beaks and feathers of every colour imaginable. They sing and twitter and talk. They caw and screech and make sweet music. They are all around us, though hardly anyone has ever seen them. So, we win, we have the best of the islands.'

But the others wanted the proof. And so Maui sang to the birds and with them, and they began to sing in response, and then the birds became visible before all the people! It was stunning, lovely, awesome and terrifying. Birds – tiny flitting flirts, soaring, gliding, wings extended, hovering, swooping. And the noise as each sang their individual song! Both peoples just stood there and saw for the first time the magnificence that had been all around them. Finally, the challenger bowed to his own people and to the Hawaiians and said, 'It is as you say. You have something that we never even imagined. This place is truly a land of enchantment and beauty unparalleled. You are free. We will return home and we hope that some of these creatures will follow us to our islands.' And there was great feasting at the skill and intelligence of Maui, who had saved the people once again.

Later that night, Maui went back to the place of the birds, along the edges between the sands and the green land, where the sweet waters meet the salt waters, where many of the birds were gathered. They looked at each other and Maui blessed them for saving the people that day, and thanked them for all that they had given up for human beings. For it would be true – human beings would not long look at them in awe and just delight in their existence. They would take them and eat them and want their feathers and songs, as they have wanted everything else that has been created. And one day, many of them would become extinct because of the human beings' mistreatment of them and lack of appreciation – these same human beings whose lives and freedom they had once saved at great price. Remember: once the birds were invisible!

Biodiversity and Extinction

It is a fact that thousands of years later, all the earth and its creatures are in mortal danger from us and have good reason to fear us. Have we learned anything since Noah?

> We have grown accustomed to thinking of ourselves as separate from creation, standing in a position of mastery. From a biblical, but also from an ecological, point of view this position cannot be sustained. As Genesis 2:7 makes plain, we are tied to the earth: since we are but a delicate mixture of soil and divine breath, a deluge of water can suffice to turn us to mud. We do not simply live on the earth, but from it and within it. The biblical assumption is that as we take care of the earth, we ourselves are taken care of; as we promote our well-being at the expense of the earth, we and the earth suffer. The ideology of mastery needs to be replaced by a much more humble understanding of ourselves, for there is more than a merely etymological connection between our humanity, the humus of the earth, and the call for humility.
>
> The forces of our political and economic life are all about the exploitation of the earth. Our consumption habits that feed on extractive production methods make a life of delight and nurture all but impossible. Where shall we begin? I don't think there is an easy answer to this question, but a clear beginning is to be found in the acknowledgement of how far we have strayed from the righteous path first walked by Noah. (Wirzba, 2000, p. 29)

The statistics with regard to the state of species of fish, birds, animals, plant life, even aquatic plants, are appalling. It is noted by the recent warnings of the United Nations concerning the global environment that 'an estimated 60 per cent of the ecosystems that support life on earth – fresh water, fisheries and the atmosphere – are quickly being degraded and depleted. They are not expected to last until 2050'.[1] It is estimated that there are thirty species lost every day in the world. That means more than ten thousand each year! In this century alone, more than half of all the known species will be gone. Originally, one of the remarkable characteristics of creation was incandescence and its birthing of new forms of life. 'God decreed that there be among the products of the earth a force which grows and bears seed so that the species should exist forever' (Nachmanides, commentary on the Torah, Genesis 1:11). We come on the scene, emerge last, and we are entrusted with all that has gone before, charged with imitating the Creator's sourcing of goodness into all things. But what we have managed to do to the earth in just the last fifty years is a horror.

Life on Earth is actually decreasing. In the past fifty years, for the first time in 100 million years outside an ice age, the actual amount of living material has gone down, by 4 per cent. God made all those fowl of the air and fish of the sea and great whales and beasts of the field and herbs and fruits and creeping things, and by taking his place and manipulating genes we've turned around and subdued every one of them...God set it up, we knocked it down. We are the winners. But why aren't we saying, 'This is good!'?[2]

Loss, diminution of creation, is a reality of life, and it is becoming every more endangered as extinction becomes a far-ranging fact. We have forgotten the ancient wisdom that all things were created for their own existence, not primarily for our use.

It wasn't simply for our use that He produced all things; instead, it was also for our benefit in the sense that we might see the overflowing abundance of His creatures and be overwhelmed at the Creator's power, and be in a position to know that all these things were produced by a certain wisdom and ineffable love...

...there is nothing that has been created without some reason even if human nature is incapable of knowing precisely the reason for them all. (Miller, 1997, p. 104)

We have presumed to find fault with God, and in our ignorance we have felt perfectly free to destroy what isn't immediately useful to us, and to mutate and genetically alter seeds, grasses, plants, fish, animals, putting in jeopardy whole biosystems of creation. Instead of diversity, we have opted for limited numbers of controlled species, chemically produced hybrids that are fast-growing, easy to harvest and artificially coloured and preserved. The produce of the earth and the beauty of the earth is seen as secondary to whatever can make a fast profit and be more easily manipulated and controlled, biologically and economically. We have forgotten that God loves diversity; as does the earth and all of creation – even human beings come in endlessly fascinating, myriad colours, shapes and forms. In spite of being schooled in basic biology, chemistry and agriculture, we forget the foundations of the interlocking interdependence of air/water, earth and sun to sustain life on the planet. And 'seeds' (zerah) are the essential ingredient, mentioned six times in the original creation story in just two verses: Genesis 1:11-12. Along with seeds are the grasses (aisev) and fruit trees (aitz peri), which are also seed-bearers. This was the description of our original diets and food for pleasure and necessity.

...In its emphasis on seeds, the Bible is offering a profound ecological message about the necessity of sustainability. The repeated phrase 'after its kind' underscores this message. From the perspective of survival and continuity, seeds are the most significant part of the plant. Seeds are the secret to a plant's ability to populate the earth and continue its family line in perpetuity. (Bernstein, 2005, p. 36)

There is a marvellous, relatively new story for children, but in reality for adults as well, called 'A Prayer for the Earth: The Story of Naamah, Noah's Wife', by Sandy Eisenberg Sasso (1996). It begins with the quote: 'Naamah was Noah's wife, and why was she called Naamah? Because her deeds were neimin (pleasing)' (Bere'shit Rabba 23:3). The story enchantingly adds to God's command to Noah, and there is a command to Naamah as well:

> Then God called out to Naamah, 'Walk across the land and gather the seeds of all the flowers and all the trees. Take two of every kind of living plant and bring each one onto the ark. They shall not be for food, but they shall be your garden, to tend and to keep. Work quickly. The rains begin tomorrow.
>
> Naamah tied an apron of many pockets around her waist and walked through all the earth's fields and gardens. Her legs grew strong, her feet were as the wings of birds, so she travelled far and never grew tired. Naamah did as God commanded. (1996, p. 8)

In her work, Naamah is aided by the wind, which shakes free cones and seeds from great redwoods and evergreen trees, and she bends to pick up acorns and gather seedlings, and finds 'every tree from acacia to ziziphus'. Then she goes through the fields, picking flowers and weeds and planting them in tiny pots, and collecting all the flowers 'from Amaryllis to the zinnia'. Next come the seeds, which she gathers in huge baskets, 'everything from apples to zucchini'. She sets up her place in the ark as Naamah's garden, with herbs, grasses, legumes, citruses, lilies, roses – not to be eaten. And during the forty days and nights, Noah and Naamah spend time in the garden, praying for the rains to stop and breathing in the beauty/the smell of all that it contains. When they are released from the ark, Naamah begins to scatter all her seeds to the winds, walking across the earth and letting all her prizes go. She plants and seeds and works hard at renewing the earth. And God is pleased with her, and pleased with Noah. The story ends with a blessing:

> God saw all that Naamah had planted and God said, 'Because of your great love for the earth, I will make you guardian of all living plants, and I will call

you Emzerah, Mother of Seed.' For a single moment, God gave Naamah's eyes the vision to see into the future and from one end of the earth to the other. She saw how the seeds were carried great distances, and how they landed safely on the soft ground. As God had promised, the dandelions were everywhere.

Naamah delighted in how the trees grew and spread umbrellas of shade over the earth. Flowers sprinkled yellow, peach and lilac over the fields.

Naamah was pleased to be surrounded by all the living plants, even the dandelions. She lay down in a grassy meadow and with each deep breath she smelled lilies, lavender and mint. A gentle wind blew through the grasses, and it sounded as if the meadow was whispering a prayer.

Naamah slept in the quiet of growing things.

God was pleased with Naamah's work. To this day whenever someone digs in the earth and plants a seed, God remembers the Mother of Seed and Naamah's garden continues to grow. (1996, pp. 31/32)

This children's story of Noah's wife and her 'ark', her greenhouse of seeds, flowers, trees, bushes, grasses and wild weeds, is essential to the recreation of the earth. Indigenous groups of the American southwest are seeking to imitate Naamah's endeavours by collecting ancient seeds stored in gourds and clay pots and nurturing their growth: varieties of corn, beans and squash – the 'three sisters', as they are called, which feed the people. Likewise, in South America and Africa, indigenous people are attempting to 'save' the seeds of their grasses: quinoa, maize, amaranth and other staples of potatoes and corn, so that they will be preserved for future generations.

It's time for some new arks to be built. It's time to reverse the process of 'subdue and dominate, rule and master' to: preserve and care for, treat with respect and tender regard, protect, sustain, encourage, aid and assist, nourish, cherish and appreciate.

The original meaning drawn from the biblical texts served to give hope and raise the spirits of a people and land decimated by war, misuse and ravage. Genesis 1:28 uses the Hebrew word *kabash* which sounds just like it is written – to put the kabash on something, to subdue and dominate, and in Aramaic the same word means to tread down, beat or make a path, again subdue. It has meant and been rigorously enforced as meaning conquer, enslave, waste and destroy. Often this was conveniently accepted and even relished because it seemingly gave credence to capitalist economic policies and encouraged individual, corporate and national greed, as well as aggression and the stealing of others' lands. But we *must read* these verbs in the context of the creation story, specifically so that we who are to 'master the world or to have dominion over it' do so in the image and likeness of the

Creator, the Sustainer of all life. For many Catholics and Christians, the notion of sin applies only to individuals, and is most severely expressed and committed in the areas of sex and personal failure. Could one be castigated for arguing that in official Church teaching and in popular practice, there would appear to be a huge lack of leadership regarding the concepts of communal responsibility, corporate accountability, systematic sin or systemic evil, with consequences that far outweigh individual misdeeds? The concept of sin that is mortal to the earth, to the environment and an affront against God is a radical idea that many in our churches resist strenuously, especially at leadership level. But it is surely a sin that cannot be ignored, for it impacts all creation down the succeeding, generations and is even more deadly than individual greed or murder.

In the Orthodox Church, one man has shed a beacon of light and become somewhat of a modern St Francis in his teaching and preaching about the environment and its religious imperatives. His title is All-Holiness, Ecumenical Patriarch Bartholomew, of Constantinople. He gave an address at an Environmental Symposium at the Santa Barbara Greek Orthodox Church in California, on 8 November 1997, entitled: 'To Commit a Crime against the Natural World is a Sin'. Here are some selections from that speech, which was startling and revelatory, and the response to a rich heritage of the East:

> ...People of all faith traditions praise the Divine, for they seek to understand their relationship to the cosmos. The entire universe participates in a celebration of life, which St Maximos the Confessor described as a 'cosmic liturgy'. We see this cosmic liturgy in the symbiosis of life's rich biological complexities. These complex relationships draw attention to themselves in humanity's self-conscious awareness of the cosmos. As human beings, created 'in the image and likeness of God' (Genesis 1:26), we are called to recognise this interdependence between our environment and ourselves. In the bread and wine of the Eucharist, as priests standing before the altar of the world, we offer the creation back to the Creator in relationship to Him and to each other.
>
> Indeed, in our liturgical life, we realise by anticipation the final state of the cosmos in the Kingdom of Heaven. We celebrate the beauty of creation, and consecrate the life of the world, returning it to God with thanks. We share the world in joy as a living mystical communion with the Divine. Thus it is that we offer the fullness of creation at the Eucharist, and receive it back as a blessing, as the living presence of God. (Tal, 2006, pp. 204–9)

The speech reads like a sermon, a preaching of the gospel of Creation, and how it is woven into the fabric of liturgy, life and ethics. He speaks of the need to impact adults and make them aware of their use and misuse of the resources of creation, of how their lifestyles and business, corporate and national choices will impact future generations. He speaks of a specific ascetic element in our responsibility towards God's creation. He says that this asceticism 'requires from us a voluntary restraint in order for us to live in harmony with our environment. Asceticism offers practical examples of conservation'. The first practice is to reduce consumption so that resources and the earth itself are left for the next generations, and to focus immediate attention on the peoples of the developing world as they struggle with environmental degradation, so that they might know, now, equality and a life that is beyond mere survival.

Next he says that it must be more than personal practice: it must investigate and confront public policies. No person, group, corporation or nation can work 'in arrogant supremacy' in the natural world, but the abundance of resources must be extended to include those most in need now. Asceticism must be seen as a communal responsibility and practice, as well as an attitude of mind and heart. Unrestrained and excessive consumption, avarice and greed, must have specific corrective practices and a vision of repentance that all embrace.

He specifically speaks of the necessity of approaching the issue of ecological damage and environmental waste as sin, and talks of how to deal with it pragmatically and religiously. His words should be the basis of a spirituality and theological teaching on sin, justice, reconciliation, repentance and restoration.

> If human beings treated one another's personal property the way they treat their environment, we would view that behaviour as antisocial. We would impose the judicial measures necessary to restore wrongly appropriated personal possessions. It is therefore appropriate for us to seek ethical legal recourse, where possible, in matters of ecological crimes.
>
> It follows that to commit a crime against the natural world is a sin. For humans to cause species to become extinct and to destroy the biological diversity of God's creation, for humans to degrade the integrity of earth by causing changes in its climate, by stripping the earth of its natural forests or destroying wetlands, for humans to injure other humans with disease, for humans to contaminate the earth's waters, its land, its air and its life with poisonous substances – are sins.
>
> In prayer, we ask for the forgiveness of sins committed both willingly and unwillingly. And it is certainly God's forgiveness which we must ask, for causing harm to his own creation.

Thus we begin the process of healing our worldly environment, which was blessed with beauty and created by God. Then we may also begin to participate responsibly, as persons making informed choices, both in the integrated whole of creation and within our own souls.

And he ends with the prayer:

...The Lord suffuses all of creation with His divine presence in one continuous legato from the substance of atoms to the Mind of God. Let us renew the harmony between heaven and earth and transfigure every detail, every particle of life. Let us love one another, and lovingly learn from one another, for the edification of God's people, for the sanctification of God's creation, and for the glorification of God's most holy Name. Amen. (2006, pp. 208–9).

Making Earth an Ark

It is time to undo what we have done, plant seeds of hope, learn genesis, protect what is endangered, stop extinction and make covenant once again with all that God has made, so that all peoples down to the seventh generation (for a start) may come to know and love the world that God has made and given to us as gift and revelation, as a place to stand upon and dwell with and live on. What follows is an ancient prayer of the church:

'The earth is the Lord's and the fullness thereof.' O God, enlarge within us the sense of fellowship with all living things, our brothers the animals to whom Thou hast given the earth as their home in common with us. We remember with shame that in the past we have exercised the high dominion of man with ruthless cruelty, so that the voice of the earth, which should have gone up to Thee in song, has been a groan of travail. May we realise that they live, not for us alone, but for themselves and for Thee, and that they love the sweetness of life.
        (Liturgy of St Basil)

We will end with a poem/prayer called 'Heart's Ease':

> A herb whose flowers and roots heal
> Chew the leaves, make tincture, tea.
> Ground up, roots pulverised –
> It is said to assuage sadness
> relieve depression
> break up the burden of sorrow.

How does it know how to do that?
Where does the hardness, the loss and lack of
the grieving ache go?
How to be heart's ease for the earth and its children?
Repair the world?
Bend the arc of one planet towards wholeness and justice?
Release peace into the very atmosphere, the soil and the waters?
Dissolve the yokes of bondage, horror, domination and violence?

We are in sore need of a breed of folks
with heart's ease growing wild everywhere
undaunted by climes and human invasions –
a spirituality of communion
eating and drinking and being heart's ease for earth and her children.[3]

Notes

1. From 'To Serve and Preserve,' an article by Ched Myers, quoting David Helton, which originally appeared in *Sojourners*, March 2004.
2. Ibid.
3. Megan McKenna, unpublished.

Chapter Four

Amos and Isaiah: The Prophets and the Land

The Ruling

Once upon a time, two men and their families came to a rabbi arguing heatedly over a piece of land that overlapped on to both of their properties. They both began by shouting and screaming at the rabbi and at each other: 'It's mine!' 'No, it's mine!' The rabbi waited a moment and let them yell. Eventually they realised he was waiting for them to stop, and so they did. The rabbi spoke to the first man, asking, 'What is your argument? Why do you say that the land belongs to you? Why should I rule in your favour?' The man pulled himself together and said, 'It has been in our family's possession for hundreds of years. We own it by right. It has been passed down to us from generation to generation. Rabbi, you yourself know what that means in the Jewish community!'

The rabbi nodded and then turned to the other man. 'And you,' he said, 'why do you say that I should rule in your favour? Why do you claim that the land is yours?' And the man pulled himself up to his full height and said, 'We have worked the land for years. They have let it lie fallow and not used it. They didn't even know it might be theirs until we started harvesting the crops, and the land was found to be rich and fertile. It has always been contested between our families, but we are the only ones to appreciate it and farm it and tend to it, as it was commanded in the Torah. So, it is ours by right!'

The rabbi stood silently and stroked his beard. Then he knelt down on the ground, put his ear to the earth and listened. He stayed in that position for an uncomfortably long time, while the two men and their families became more and more impatient. 'What are you doing?' they demanded of him. He looked up at them and said, 'I have heard both your sides of the argument and now I am listening to the earth's version of the truth of the situation.' Finally, the old rabbi dragged himself back up on to his feet. He stood silent a moment and then solemnly gave his ruling, 'This is my decision: the land has told me that it does not belong to either of you, or to anyone. It is you who belong to the earth. Remember that. Now both of you go home and listen to the land you stand on, which feeds you and gives you shelter.'

This ancient story, honoured within the Jewish community, reveals the power and importance of the land in Israel and in the Jewish religion. Land is not a mere thing, a commodity, something to be bought and sold. The people have a relationship with the land, a relationship that is mutual. When God covenants with the people, the land is an equal member of that covenant, and it must be treated with respect, and the law must be obeyed in relation to it. When that relationship is abused or forgotten, it is often an indicator that the people are no longer faithful to God's demands of the covenant and that the land and the poor of the land are suffering as a consequence. And with that development, the prophets are sent to rectify the injustice and reclaim the land for the poor and for God.

Perhaps the two strongest prophets in regard to issues of the land, the earth and its waters and resources, are Amos and Isaiah.

Amos

Amos is described as a shepherd of Tekoa and a dresser of Sycamore trees, taken from his flocks and his orchards to address the people with the Word of God. He appears out of nowhere in the reign of Jeroboam II in Israel, around 760 BCE. Both the kingdoms were enjoying a rare period of peace and prosperity, but the rise in economic security and material comfort was bought at a price, one that broke the covenant. It came at the price of its own people, the poor, the peasants, those who worked the land and lived from it. The people had been warned that they were never to replicate the treatment they had received in Egypt, with vast gaps between the rich and the poor, between the landed and the landless, those free and those enslaved by the powerful elites of society. But Israel was indeed imitating its neighbours and its task-masker of old, Egypt. Amos describes himself as 'taken' by God from his work to become a nabi-prophet and to speak on behalf of those who had everything taken from them by those in power: their land, their livelihood, their dignity, their hope and their possibility of a future. He was to speak on behalf of Yahweh God, who had had enough of this unlawful taking. Amos appears and speaks the Word to the Northern Kingdom. And the Word does not come quietly. Amos announces his presence and the glance of God upon the people with ferocious words.

He proclaimed:
The Lord roars from Zion,
Shouts aloud from Jerusalem;

And the pastures of the shepherds shall languish,
And the summit of Carmel shall wither.
>   (Amos 1:2)

Amos likens Yahweh to a roaring lion coming out of Jerusalem in search of his land and people, specifically Carmel. Carmel is a place in the mountainous, fertile region of the Northern Kingdom (around Haifa today), but in Hebrew the word also means farmland, an orchard and, especially, a vineyard. The first two chapters are oracles against the other nations surrounding Israel for the evils they have done – and Israel is well aware of the other nations' sins. The evils that are catalogued and denounced are important to note. Brutality and military excess, brutal carnage in battle and afterwards is held against Damascus/Aram. Philistia/Gaza is rebuked for its destruction of an entire people, whom it reduced to slavery. Tyre is held accountable for its kinship and covenant with Israel, but also for its practice of slavery. Edom (considered the descendants of Esau, Jacob's blood brother) is rebuked for holding on to the blood feud for so many generations. The Ammonites are described in horrific detail: 'They ripped open the pregnant women of Gilead in order to enlarge their own territory' (1:13). Moab desecrates the dead.

After building up the crowd into a self-righteous group raging against the sins of their neighbouring nations, Amos turns on Judah, 'the other kingdom', for 'having spurned the Teaching of the Lord and not observing His laws'. Last is Israel, not just the Northern Kingdom but also the people of Israel, the Lord's inheritance. Amos is detailed and specific in listing their crimes against God, the land and the poor:

> Because they have sold for silver
> Those whose cause was just,
> And the needy for a pair of sandals.
> [Ah,] you who trample the heads of the poor
> Into the dust of the ground,
> and make the humble walk a twisted course!
> Father and son go to the same girl,
> And thereby profane My holy name.
> They recline by every altar
> On garments taken in pledge,
> And drink in the House of their God
> Wine bought with fines they imposed.
>   (Amos 2:6-8)

Their crimes are social, in relation to one another; but worse, they are crimes against the powerless. They are oppressing their own people, beggaring them, and taking from them pledges, cloaks, fines, which they use themselves and use in worship of God! There are sexual and cultic sins, but what is emphasised is what they are doing to their own people. They are not God's people anymore – their practices make them like the others of the earth. The land and the poor of the land are insulted, used and disdained. How could this have happened to God's chosen people?

D.N. Premnath in his book, *Eighth Century Prophets: A Social Analysis* (2003), describes the process of how Israel came to be as her neighbouring nations. The ten steps in the process are crucial, not only for the past history of Israel, but for all the developing world. Poor and developing nations today find themselves in the same situations in relation to the rest of the first and second worlds, with their elites of the powerful, the wealthy and those with military control. Basically, he is answering the question: 'How do the poor become poor?'

1. The initial step moves the basis for the economy from the needs of the whole to the wants of the few.

2. This step is pushed along by the growth of urban centres. Initially there is protection for all, for the land, the crops. This degenerates into exploitation.

3. A militarisation cycle is set up, with the military connected to political power and siphoning off the socio-economic benefits, pumping them again into the military.

4. This step and the next bring the people of the land into the vicious and greedy circle of the powerful elites. Premnath calls these steps the 'extraction of excess' and the 'lifestyle of the upper class'. The farmer, the poor, would be taxed to support the lifestyle of the wealthy to strengthen the hold of the military.

5. Luxury abounds, and leisure, the 'unproductive use of time', is coupled with a disdain for physical work. The poor live to provide for the lifestyle of the rich.

6. With the next three steps, the people sink into poverty. If the weather held and the crops were good, the people would at least not starve. But at this point they are forced to plant speciality crops.

7. With these speciality crops, the staples of the food supply are grown minimally, and food supplies and daily sustenance drops.

8. Something untoward happens – extreme weather, drought, a bad crop – and the peasants/poor are forced into debt, and have to use their property as collateral, or even sell their children into slavery.

9. Their property is sold to creditors (part of the elites) and there is no recourse with judges (also in the upper class).

10. The poor continue to sink into poverty, debt and loss of land, while the rich continue to become richer and disdainful of the majority of the people.

Amos comes down on them hard with specifics: they take the poor person's garment in pledge (their covering and only shelter sometimes) and do not return it (Amos 2:8); they set the scales for cheating (Amos 8:5); and extort their goods and property, or outright rob them (Amos 3:10). They have forgotten that care for the poor and right use of the land is woven as a motif throughout every piece of the covenant since the giving of the Law:

> If, however, there is a needy person among you, one of your kinsmen in any of your settlements in the land that the Lord your God is giving to you, do not harden your heart and shut your hand against your needy kinsman. Rather, you must open your hand and lend him sufficient for whatever he needs…there will never cease to be needy ones in your land, which is why I command you: open your hand to the poor and needy kinsman in your land.
> (Deuteronomy 15:7, 8, 10)

Amos denounces the injustices in the land and then he announces the justice that is to come. He reminds them of how often God warned them, threatened them, and how ruin could so quickly come upon them; but they did not take heed in the past and they are not listening and obeying now. In one line, he describes them as 'turning justice into wormwood', which is bitter. 'Justice is supposed to be sweet, but they turn it bitter and by doing so they embitter the life of the poor' (notes of the *Jewish Study Bible*, p. 1185). Perhaps the most famous and oft-quoted line of Amos is this: 'But let justice well up like water, righteousness like an unfailing stream' (Amos 5:24). Yahweh wants the people, those in power, to imitate the power of the waters of the earth. But the people live their lives and are 'not concerned about the ruin of Joseph' (6:6b). They are too busy idling away their time, playing musical instruments and deciding what they will eat, drink and wear as they lie around on their couches and anoint themselves. It is a devastating picture of hedonism, materialism and insensitivity to the plight of the majority of the people in their land.

God sees that this is not good, and by God's word will come reversal:

> 'I will never forget any of their doings.'
> Shall not the earth shake for this
> And all that dwell on it mourn?
> Shall it not all rise like the Nile
> And surge and subside like the Nile of Egypt?
> And in that day declares my Lord God –
> I will make the sun set at noon,
> I will darken the earth on a sunny day.

...A time is coming – declares my Lord God – when I will send a famine upon the land; not a hunger for bread or a thirst for water, but for hearing the words of the Lord. Men shall wander from sea to sea, and from north to east to seek the word of the Lord, but they shall not find it.
(Amos 8:7b-9, 11-12)

The heavens and the earth itself will portend what is coming, the reversal of the prosperity and false peace and the injustice of rich and poor in God's land, among God's people. A solar eclipse will herald the day of the Lord, and a reversal of the natural order portends that this is already a reality among them, through their behaviour and disdain of their own people. Their worship of Yahweh is empty, the Torah is forgotten now and it will be again in the times to come. There will be an end to life as they have devised it through injustice and misusing the land and the poor. But God 'will not wholly wipe out the house of Jacob – declares the Lord' (9:8b). There will be a remnant that will come back, and hope will be instilled in the people and the land once again. The promise is laid out like the harvest in the fields:

A time is coming declares the Lord –
When the plowman shall meet the reaper,
And the treader of grapes
Him who holds the [bag of] seed;
When the mountains shall drip wine
And all the hills shall wave [with grain].

I will restore My people Israel.
They shall rebuild ruined cities and inhabit them;
They shall plant vineyards and drink their wine;
They shall till gardens and eat their fruits.
And I will plant them upon their soil,
Nevermore to be uprooted
From the soil I have given them
said the Lord your God.
(Amos 9:13-15)

Most exegetes believe that this last glowing portion of a time when the land gives back so much that harvest and seeding overlap one another, and 'nevermore' will they be uprooted, was written much later, after the destruction of the kingdoms of Israel, the exile to Babylon and the return of the remnant that will begin again. The Northern Kingdom was destroyed as prophesied in Amos 9:8 because they did not heed the words of the shepherd and the vine-dresser from Tekoa. But the description echoes much that will come later in the prophets' promises: a time of prosperity and peace that is truthful and shared by all.

Amos is the prophet of the poor and the land, and his words need to resound today in every nation where the world is divided into first, second, third and now fourth worlds because of inequality, greed, misuse and robbery of resources. Amos declares to one small nation that all the nations are held accountable by God for what they do, and judgement will be rendered on those who claim to belong to God, who has created and ordered the universe (4:13; 5:8; 9:6) and who set the stars in place and holds sway over the seas (5:8-9). This God of creation does not want empty worship that fulfills the rubrics, offers designer sacrifices and uses all the correct words, with ostentatious liturgy. What God wants is justice!

If God is the Creator of all the earth, and all the earth belongs to God, then all nations are accountable to God. We are all children of the same God, siblings in the same global family. In the words of Amos, we are bluntly told that God expects, even demands, that we treat one another without rivalry, but with *raachma* – brotherly and sisterly love, marked by pity and compassion for the needs of others. Care for the weak and the poor, especially those bound to the land, to the food chain and to the sustaining of the rest of the population, is of ultimate importance.

In an essay by Christoph Uehlinger entitled 'The Cry of the Earth? Biblical Perspectives on Ecology and Violence', the liberation theologian Leonardo Boff underlines the unique significance of the land for God and for the human race:

> The language of the Hebrew Bible knows more than twenty verbs for crying and groaning, moaning and lamenting. Although some of them occur only very infrequently, this is a clear indication of the significance of distress and lament in the First Testament. Israel's history as the people of Yahweh began with the cry of distress of exploited foreign workers (Exodus 2:23f; 3:7, 9; Deuteronomy 26:7). This confession – which is not a historical but a religious statement – is meant to give the history of Israel a special significance. In it the cry of the poor will not remain unheard: If a stranger, a widow or an orphan cries out to me, I will surely hear their cry (Exodus 22:20, 22). (Boff and Elizondo, 1995, p. 44)

This is the cry of the people and the cry of the earth as well. It is heard in Exodus, Amos, Isaiah, the Book of Job and throughout the Hebrew scriptures. In his time, Jesus will weep over the city of Jerusalem and try to tell the people that their beloved Temple and city will be crushed into the ground (Luke 20:43-44), as well as reminding his disciples that the blood of the prophets and martyrs cries out from the ground, from Abel to the present day (Matthew 23:34-36). The fate of the people, the poor and the prophets, is intimately tied to the land and to the Law, as well as to the gospel's pronouncement of the good news of God. Jesus' presence, bringing the kingdom of justice and peace, is felt and known first by the poor. This is one of the reasons why Jesus deliberately heals and frees, liberates those bound by sickness, slavery and destitution, on the Sabbath. This is true worship and obedience to the Law. This is the imitation of the God of the Exodus that must be the mark of all true followers.

Yet from Amos to the current era, 'the poor continue to be the most threatened beings in creation':

> Recent data suggest that total world profits are sacrificing the populations of Hiroshima and Nagasaki every day. Progress is immense, but deeply inhuman. Its focus is not human beings and peoples with their needs and preferences, but merchandise and the market to which everything has to be subject.
>
> In this context, the most threatened beings in creation are not the whales, but the poor, condemned to an early death. UN statistics indicate that fifteen million children die every year before finishing their fifth day of life, from hunger or the diseases associated with hunger. 150 million are undernourished and 800 million live permanently with hunger.[1]

While these statistics are more than fifteen years old, their validity is no less real today, when it is estimated that around twenty-five thousand people die each day from preventable starvation. Jesus was born into this world, in the bottom part of the social structure, in occupied territory, and he lived that way for his entire life, under the eye and the heel of Rome. It is equivalent to living in the West Bank of Palestine today, virtually living in a huge open-air prison, without sufficient access to clean water, food, medical help or work, let alone protection and a sense of daily well-being. And it is the same in so many parts of the world that are not developing but are being left behind, or exploited beyond recovery, by the wealthier nations in their globalising greed.

God is the last arbiter of justice, and God's demand to treat one another with integrity extends not alone to the poor but to our enemies also. We are not allowed to use excessive force, abuse or brutality, and certainly never under the spurious guise of 'spiritual' justice, using the name of the Creator to exact death and horror with others of the human family. All of us, believers and unbelievers alike, will be held accountable, according to Amos. Amos comes down hard on religious people who continue to worship without doing justice, and on those who destroy creation, the land and the poor, and still think they are practising believers. Three hundred years after Jesus, there is another preacher, Basil (330–379), who is a monk and the Bishop of Caesarea in Cappadocia and a doctor of the Church, who echoed Amos' words to the Christians of his day.

What will you answer the sovereign judge, you who cover your walls and do not cover the one who resembles you? You who decorate houses and don't even look at your brother who is in distress?...you who bury your gold and do not come to the aid of the oppressed?

Tell me, what belongs to you? From whom did you receive everything that you carry through this life?...Did you not come out of your mother's womb naked? And won't you also return to the earth naked? (Job 1:21) From whom did you get your present goods? If you answer: by chance, you are an ungodly person who refuses to know his creator and to thank his benefactor. If you agree that you got them from God, then tell me why you received them.

Is God unjust in sharing out unequally the goods that are necessary for life? Why do you have an abundance and that person there is destitute? Is it not solely so that one day you might receive the reward for your kindness and your disinterested management, while the poor person will attain the crown promised to patience?...The bread that you are keeping belongs to the person who is starving; the coat that you are concealing in your trunks belongs to the person who is naked...Thus, you are committing as many injustices as there are people whom you could help.[2]

POVERTY IS NOT INEVITABLE: POVERTY IS PLANNED. POVERTY IS THE BRUTAL REVELATION THAT THERE IS NO PITY IN THE LAND.

MITAKUYE OYASIN – all my relations, the greeting/blessing of the Lakota people. The blessing includes everyone who was ever born, or even unborn, in the universe, and everyone who will ever be born and every single creature and thing in the universe. It's an immense blessing uniting earth/sky and human beings and all things – MITAKUYE OYASIN. I greet you.

Amos is trying to teach the people that they are all connected, all related, but that realisation will be a long time coming to fruition. Many indigenous peoples know this mysterious Truth of the oneness of all things, so that all must be honoured and treated with respect. Oddly enough, religious people of many traditions – Judaism, Christianity, Islam, even Buddhism (except for the practice of the Bodhisattva, who gives up nirvana until all sentient beings are saved) – have been very slow to appropriate it and integrate it into the rest of their practice as believers. On the other hand, there have been individuals for whom this reality has always been the only reality and they have sought to express it to others. Adlai Stevenson, in his last speech as the United States ambassador to the United Nations in 1965, said:

> We travel together, passengers on a little space ship, dependent upon its vulnerable reserves of air and soil, all committed for our safety to its security and peace, preserved from annihilation only by the care, the work, and I will say the love we give to our fragile craft. We cannot maintain it half fortunate and half miserable, half confident, half despairing, half slave to the ancient enemies of mankind and half free in a liberation of resources undreamed of until this day. No craft, no crew can travel safely with such vast contradictions. On their resolution depends the survival of us all. (Tal, 2006, p. 168)

Amos has introduced the joint concepts of creation and redemption, and the prophet Isaiah will continue to interweave the realities of both for all, including humanity and the earth itself. But first there is a story to be told. There is an old tradition in Judaism and in Christianity that it is among the poor that you find the faithful of the earth and those who bear the secrets of wisdom – that the poor are somehow the privileged place of revelation and knowledge of God. The story told below from the indigenous Indians of Mexico – called 'The Harvest Birds' or, in Spanish, 'Los Pajaros De La Cosecha' (it is a bilingual book for children) – is a bit of that wisdom.

> Once upon a time, there was a poor man, Juan Zanate. That wasn't his real name, but that was what the people called him because there were always birds flying around him – zanate birds (black birds, like crows). He loved the birds and the land and the trees and dreamed of having land of his own. But when his father died and the land was divided, there was only enough for his two older brothers. So Juan worked for others and dreamed on. He tried to borrow land, but they mocked him – what would he know about farming?
>
> Juan was ashamed that he had no land and he would often sit under his favourite tree, thinking and dreaming. It was a tree full of zanate birds! In fact, he was there so often that one bird in particular came to rest on his shoulder whenever he sat there. Juan named him Grajo. Sometimes the bird would stay with him as he walked, sitting on his hat!
>
> One day, Juan decided to go to the elder of the town and ask him how he could get some land to farm for himself. As he walked towards the town, the birds whirled around his head for the first part of his journey, but they

stood on fence rails and in the trees when he came near to the town and the people. Juan eventually found the old man, who greeted him with a smile and said, 'Hmmmmm, you've been sitting under your tree again.' Juan was taken aback – how could he know that? But the old man just laughed and said, 'As you get old, Juan, you learn many things by observation and silence – and the birds have left their mark on your hat!' Juan poured out his heart, 'How can I prove to you and the others that I can farm? Please, will you lend me a piece of land that you're not using and I will show you that I am good with the land.' The old man took pity on him and said, 'I will help you and lend you some land, but if you fail, then you must work for me for free for as many days as you have worked the land for yourself.' Juan thought about that, but he was sure that he could farm, and so he agreed to the terms.

He was overjoyed – he had his own piece of land to work. He ran around telling everyone that he now had his own land. Of course, they mocked him, saying, 'You're so stupid, nothing will grow on your land; better work here for us and forget your dreams.' But Juan would not be put off. He immediately went to work on preparing his land for seeding. The plot of land was small and there wouldn't be much of a harvest, but Juan decided that didn't matter. He thought to himself, 'Ah, my head is small, but it's big enough to hold many, many dreams.' As he worked, the zanate birds would fly around him, singing and encouraging him. Eventually, the land was ready, but he had no seeds, and no money to buy them. So he went to the store and asked for seeds in exchange for work. He spent many hours cleaning the store and fixing up the seeds and corn, beans and squash to be displayed, and then he was allowed to choose seeds for his own planting.

The birds flew all around him as he planted, but they were his friends and he saved some seeds for them, knowing from experience that they too were hungry and, if he fed them, they wouldn't steal his seeds before they had a chance to grow. Grajo sat on his shoulder and Juan could swear he told him what to do, how deep to plant, how much space to put in between and to go slow. He worked slowly and patiently each day, surrounded by the birds. He prayed for rain, and sometimes carried water to his plants. But as the plants grew, so too did the weeds. He spent hours pulling them up, to give his plants breathing space. He thought he heard the birds telling him not to throw away the weeds, so he planted them along the edge of his small field. When the other farmers heard about this, they laughed at him again.

Then the harvest time came. The other farmers waited to see what Juan would bring in – if anything. They were stunned when they saw Juan's crops – his ears of corn were ripe, large and sweet white, his squashes were big and colourful, and his beans were long and of so many varieties. How did so much come from that little piece of land he had borrowed? They had to admit: Juan knew how to farm; he knew the land. When they asked him how he did it, Juan smiled and said, 'It was the birds who taught me. I was very quiet and I listened and I observed them. I've been learning the language of the land!' Suddenly everyone wanted Juan to work with them in their fields. But the old man was there too and he said, 'No, I'm giving Juan the land that he has worked. It is his now.'

The harvest reaped plenty and Juan bought many things he'd never had before, but needed, along with seed for planting, a knife to whittle, a new digging stick and extra grain/seeds for his companions and friends, the birds. As the old man walked back with him to his field, he asked him, 'How did you do it? How did you learn?' Juan was proud to tell him, as his friends the zanate birds flew around him, landing on his shoulders and on his hat: 'It was the birds who taught me, and this is what they said: "All plants are like brothers and sisters. If you separate them, they become sad and won't grow. But if you respect them and leave them together, they will grow happily and be content." They taught me that the three sisters – corn, beans and squash – grow better together, as each needs something that the other has already, so I planted them together, not separately. I replanted all the weeds around my field to protect it from hard rains and hail and the waters and rocks coming down from the mountains, so that my soil would not erode and wash away. And I fed my friends the birds so that they wouldn't eat my seeds and destroy my harvest. Now I can't wait to plant again and see what else they have to teach me about the land. Come, let us eat. We will rest under my tree and share our feast with my friend Grajo and his friends – I'll introduce you all to one another.'[3]

Isaiah

Isaiah sings! His words stream forth at times like water in the desert. His allusions and images are rife with weather, with observations of the desert, the forest, the mountain, the valleys. Isaiah uses all of creation to speak of the Creator, who seeks to reveal promise and hope for the future. He even uses metaphors, borrowed from the daily wonders of creation, to speak of God's Word:

> As the heavens are high above the earth,
> So are My ways high above your ways
> And My plans above your plans.
> For as the rain or the snow drops from heaven
> And returns not there,
> But soaks the earth
> And makes it bring forth vegetation,
> Yielding seed for sowing and bread for eating,

So is the word that issues from My mouth:
It does not come back to Me unfulfilled,
But performs what I purpose,
Achieves what I sent it to do.
Yes, you shall leave in joy and be led home
Secure.
Before you, mount and hill shall shout aloud,
And all the trees of the field shall clap their hands.
Instead of the brier, a cypress shall rise;
Instead of the nettle, a myrtle shall rise.
These shall stand as a testimony to the Lord,
As an everlasting sign that shall not perish.
          (Isaiah 55:6-13)

This portion of Isaiah is towards the end of what is referred to as Deutero-Isaiah or Second Isaiah, chapters 40–55, which weaves together the remembrance of the God of creation and the God of the Exodus and how that God is present and working in history, now among the people, in Israel, in Babylon, in exile and in the whole of the world.

There are five passages in Isaiah that are often referred to as Isaiah's creation stories: Isaiah 40:12-31; 41:1-5; 41:17-20; 42:5-9; 43:1-8.

Isaiah 40:12-31

This is the section of Isaiah that famously begins: 'Comfort, oh comfort My people.' We hear it read during the Advent season and in Lent, releasing the people from their mourning and telling them to turn and catch the presence of the Lord coming towards them, and that 'all flesh, as one, shall behold – The presence of the Lord will appear' (40:5). These prophecies of the beginning of Second Isaiah were written for the exiles, still in Babylon, before the Persian emperor Cyrus announces the decree that they will be allowed to go back home to Israel, to Zion. The people are reassured with a description of their God, the God who created everything. No other gods have any power in relation to the God of all creation. Surprisingly, rather than their God coming as a mighty conqueror, which they have all too vivid recollections of in their immediate past experiences, their God comes as a shepherd. This is the paradoxical God who will set them free and give them a life on their land again.

Behold your God!
Behold, the Lord God comes in might,
…Like a shepherd He pastures His flock:
He gathers the lambs in His arms

And carries them in His bosom;
Gently He drives the mother sheep.

Who measured the waters with the hollow of His hand,
And gauged the skies with a span,
And meted earth's dust with a measure,
And weighted the mountains on a scale
And the hills with a balance?
Who has plumbed the mind of the Lord,
What man could tell Him His plan?
Whom did He consult, and who taught Him,
Guided Him in knowledge
And showed Him the path of wisdom?

The nations are but a drop in the bucket,
Reckoned as dust on a balance;
The very coastlands He lifts like motes.
Lebanon is not fuel enough,
Nor its beasts enough for sacrifice.
All nations are as naught in His sight;
He accounts them as less than nothing.

To whom, then, can you liken God,
What form compare to Him?
(Isaiah 40:9c, 10a; 11-18)

This is God! There is no other who is the Creator. There is no God like the one God! This God of Israel is incomparable! This God has made all things and preserves them. This God will act on their behalf, and no one, no nation, will be able to stand against the decision to lead the people back home, and set them free. In Yahweh God, the God of Creation and the God of the Exodus, the God of freedom and hope are one. God protects them and is with them – in exile, in Babylon, in defeat, in their unfaithfulness, when they worship in truth and when they remember the covenant that was made with them.

God's wisdom and knowledge is nothing at all like the wisdom of the nations and their petty human-made gods. Their actions in history and the rise and fall of their plans and empires are all short-lived and empty in the face of the enormity and never-ending mysteries of creation. Yahweh God is not only the God of creation, but the God of history and of all nations, whether they know it or not, and all history will serve the God of creation.

This will be attested to by the fact that a pagan, the Persian ruler Cyrus, will be inspired to set the prisoners in exile free and send them home to rebuild their lives and worship their God. In Isaiah 41:1-5, Yahweh God summons the nations, the coastlands, to appear before a court of law, and declares that it is Yahweh God who has roused 'a victor from the East, [and] summoned him to His service'. It was God who delivered the other nations into God's power, so that Cyrus would serve God in letting his people go home. God has called the people to God, chosen them and not rejected them, and once again they will see what their God does for them. God the Creator continually cares for the universe and all of creation, and continually cares for the people in their distress and needs. God calls on the people to witness to God's words and follow in God's deeds:

> The poor and the needy
> Seek water, and there is none;
> Their tongue is parched with thirst.
> I the Lord will respond to them.
> I, the God of Israel, will not forsake them.
> I will open up streams on the bare hills
> And fountains amid the valleys;
> I will turn the desert into ponds,
> The arid land into springs of water.
> I will plant cedars in the wilderness,
> Acacias and myrtles and oleasters;
> I will set cypresses in the desert,
> Box trees and elms as well –
> That men may see and know,
> Consider and comprehend
> That the Lord's hand has done this,
> That the Holy One of Israel has wrought it.
>   (Isaiah 41:17-20)

There are allusions to the Exodus and how God once brought them out of Egypt, through the desert, feeding them and providing them with water in the wilderness. God will once again provide for the people, leading them now out of exile, if only they will learn to trust in and rely on God and not resort in despair to making idols out of wood and stone with their own hands. Those gods simply don't exist. The true God, however, the only God, is always creating. The one true God will make the desert a place to live in and order the waters to move and to bring forth life, and the earth will respond with trees that grow in arid land. The original abundance and profligate life will return.

Isaiah 42

This song of Isaiah is called the Servant Song, describing the servant whom God has chosen, in whom God takes great delight. It is debated whether this refers to Israel itself, to the Messiah to come, to Jesus the servant of God, or to all those called in baptism to be the singing, suffering servants of God, faithful to living so as to give delight to God and to teaching the truth of how to be human to all the nations. The singular marks of this servant are gentleness and tender regard for all that is, especially those bruised, broken, struggling and without a voice in the world. This is God's speech. It is meant to strengthen and encourage Israel to remember who their God is and to show obedience.

Thus said God the Lord,
Who created the heavens and stretched them out,
Who spread out heaven and earth and what it brings forth,
Who gave breath to the people upon it
And life to those who walk thereon:
I the Lord, in My grace, have summoned you,
And I have grasped you by the hand.
I created you, and appointed you
A covenant people, a light of nations –
Opening eyes deprived of light,
Rescuing prisoners from confinement,
From the dungeon those who sit in darkness.
I am the Lord, that is My name;
I will not yield My glory to another,
Nor My renown to idols.
See, the things once predicted have come,
And now I foretell new things,
Announce to you ere they sprout up.
Sing to the Lord a new song,
His praise from the ends of the earth –
You who sail the sea and you creatures in it,
You coastlands and their inhabitants.
(Isaiah 42:3-10)

The servant of God, God's people, should not act like the other gods made of silver, gold and bronze, which are heartless, without pity, useless and unresponsive to those in need. Israel must act like the true God. If Israel obeys and returns to the ways that God is teaching, then nations, all peoples, will learn of the truth from them. They exist as a people, as God's own chosen ones, by God's grace, not by their own power. They will thrive, like the fecundity of the land and water in desert places, if only they will imitate the Creator who has made them, sustains them, and to whom they belong. They will be light to the nations – like the light of that first day, hidden for so long, but coming into the world in the Word of God, in the Torah, in the Messiah to come, in the people who reflect this light of God in their actions and worship.

All the references to 'I' in God's speech reveal what we are to imitate. God expects us to be like the hovering servant, seeking to keep the slightest bit of life in existence and to breathe life into those who are nearly dead, sharing our own life with those most in need of it. This is the tradition of other religions as well, as reflected in this prayer from India:

> May I become at all times, both now and forever
> A protector of those without protection
> A guide for those who have lost their way
> A ship for those with oceans to cross
> A bridge for those with rivers to cross
> A sanctuary for those in danger
> A lamp for those without light
> A place of refuge for those who lack shelter
> And a servant to all in need.
> For as long as space endures,
> And for as long as living beings remain,
> Until then may I, too, abide
> To dispel the misery of the world.[4]

Isaiah 43:1-8

The last piece from Second Isaiah is sometimes called an oracle of salvation and is meant to give comfort and hope to those still in exile. It uses the verbs from the creation stories in Genesis 1 and 2 and refers back to the Exodus account, drawing together the God of Creation and the God of Freedom and Liberation. The people heard many negative, terrifying prophecies in the past, and they came true – and now they hear positive, life-giving prophecies, and these, too, will come true. The people, the land and all creation belong to God, and though the people, and vicariously the land and its inhabitants, suffer, God stays with them, and one of the works of God that we are to imitate is to ingather from all the ends of the world; to gather the lost and exiled, the ones who feel abandoned: refugees, migrants, those unwelcome and scattered on earth. It is horrifying to note that, even today, more than one-third of the world's population is wandering, without a home, status or dwelling place, caught on borders, many in deserts unfit for human habitation. But here is what God is going to do, in spite of what history attempts to undo:

Fear not, for I will redeem you;
I have singled you out by name,
You are Mine.
When you pass through water,
I will be with you;
Through streams,
They shall not overwhelm you;
When you walk through fire,
You shall not be scorched;
Through flame,
It shall not burn you.
For I the Lord am your God,
The Holy One of Israel, your Saviour.
I give Egypt as a ransom for you,
Ethiopia and Saba in exchange for you.
Because you are precious to Me,
And honoured, and I love you,
I give men in exchange for you
And peoples in your stead.

Fear not, for I am with you:
I will bring your folk from the East,
Will gather you out of the West;
I will say to the North, 'Give back!'
And to the South, 'Do not withhold!
Bring My sons from afar,
And My daughters from the end of the earth –
All who are linked to my name,
Whom I have created,
Formed, and made for My glory –
Setting free that people,
Blind though it has eyes
And deaf though it has ears.'
                    (Isaiah 43:1-8)

This is the hope of Israel, but with Jesus it is the hope of all the earth. This universality, this communion and oneness of all living things and the earth, is a hope for many in the human family. It is found in those who don't believe in a particular religion and in those scattered throughout the East and the West. This is the way others speak their hope today:

Great ideas, it has been said, come into the world as gently as doves. Perhaps then, if we listen attentively, we shall hear amid the uproar of empires and nations, a faint flutter of wings, a gentle stirring of life and hope. Some will say that this hope lies in a nation; others in a person. I believe rather that it is awakened, revived, nourished by millions of solitary individuals whose deeds and works every day negate frontiers and the crudest implications of history. As a result, there shines forth fleetingly the ever-threatened truth that each and every person, on the foundation of his or her own sufferings and joys, builds for all.[5]

The Art of Peace functions everywhere on earth, in realms ranging from the vastness of space down to the tiniest plants and animals. The life force is all-pervasive and its strength boundless. The Art of Peace allows us to perceive and tap into that tremendous reserve of universal energy.[6]

In this last quote, the word 'peace' surfaces. It means wholeness, holiness, balance and harmony, at-one-ness, communion. These passages of Second Isaiah were directed towards a people broken and bruised, long in exile and longing for home. Now these passages belong to all the world, its peoples and geographies – all need this life, this hope, this encouragement. Peoples of all faiths must begin to practise and live as servants who bring delight, life and communion to all, with dignity, respect and freedom – this is the divine care of Yahweh God that we are called to imitate as the only truth, the only wisdom. In the early days of the church, Ephrem of Syria preached this short sermon about living with the heart of our God:

An elder was once asked, 'What is a compassionate heart?' He replied, 'It is a heart on fire for the whole of creation, for humanity, for the birds, for the animals, for demons and for all that exists. At the recollection and the sight of them such a person's eyes overflow with tears owing to the vehemence of the compassion which grips his [or her] heart; as a result of his [or her] deep mercy his [or her] heart shrinks and cannot bear to hear or look on any injury or the slightest suffering of anything in creation.[7]

It has been thousands of years, but the story continues to be told and a people continue to hear of the wonder of their God's compassion for them. It still needs to be told over and over again, so that all people hear the blessing and the promise of what creation was meant to be and who we are meant to be in imitation of our God. Isaiah tries to use language that is equal to the book of creation, to lure his people back into the presence of God who is everywhere, to give them eyes to see and ears to hear once again the Word written in the Law, the land and all that speaks in nature. It is a task set before all of us, a necessity if we are to change and return to the trajectory of creation's original blessing of goodness, if we are to save our home. William Sloane Coffin answered a question someone asked him about what they had to do to be saved. His reply startled the one who posed the question. He replied: 'The most urgent religious question is not "What must I do to be saved?" but rather "What must we all do to save God's imperiled planet?"' That is our situation today.

We will return in Chapter 7 to Isaiah the prophet to look at his vision of the 'new heaven' and the 'new earth' that will come about through the long-awaited Messiah, Jesus, beloved child of the Father, who lives in the power of the Spirit. For now, to end this chapter, let's listen to a story I first heard while I was in Peru a few years ago, which will remind us of our connection to the land. I've given it the name 'Jigsaw Puzzle World'. It is disarmingly simple.

Once upon a time there were two young children. They were sent home from school with a huge cut-out map of the world on newsprint. There were hundreds of pieces, with all the countries/nations, seas, but all cut up. Their homework was to put it all together and construct a map of the world. They worked at it for hours, but became frustrated, angry and tearful. They complained to their parents, 'We don't even know what the world looks like. How can we ever put it together? There are so many pieces. It's impossible. We can't do it.'

The parents looked over the puzzle. What the children said was true. There were hundreds of pieces, small and large, of every country in the world. It would be a daunting task to complete, even for adults. But then one of the parents noticed that there seemed to be another picture on the other side of the pieces. They looked at them intently for a while and then they suggested to the children that they turn over all the pieces to see what was on the other side. When they did this, they began to get excited, exclaiming, 'Yes, look! I see feet and hands, heads, arms and legs, all kinds of clothes. We can put these together.' And they did! They matched feet and clothes, heads and hats/scarves, hands and arms, and began to put together a whole world of people, dressed in their native clothes and headdresses, and all holding hands. It didn't take that long at all. The children were delighted.

Then the parents smiled and said, 'Be careful now and turn over the puzzle.' When they did so, they couldn't believe what had happened: the whole world had come together! They saw and learned the lesson. When you get all the people together as one, then the whole world comes together too.

We must learn the lesson of the rabbi who sought to teach his people: 'The land, the earth, does not belong to us. We belong to the land. It lays claim to us.'

Notes

1. Human Development Report UNDP, Oxford, 1990.
2. Homily 6 against wealth, quoted in *The Daily Gospel on Line*, commentary of the day, 31 May 2006.
3. Based on the book by Blanca Lopez de Mariscal, Children's Book Press, Emeryville, Calif., 1995, a folktale from Oaxaca, Mexico. (Note: zanate birds are black birds, like crows, ravens and grebels.)
4. Shantideva, a card from Chennai, India, given as a gift.
5. Albert Camus, French philosopher and writer, from a poster in a college dormitory decades ago.
6. Morihei Ueshiba, Japanese founder of aikido martial art, from the wall of an Aikido practice-area.
7. *Hymns of Paradise* (Syriac edition: E. Beck in CSCO, vols 174–175 [1957]; English translation [with Commentary on Genesis, section 2]: trans. S.P. Brock. Crestwood: St Vladimir, 1990).

Chapter Five

Trees

The full phrase for the title of this book is 'Harm not the earth, nor the seas, nor the trees', and so trees deserve a chapter of their own. We have already been introduced to the Tree of Life and the Tree of the Knowledge of Good and Bad in the garden in Chapter 2 of Genesis, and to all the trees that were created on the third day.

So let's listen now to a story from the Native Americans of the Northeastern Woodlands of North America. This story has a number of variations and is called 'Why Some Trees Are Always Green' or 'Once The Trees Could Walk', but all variations spring from the same source and are rich in symbolism and wisdom.

Once upon a time, long before there were any two-leggeds, the trees could move. They could walk! Oh, they didn't move fast like the animals and they didn't seed on the wind, but they did actually move, very, very slowly. They could shift and face the sun at a different angle instead of waiting for it to come around to them. They could move closer to water, or up and down the side of a mountain, or into the shade of a canyon wall. They could decide to be closer together or to stay further apart in a wide-open field. They mostly moved around in spring and summer, then they usually settled in for the fall and winter months. It was indeed a spectacle to watch – to catch a glimpse of a great oak or willow or even a redbud as it took a step, leaned and moved, shifting its bulk or bending its branches. You could learn a great deal by sitting or standing very still and patiently watching them take their sure but slow-motion steps. They were free to move about in their stately, solemn ways.

This was the way of things for many generations. The animals and birds were used to the shifting of the trees, learning from their movements to expect something a little different all the time. Then one year something changed. No one knows exactly what happened, or what caused the change, but the trees started fighting. First it was complaints, annoyance and harsh words – one wanted to be in a part of the sun that another was already in, or one wanted to be nearer to the stream, or one wanted the shade, or to be closer to other trees. Then suddenly everything became aware of a low murmur, a grumbling among all the trees: the oaks, poplars, beech, maples, willows, redbuds, dogwoods, the hickory and the elms. Even the smaller trees and bushes seemed to be joining the din. And it grew louder and louder. The only ones that weren't complaining were the fir trees, the pines, the cedars and the spruce. They were conspicuously quiet. They, of course, had sticky needles and pointy edges and they weren't really welcome among the other trees, so they often kept to themselves or stood alone on a hillside or at the entrance to a valley.

Well, it got worse. The trees shook their branches threateningly and their leaves were scattered far and wide. They leaned and listed towards the other trees, wailing and howling, shoving the others aside if they could. The animals and birds didn't know what to do. They scurried out from under the once-sheltering branches to watch their nests swaying precariously in the limbs of the trees. All the trees seemed to be so angry and discontented with where they were standing.

Then the Great Spirit, Gitchie Manitou, saw all that was happening and heard the whining and howling, the arguing and pushing around, even the crashes of great branches and some trunks falling to the ground in the forests. This was not as it was meant to be. This was chaos, a mess, and disorientating for all the other creatures that lived with the trees. The Great Spirit cried out, 'Enough! What are you doing to one another? What are you doing to yourselves? I have given you so much: beauty, elegance, stateliness and dignity, and the freedom to explore the earth that you are rooted so firmly in. You have leaves and fruit, some even flowers. You have so much life. Why are you jealous and fighting and without gratitude?'

The Great Spirit's voice sounded like thunder claps through the valleys and woods. There was power and anger in the sound and, if you listened, there was also great sadness. The Great Spirit spoke again, 'This must stop. From now on, you will be rooted firmly in the ground and you will grow only where you are planted. Your seeds may take flight on the wind and be seeded elsewhere by the birds and animals, but you will not move again, except in the wind and air currents. And because you fought, dropping your leaves and stripping others of theirs, every year you will lose all your leaves and stand shivering in the cold through the winter. You will still know a short moment of shining colours of glory, but you will also know a little of dying, and your leaves will fall in great heaps beneath your branches. If only you could have been satisfied with all that I gave you. But every spring you will come back to life again and your leaves will grow fresh and green and you will breathe deeply and know that you are alive again.'

Then, turning to address the very silent firs, pines, cedars and spruce, the Great Spirit spoke in a soft and gentle voice, well-pleased with their refusal to join in the discontent: 'You, my peaceful pines and secure-in-your-place spruce, my contented cedars and faithful firs, you will stay green for ever. You will not die in winter, but stand upright and carry the beauty of the snow, and provide safe haven for the birds and animals. You will be called evergreens and your beauty and your grandeur will evoke a silence in the forest that the other trees will be able to hear. That silence and evergreen will serve to remind them to be thankful and not to fight, and that they will one day stand fully clothed in their beauty once again.'

You who walk in the forests and see the trees in all the seasons of the year, take heed and learn to be grateful and content.

There is a Jewish saying: 'Creation was the first book that God wrote and we can read it everywhere and at all times.' The world of trees teaches us, as does all of creation. Perhaps trees teach us more than other aspects of creation, since many of our greatest stories revolve around trees: our human journey begins in a garden with trees; Jesus' life takes him from a garden in Gethsemane to death on a tree; our greatest written story ends in the last chapter of Revelation with trees whose leaves are for the healing of nations.

There are myriad species of trees, all seeded on the third day or third stage of creation to cover the earth, to stand their ground, giving fruit and flower, shade and support, and bearing seed within them. In Genesis 2, the Creator God plans and plants a garden with trees that are lovely to look at, to smell and eat of, pleasant and good, a feast for the eyes and soul, and sustenance for the body. In the heart of the garden are planted two specific trees, unnamed as to the species: the Tree of Life and the Tree of the Knowledge of Good and Bad. The notion of a Tree of Life appears in many religions and ancient stories, as a tree that bore in its seed the possibility of eternal life for the one who ate it. In the Book of Proverbs, the woman Wisdom is described as 'a Tree of Life to those who grasp her, and whoever holds onto her is happy' (Proverbs 3:18).

The person who knows and chooses the good and refuses the evil is like the Tree of the Knowledge of Good and Bad. Adam is told in the garden that if he eats of the Tree of the Knowledge of Good and Bad, he will also know death. There is no mention made of what happens if he eats of the Tree of Life. Oddly enough, Adam and Eve are not tempted to eat of that tree. They both know what is good and what is bad, perhaps a way of saying that they now know consciousness of themselves and of others. They know experience and its consequences, and part of that level of awareness means knowing what it is to be mortal, to know death as the normal end to being born as human beings. In Genesis 3, Yahweh God wonders inwardly whether those he has created who have eaten of the Tree of Knowledge, and, if so, perhaps they will disobey again and reach out for the Tree of Life and live for ever. So humanity is banished from the garden of Eden.

At the eastern gate of the garden of Eden (where the sun rises), an angel is placed with a flaming sword to guard the way to the Tree of Life (Genesis 3:22-24). There are many medieval stories about that angel. Some say that the sword is the sun rising every morning, heralding dawn and another day of life. The sword is also thought to blind with light so as to hide the tree that bears the fruit that could make one live for ever. Traditionally, the angel is Michael, who was sent to guard the vulnerable humans from the anger and jealousy of the angel Lucifer, who fought in heaven and was cast down to earth. Michael is told that Lucifer, whose name is now Satan (which means the Hinderer, the Adversary), will try to keep those whom God has created out of heaven, since he himself is exiled to earth as a consequence of his actions. Michael watches for Lucifer, but he is expecting a creature of light like himself to enter the garden and attack Adam and Eve, and so he does not notice when the angel exiled from the light enters the garden as a serpent. He fails to protect the human beings that Yahweh God has created and finds so very good. Michael is heartbroken and crestfallen. And so it is he who finds himself stationed at the eastern edge of the garden of de-light (*Gan - eden*, the garden of light is the Hebrew name for Eden) to hinder any human being from re-entry. They will not be able to reach for the tree's fruit in this world.

Michael watches these vulnerable human beings and his heart pities them. They struggle with the darkness, with the passage of time, night and day, clinging to one another. They struggle to find food, shelter and comfort, to survive in this new and strangely unknown, even hostile world they now dwell in, and he begins to think about whether he can do something for them to make their lives easier. He has learned much during his time as sentry to the garden and he decides that he will help them to live more gracefully. He takes his sword and inverts it, turning it into a plow, and he teaches the humans how to plow the land, to plant food and so live with harmony, as the seasons and light come and go. Michael and all the other angels have learned that you cannot fight evil on earth as you do in heaven – with war, with swords and with power. On earth, you must fight evil and deprivation with food, with sustenance and with life. So Michael the Archangel becomes the patron of farmers, of prophets and of peace-makers, of all those intent on turning back the chaos that evil creates and restoring the harmony and wholeness of the earth that Yahweh God created as good.

Throughout the history of Israel and the people's growth in awareness of being a people bound and covenanted to Yahweh God, the image of the tree is central: one knows and eats of the Tree of Knowledge of Good and Bad daily. One must choose to obey or to disobey the Word of God revealed to the people. The first psalm of the 150 psalms is the opening image of those who gather to sing and pray the praises of God in worship and in public acknowledgement of the covenant that binds them and separates them out from the other nations. It uses the symbol of a tree – the kind of tree a person and a nation chooses to become.

> Happy is the man who has not followed the
> counsel of the wicked,
> or taken the path of sinners,
> or joined the company of the insolent;
> rather, the teaching of the Lord is his delight,
> and he studies that teaching day and night.
> He is like a tree planted beside streams of water,
> which yields its fruit in season,
> whose foliage never fades,
> and whatever it produces thrives.
>
> Not so the wicked;
> rather, they are like chaff that wind blows away.
> Therefore the wicked will not survive judgement,
> nor will sinners, in the assembly of the
> righteous,
> For the Lord cherishes the way of the righteous,
> but the way of the wicked is doomed.
>
> (Psalm 1)

This is the choice laid before each of us: to choose now to undo the chaos and to rebuild and replant, to live as trees planted by running waters, and to obey the Word of the Lord God Yahweh, or to choose to undo life and to tear down what is lifegiving and good, and to break faith with the Word of the Lord. All of the stories and the Scriptures of the Bible seek to remind us of who we are, what we are created and born to be: very good, made in the image and likeness of God. This is the way Meister Eckhart, a Dominican mystic, put it:

> The seed of God is in us.
> Now the seed of a pear tree
> Grows into a pear tree
> And a hazel seed
> Grows into a hazel tree.
>
> A seed of God
> Grows into God.

The Scriptures make the consequences of choosing to do evil and undo creation clear. In Isaiah 44:9-20 there is a short parable, a tale of idol-making, where the prose of the piece, in the midst of poetry, shows clearly the difference between making something that is good and something that is worthless, and the effects each has on the maker. There are two idol-makers: one an iron-forger and the other a carpenter (a 'craftsman in wood'). The story begins with a number of insulting statements, condemning the men for their stupidity in making false gods:

> The makers of idols
> All work to no purpose;
> And the things they treasure
> Can do no good,
> As they themselves can testify.
> They neither look nor think,
> And so they shall be shamed.
> Who would fashion a god
> Or cast a statue
> That can do no good?
> Lo, all its adherents shall be shamed;
> They are craftsmen, are merely human.
> Let them all assemble and stand up!
> They shall be cowed, and they shall be shamed.
> (Isaiah 44:9-11)

The description that follows of the idol-makers shows that all their hard work comes to naught and that they are left hungry and with nothing for all their labours. The first idol-maker is an ironsmith and he is dealt with in few words:

> The craftsman in iron, with his tools,
> Works it over charcoal
> And fashions it by hammering,
> Working with the strength of his arm.
> Should he go hungry, his strength would ebb;
> Should he drink no water, he would grow faint.
> (Isaiah 44:12)

But why so quickly pass over the ironsmith? The history of Israel and its experience at the hands of other nations echoes a warning against anything that has to do with the forging of metals. To be described as closely connected to living by the sword or making iron would be a high insult. Remember this description of what Yahweh God has done for them in the past:

> And when you look up to the sky and behold the sun and the moon and the stars, the whole heavenly host, you must not be lured into bowing down to them or serving them. These the Lord your God allotted to other peoples everywhere under heaven; but you the Lord took and brought out of Egypt, that iron blast furnace, to be His very own people, as is now the case.
> (Deuteronomy 4:19-20)

The first association for the Israelites with forging and iron-smithing is that this is the curse and the work of the land that made them slaves, seeking to destroy them; whereas their God, Yahweh, is the liberator of the slaves and does not take delight in what other nations do, either to impress their idols and gods or to conquer the earth. As early as Genesis 14:1, there is a description of who has made war on others – and the only one to survive comes to Abram, the Hebrew, who 'was dwelling at the terebinths [oaks] of Mamre' (Genesis 14:13). There is a long precise description of the warring tribes and kings, because it is believed that this is the beginning of what we call war; this is the note that accompanies this passage in the Tanhuma:

> 'Now when Armraphel king of Shinar, Arioch king of Ellasar, Chedorlaomer king of Elam, and Tidal king of Goiim made war...' (Genesis 14:1)
> Before their time there had been no war in the world, and it was they who came and introduced the sword and started to wage war. God said, 'You wicked ones, you have introduced the sword, let the sword enter your own heart.' (See Klagsburn, 1980, p. 382)

The prohibition against killing that is part of the covenant of Noah is rigidly enforced in certain areas of Israelite religious life. It even impinges drastically on King David: David intends to build a Temple for the Ark of the Covenant, the dwelling place of God, but he is not allowed to; he dreams of it and plans its design (given by Yahweh in a dream, traditionally), but he is not allowed even to begin to build it. The reason is that he has wielded the sword and killed too many people.

It is written:

> David said to Solomon, 'My son, I wanted to build a
> House for the name of the Lord my God. But the word
> of the Lord came to me, saying, "You have shed much
> blood and fought great battles; you shall not build a
> House for My name for you have shed much blood on
> the earth in My sight."'
>> (1 Chronicles 22:7-8)

The God of Life will not allow anyone who kills, who sheds blood and makes war upon the good earth and the people created in the image of God, to build any temple to God's name. It is unthinkable, an insult and abomination, to conceive that the two can be enacted by the same person. Even the great David is disqualified. Tainted hands that kill, even where the wars were considered righteous or necessary, cannot build what is holy in the sight of God.

The fate of the ironsmith is simple: he labours at a hot forge, is left thirsty and hungry, and after making a dead idol, he feels him empty and distant from Yahweh God. The story of the carpenter, however, is more detailed, perhaps because it is connected once again to trees. The carpenter starts out imitating God and then goes astray, and creation goes awry as well. Here is the carpenter's work in the beginning:

> The craftsman in wood measures with a line
> And marks out a shape with a stylus;
> He forms it with scraping tools,
> Marking it out with a compass.
> He gives it a human form,
> The beauty of a man, to dwell in a shrine.
> For his use he cuts down cedars;
> He chooses plane trees and oaks,
> He sets aside trees of the forest;
> Or plants firs, and the rain makes them grow.
> All this serves man for fuel.
> He takes some to warm himself,
> And he builds a fire and bakes bread.
> He also makes a god of it and worships it,
> Fashions an idol and bows down to it!
> Part of it he burns in a fire:
> On that part he roasts meat,
> He eats the roast and is sated;
> He also warms himself and cries, 'Ah,

I am warm! I can feel the heat!'
Of the rest he makes a god – his own carving!
He bows down to it;
He prays to it and cries,
'Save me, for you are my god!'
(Isaiah 44:13-18)

The passage drips with cynicism, mocking the man's stupidity, even though he knows how to plant, to harvest, to make fire, to cook, to warm himself, even to work with the knowledge of a compass, and appreciate beauty and understand that trees last and provide shelter. But then he becomes just plain stupid, acting like the idol he has made himself. It's a waste of the tree, the wood, his energy, his skills and time. The writer of Isaiah 44 continues with his judgement on the carpenter:

They have no wit or judgement;
Their eyes are besmeared, and they see not;
Their mind, and they cannot think.
They do not give thought,
They lack the wit and judgement to say:
'Part of it I burned in a fire;
I also baked bread on the coals.
I roasted meat and ate it –
Should I make the rest an abhorrence?
Should I bow to a block of wood?'
He pursues ashes!
A deluded mind has led him astray,
And he cannot save himself;
He never says to himself,
'The thing in my hand is a fraud!'
Remember these things, O Jacob,
For you, O Israel, are My servant:
I fashioned you, you are My servant –
O Israel, never forget Me.
I wipe away your sins like a cloud,
Your transgressions like mist –
Come back to Me, for I redeem you.
(Isaiah 44:18-22)

This is the writer's opinion of those who worship other gods of their own making and choosing: they are as dumb as the blocks of wood they carved them out of and as senseless and inert. Unfortunately, the possibilities of change are limited: 'The carpenter, being warm and well fed, has no immediate reason to suspect that his idol-making ways will lead to anything bad'.[1] But what does all this have to say to us in the twenty-first century? Sadly, it has all too much to say. We have not learned much in nearly two and a half thousand years. We look at iron and ores, oil, natural gas and nuclear material merely as resources, raw possibilities, there at our disposal. The story is very close to present reality.

> But someone goes hungry and thirsty and is exhausted and wearied by working with such materials. Trees grow from the ground, while iron, coal, oil and all other raw materials remain in the ground, and getting them out is expensive, dirty, dangerous and wasteful (particularly so for methods such as strip mining and mountaintop removal). Further, those that do the bulk of the work tend to get paid the least. Entire towns in West Virginia owe their continued existence to coal mining, to the point where children are sometimes discouraged from learning too much, lest they become dissatisfied with their expected profession as coal miners. There is more than one kind of hunger that result from all this.
>
> We do not fare much better in harvesting trees. Also dangerous and low-paying as a profession, deforestation is wasteful in many ways, from the not-so-well-thought-out (even if we matched harvesting tree-for-tree with planting new seedlings, it would take decades for the new trees to grow to a useful size: a generation of our own children will have few or none) to the utterly absurd (twenty-five million trees per year are destroyed to satisfy China's desire for disposable wooden chopsticks).[2]

These realities are duplicated in country after country, with mining for copper, alloys, tin, basalt, coal, iron ore for steel, oil and natural gas and with deforestation on massive levels. We live as though there will be excess and abundance no matter what we do and no matter how much we waste in 'idol' making – just as the carpenter uses half of the tree for warmth, cooking and shelter, and wastes the other half mindlessly; uselessly; and then, after fashioning it with his own hands, he bows down and worships it, pleading for it to respond and save him! Our idols today have many names and faces. One example is our pursuit of weapons: in the last year alone, over eight hundred billion dollars were spent in the US on weapons, war on other countries, security and espionage. As we bow down to idols to save us, we use what would have been the legacy and heritage of our children and grandchildren worldwide. We do not see nuclear weapons and power as dangerous or, as Isaiah calls it, an 'abomination' (the word 'bomb' is embedded in it, oddly enough) or an 'abhorrence', and we stupidly refuse to look seriously at alternative sources of energy that can creatively provide what we need: solar, wind power and alternative fuels.

Nuclear weapons are singular to the last generation; they are our responsibility, our hellish contribution to technology, insecurity and fear. In a fraction of a milli-second, we stand poised and ever-ready to annihilate creation. We live in arrogance before the God that made us and shared power with us to care for the earth. Anti-nuclear campaigner David Lange makes these important points about the absurdity of 'the nuclear deterrent':

> There is a quality of irrationality about nuclear weapons, which does not sit well with good intentions. A system of defence serves its purpose if it guarantees the security of those it protects. A system of nuclear defence guarantees only insecurity. The means of defence terrorises as much as the threat of attack…
>
> The weapon has its own relentless logic, and it is inhuman. It is the logic of escalation, the logic of the arms race. Nuclear weapons make us insecure, and to compensate for our insecurity we build and deploy more nuclear weapons. We know that we are seized by irrationality and yet we persist. We all of us know that it is wholly without logic or reason to possess the power to destroy ourselves many times over, and yet in spite of that knowledge the nuclear powers continue to refine their capacity to inflict destruction on each other and all the rest of us. Every new development, whatever its strategic or tactical significance, has only one result; and that is to add to an arsenal which is already beyond reason. (Tal, 2006, pp. 79–80)

This issue of security is central. It is deeply reflective of who and what we actually worship. We must ask ourselves: what is the root source of our security? Is it God? Is it our community of believers in this God of Jesus Christ? There is a saying I have heard often in my travelling, which goes: 'Call God by whatever name you wish: God's Name is Truth. God's Name is Peace.' The arms race to collect ever more and ever new weapons is idol-making of massive proportions, and the worship of evil, of violence and of death. It is the choice to live daily with the reality of returning earth and all its inhabitants to primeval chaos and nothingness, to spit in the face of the Creator and to wipe creation from the face of the deep. It is anti-life, anti-good and anti-God.

I have lived in New Mexico for the last twenty-two years, and I have lived in the shadow of Los Alamos, the site of the detonation of the first nuclear bomb. The first mushroom cloud rose and hovered over the desert. One of the makers of the bomb, physicist J. Robert Oppenheimer, is said to have commented on the explosion with the words: 'Now I am become Death, the destroyer of world' (from the Bhagavad Gita). This event happened months before I was born, and it was followed by the bombing of Hiroshima and Nagasaki in Japan.

The first sin was fratricide. The last sin will not be genocide, which we are very good at, but earthicide, planeticide We will manage, as we choose to eat of the fruit of the Tree of the Knowledge of Good or Bad, not only to uncreate our planet but, most likely, to wrench our planet out of orbit and create a huge explosion/hole to replace this beautiful floating creature called earth.

On the other hand, in the 1960s when I was in my early twenties, I stood in a muddy field in Central Park, New York City, and watched human beings walk on the moon and send back the most amazing pictures from outer space, and I listened to astronauts become poets in their assessment of the planet we live on. Lewis Thomas wrote about what we had all seen in those pictures: 'The astonishing thing about the earth, catching the breath, is that it is alive. The photographs show the dry, pounded surface of the moon in the foreground, dead as an old bone. Aloft, floating free beneath the moist, gleaming membrane of bright blue sky, is the rising earth, the only exuberant thing in this part of the cosmos.' This reflects what it means to have to choose to eat the fruit of the Tree of Knowledge of Good and Bad. The significance is not in the initial choosing – it is in the daily choice of which fruit we will eat, which tree we will reach for – good or evil.

Trees in the New Testament

There are so many stories of trees in the gospels. The symbol of the Israelites sitting under their own fig tree or drinking wine from their own vineyard is an image of Israel at peace, of a time of abiding justice, with the presence of God filling the land. It heralded the presence of the Messiah, the long-awaited one, a human being who would be the presence of God and the wisdom of God among the people, so strongly that all the other nations would see the light of Israel and stream towards Jerusalem as the source of justice and peace. In chapter 1 of John, as Jesus is gathering the first of his disciples together, he calls Philip to come and follow. Philip goes to look for Nathanael, to come and see what he has found in Jesus. As Nathanael is walking towards Jesus, Jesus greets him with the words, 'Here is truly an Israelite in whom there is no deceit!' Nathanael asks him, 'Where did you get to know me?' Jesus answers, 'I saw you under the fig tree before Philip called you' (John 1:47-48).

Jesus tells stories of a fig tree that does not produce fruit, and is to be cut down and thrown out as rubbish. As he walks into the city of Jerusalem the week before he dies, he curses a fig tree that has no fruit on it. There is the parable of the mustard seed, planted in a vineyard, which becomes a sheltering tree for all the birds of the air – a symbol of what the kingdom of God on earth might look like and who might find sanctuary within it. The tax collector Zacchaeus, being very short of stature, runs on ahead of the crowd and climbs a sycamore tree in order to see Jesus. He perches in the branches, like a strange bird, until Jesus stops at the foot of the tree and looks up, and tells him to come down, and invites himself to dinner at Zacchaeus' house. Imagine Zacchaeus in all his finery and robes getting out of that tree in front of everyone, and Jesus looking on in delight. It seems tree-climbers tickle Jesus' fancy: this is the only occasion on which Jesus invites himself to dinner at anyone's house!

Jesus is born of the root of Jesse, the tree of David, the ancestral tree of history and family, a tree that each of us is born of. Of course, there is the wood of the cross that becomes the Tree of Life for all peoples, watered by the blood of the broken Lord, who died with his own limbs stretched like branches and his body hung between earth and heaven. Along with gardens, trees figure strongly in our stories, our salvation and our faith. We need to look at a few more closely.

Let's go back to that image of the Tree of the Knowledge of Good and Bad and look at Jesus' parable of the fig tree that does not produce fruit. It is found in Luke and it is read on the Third Sunday of Lent, cycle C. It is a call to 'repent, and change', warning that 'now would be a good time to bear fruit and become what you are'. Prior to the parable's telling, Jesus has been told the story of some Galileans who were butchered by Pilate, their blood mixed with the sacrifices they were going to offer in the Temple. It was the understanding that if you died without a chance to make sacrifices, or atone for what you had done, you died a terrible death, as a sinner. But Jesus ruthlessly questions them: 'Do you think that because these Galileans suffered in this way they were worse sinners than all other Galileans? No, I tell you; but unless you repent, you will all perish as they did' (Luke 13:1-5). To drive his point home, he uses another image of those who died when a tower fell on them, giving them no chance to prepare for death. He reiterates the necessity of repenting *now*, as all of us are just like those people. They are not any worse offenders than we are, and the way we die (we will all die) is not the issue. What is important is what we are doing in our lives today. The image that might be used in the present, as harsh as it is, would be of those caught in terrorist attacks, or killed as 'collateral damage', trapped in the crossfire of those who hate and kill. Aren't all of us just like them, human, with the same fears and the same desire to cling to life? It is in light of this conversation that Jesus is having with the people around him, that he tells the parable:

> A man had a fig tree planted in his vineyard; and he came looking for fruit on it and found none. So he said to the gardener, 'See here! For three years I have come looking for fruit on this fig tree, and still I find none. Cut it down! Why should it be wasting the soil?' He replied, 'Sir, let it alone for one

more year, until I dig around it and put manure on it. If it bears fruit next year, well and good; but if not you can cut it down.'
(Luke 13:6-9)

It is a confusing and complex parable for people who don't know a lot about fig trees and when to harvest them. Even for those familiar with such trees, it is still a challenge. The parable appears half-way through Luke's gospel, and at a time when Jesus and his words are being rationalised, misinterpreted and ignored. Like the man in the parable, Jesus' patience is running thin. This is the first in a long run of parables, in the chapters to come, about the necessity and immediacy of repenting, of changing drastically, of accepting Jesus' presence and words and turning to live in the kingdom of abiding justice that reaps a harvest of peace.

But first, a few notes on fig trees. Palestinian fig trees bear fruit for about ten months of the year, so an owner could expect to get figs pretty much all year long. However, it takes about three years after planting for fig trees to produce the first fruit. And in Jewish tradition, the first three years of fruit was considered forbidden:

> When you enter the land and plant any tree for food you shall regard its fruit as forbidden. Three years it shall be forbidden for you, not to be eaten. In the fourth year all its fruit shall be set aside for jubilation before the Lord; and only in the fifth year may you use its fruit – that its yield to you may be increased; I the Lord am your God.
> (Leviticus 19:23-25)

Now the owner in the parable has come for the last three years – so it's nine years since planting and it looks hopeless. The fig tree gives no fruit. Root it out! The owner describes it as 'wasting the soil'...other translations say 'cluttering up the ground'...meaning that it is sucking nutrients and water out of the soil so that the vines will have less. But the owner finds himself being urged by his gardener to have mercy and give the tree yet another year, and another chance to bear fruit. The gardener suggests some things to help it along! Now usually you might think of more or less watering, adding some fertiliser or new soil, or checking for bugs, but the suggestions offered by the gardener are radical: dig around it – a nice way of saying chop up the soil around it and hack away at the roots; and then put manure on it – a nice way of saying dump a lot of shit on it! Those listening would have been howling with laughter, while at the same time insulted and indignant. This is called 'insult humour', common in Israel, and Jesus is a master at it (see Pilch, 1997 pp. 55–7). Some exegetes say that this is about the leaders of the Jewish community, but Jesus has just gotten through telling them that everyone, individually, must repent and listen to his words, and change so that their lives bear fruit. Still, Jesus is definitely playing with the meanings of words. Israel has always been God's cherished vineyard (the parable of Isaiah 5:7), and this fig tree in the vineyard is the symbol of abiding justice that leads to peace. This is what John Pilch says about the wording:

> Moreover in Aramaic there is a wordplay between 'dig it out' and 'let it alone' (also the word for forgiveness), which makes the parable and its point very easy to remember. Judgement (dig it out)? No, mercy and forgiveness (let it alone)! The tree cannot lift itself by its roots. They (the leaders) need the intervention of an outsider, the gardener, God himself! (1997, p. 57)

I would say that the gardener is Jesus, the vineyard owner is God, and the people and the leaders are a mixed bag of folks – some responding to Jesus and some rejecting him. But Jesus' exhortation is for everyone. Jesus is telling us: look to yourselves! Forget about looking at your enemies and judging them so harshly! Now is the time for *you* to repent and to begin bearing fruit. God, Jesus and the Spirit have been seeded in us, and they keep coming year after year, expecting to see the fruit that we bear yearly, every month of the year, in our lives. What kind of fruit are we bringing forth for the world to eat? Is it the fruit of the kingdom of God: justice, peace, compassion for victims of violence, tender regard for the poor, generosity for the desperate, mercy, forgiveness, reconciliation, unity, sharing, abundance of life for all? Or are we individually and in our groups merely a drain on others, sucking the life out of them? Are we in need of a little shock treatment – some alkaline poured on us or our roots chopped up? This is much like shocking people back into consciousness and life after a heart-attack. Jesus is trying to do that with those who listen to him but do not necessarily respond to his words. Earlier in Luke's gospel, Jesus talks about good and bad trees and their fruits:

> No good tree bears bad fruit, nor again does a bad tree bear good fruit, for each tree is known by its own fruit. Figs are not gathered from thorns, nor are grapes picked from a bramble bush. The good person out of the good treasure of the heart produces good, and the evil person out of evil treasure produces evil; for it is out of the abundance of the heart that the mouth speaks.
>
> (Luke 6:43-45)

Jesus is interested in who we are at heart, at the core of our roots. The parables are about unmasking us all and revealing our true natures, as well as about revealing the nature of God and how far we are from living in the image and likeness of the One who has made us.

Jesus is speaking about personal conversion and holiness, but as a Jewish prophet, he is also using the image of trees to tell stories that are bluntly political and economic in their intent. In the gospel of Mark, one of the last things that Jesus does before going into the city of Jerusalem to celebrate the Passover and to die, is to curse the fig tree that he encounters along the road. It appears heartless, or even petty, but in light of the other parable and its connection to bearing fruit for the kingdom of God, it is a powerful symbol of the deadness of the leadership of the Jewish religion and nation and its collusion with evil (the Roman occupying forces), which has sapped the very life of the people. This parable is directed like an arrow in motion, aimed at the heart of the Jewish leadership:

> On the following day, when they came from Bethany, he was hungry. Seeing in the distance a fig tree in leaf, he went to see whether perhaps he would find anything on it. When he came to it, he found nothing but leaves, for it was not the season for figs. He said to it, 'May no one ever eat fruit from you again.' And his disciples heard it.
> (Mark 11:12-14)

Just as Jesus is hungry, so God is hungry for the fruit of our lives: worship, justice for all, equality and sharing, no poor in the land, the promise of the law and the covenant – but there is no fruit. Even if it was not the season for figs, there should have been something there! But there was nothing. This parable is broken up into two segments: what begins in the words above and what follows after Jesus' entrance into Jerusalem, with the story of driving the money changers out of the Temple because they have desecrated it with cheating the poor in money exchanges and offerings, and making a profit out of the worship of Yahweh. The temple economy is bereft, empty and hollow, as dead as any fig tree on the road. The leaders hear of what Jesus has done and they are already looking for a way to kill him – in the tradition of the prophets. The story continues:

> In the morning as they passed by, they saw the fig tree withered away to its roots. Then Peter remembered and said to him, 'Rabbi, look! The fig tree that you cursed has withered.' Jesus answered them, 'Have faith in God. Truly I tell you, if you say to this mountain, "Be taken up and thrown into the sea," and if you do not doubt in your heart, but believe

that what you say will come to pass, it will be done for you. So I tell you, whatever you ask for in prayer, believe that you have received it, and it will be yours. Whenever you stand praying, forgive, if you have anything against anyone; so that your Father in heaven may also forgive you your trespasses.'

(Mark 11:20-26)

This piece takes the reality of the curse, and hence the power of the Word of God, which a solitary fig tree experienced, and extends this power outwards. Jesus has a tendency to tell a parable and then act it out himself – giving a visual and vital experience of his spoken words. He has driven the money changers out of the Temple, symbolically cleansing the heart of the people, renewing the covenant, and judging those who have betrayed the heart of the Law and the promise of God. He has revealed the reality of religious worship and practice: it is dead and bears no fruit.

Then Jesus extends the parable in words that must be practised faithfully by all his followers. Do we have faith? Do we doubt? What's in our hearts? For many people, the heart is the place of the will – where we choose either to act truthfully, with integrity, for goodness, or to act in ill will towards others. Is it harder to tell a mountain to be uprooted, move and drop itself into the sea? Or is it harder to will the goodness, the forgiveness of God and God's mercy upon all peoples? This is the fruit of Jesus' words and works, the reality of the kingdom of God among us, and what constitutes true worship of God. Before we worship, alone or with one another, we must forgive, as we have been forgiven. This is the innermost core of the good news of God. All fruit begins with forgiveness, with mercy, with another chance – over and over again – the fruit of hearing the Word of God.

There is an old Chinese story, called simply 'The Old Tree', that is worth reading for its wisdom. It is from the collected works of Chuang-Tzu, an ancient Chinese sage.

Once upon a time, a carpenter and his apprentice were walking in the forest, looking for trees to cut down to make furniture for a wealthy patron. They walked past a great old tree that stood next to an ancient earth altar. The apprentice was in awe of the tree – its height, its girth, its age and beauty – and he stood with his head tilted back as he gazed up at it. The carpenter was impatient and prodded the young man to move along, saying, 'Yes, it's old and huge, but it's also useless. The wood is so old that you couldn't use it for anything – for making furniture or for building ships, or even for making an axe handle or tools.' And so they continued on through the woods, looking for trees that were useful.

That night, the great old tree came to the carpenter in a dream. In a voice that was both sad and angry, it said, 'You of all people should know that there are things more important than being useful. You should not have compared me to other trees, to those that bear fruit or to those that have hard woods that you can immediately find a use for, or cut and sell, even for firewood. Go back into the woods and look at those trees that you think are so useful. They are short lived. They may provide fruit and fuel, but they are easily broken in a wind or cut by anyone passing by. And most of them are very young. Look at me! I am old. I just stand here. No one thinks to chop me down because they wouldn't know what to do with me. You call me useless, but I've been here a long time and I stand beside an altar. I stand witness. I accompany those who come to worship, to visit, to seek solace, to find their footing on the earth again. I am here, and that is reason enough. There is so much you and other humans do not even dream about.'

The next morning the carpenter went back to his apprentice and took him to the woods once again. As they stood together before the great tree, the carpenter told the young man about the dream, confessing that he had taken the tree and so much of life for granted, forgetting how important it is to have a place, a holy place, on which to stand. 'You were right,' he said, 'to stand in awe before the ancient one and to appreciate its years, and to know that it had stood faithfully by the old altar long after human beings had deserted it.' And they stood there a long time, learning from the ancient tree.

There is another parable in Luke's gospel about a mustard seed that grows into a 'sheltering tree'. It is followed immediately by an account of Jesus preaching in a synagogue on a Sabbath and healing an old woman who has been bent double for eighteen years. After he lays hands on her, she stands upright and loudly praises God. Following the altercation that is caused by his healing on the Sabbath, Jesus goes back to his preaching and tells this short story:

> What is the kingdom of God like? And to what should I compare it? It is like a mustard seed that someone took and sowed in a garden; it grew and became a tree, and the birds of the air made nests in its branches.
> (Luke 13:18-19)

So short, so pithy, and it is dropped out there, like that seed planted in a garden! In other translations, the mustard seed is planted in a vineyard! And all the species of blackbirds, crows, ravens, grackles and grebes come and find 'shelter in its branches'. The image of the sheltering tree has a long history in Israel, beginning with this parable that is found in the Book of Judges:

Once the trees went to anoint a king over themselves. They said to the olive tree, 'Reign over us.' But the olive tree replied, 'Have I, through whom God and men are honoured, stopped yielding my rich oil, that I should go and wave above the trees?' So the trees said to the fig tree, 'You come and reign over us.' But the fig tree replied, 'Have I stopped yielding my sweetness, my delicious fruit, that I should go and wave above the trees?' So the trees said to the vine, 'You come and reign over us.' But the vine replied, 'Have I stopped yielding my new wine, which gladdens God and men, that I should go and wave above the trees?' Then all the trees said to the thornbush, 'You come and reign over us.' And the thornbush said to the trees, 'If you are acting honourably in anointing me king over you, come and take shelter in my shade, but if not, may fire issue from the thornbush and consume the cedars of Lebanon!'

(Judges 9:8-15)

In this story, the people are interested in finding a king for themselves, like they have in other countries. The first three trees are useful but the last is not, and is even seen to be aggressive and destructive. The thornbush's fruit is inedible and the thornbush warns the others that if they 'take shelter in its shade' (of which there is little or none) it will turn on them and utterly burn them out, along with the great towering cedars of Lebanon. The parable is a warning about leadership that is aggressively destructive, bringing ruin to what is truly great, long lasting, useful and beautiful, the opposite of what will give 'shelter from the shade'.

This image is repeated a number of times by the prophet Ezekiel. In chapter 31, as Ezekiel tells the history of the Pharaoh of Egypt and his hordes, he says that Assyria 'was a cedar in Lebanon with beautiful branches and shady thickets, of lofty stature, with its top among leafy trees'. He continues with the praise:

It exceeded in stature all the trees of the field; its branches multiplied and its boughs grew long...[and] in its branches nested all the birds of the sky; all the beasts of the field bore their young under its boughs and in its shadow lived all the great nations' and even the 'cedars in the garden of God could not compare with it...all the trees of Eden envied it in the garden of God
(Ezekiel 31:1-9)

After all this praise, its end is as ruthless as its wickedness and arrogance: it 'was cut down and abandoned' and was left as a reminder that no other nation should follow in its wake, or else they too would all 'be consigned to death, to the lowest part of the netherworld, together with human beings who descend into the Pit' (Ezekiel 31:10-14). The image of the nation falling is depicted as a great tree being felled in a forest, and the utter destruction and shattering of every limb and branch as it comes crashing down. The parable is an earlier version of the warning of what will come in justice to those nations that tower above others on the earth. It is a dire warning to the nations that dominate the world today, heedless of the consequences of their actions.

Earlier in Ezekiel, there is another parable. In chapter 17, there are two accounts of great eagles that come to Lebanon and seize the top of the cedar, pluck it off and transplant it. The first transplants it in a city of merchants, then the other eagle comes and bends the roots in his direction. Both will wither and die. The first eagle is Babylon and the second is the Pharaoh, whom Zedekiah turned in his revolt against Nebuchadnezzar. Both will know end and destruction, but God promises to uphold the cedar of Lebanon, which is Israel. People forget that God is witness to the politics, the economics, the nationalism, the wars and brutality, the slavery and the rape of the land and the people of all nations. This is the promise, the hope, of what God will do for the people – for Israel, for Christians and for all who seek the truth and the revelation of God:

> Thus says the Lord God: Then I in turn will take and set [in the ground a slip] from the lofty top of the cedar; I will pluck a tender twig from the tip of its crown, and I will plant it on a tall, towering mountain. I will plant it on Israel's lofty highlands, and it shall bring forth boughs and produce branches and grow into a noble cedar. Every bird of every feather shall take shelter under it, shelter in the shade of its boughs. Then shall all the trees of the field know that it is I the Lord who have abased the lofty tree and exalted the lowly tree, who have dried up the green tree and made the withered tree bud. I the Lord have spoken, and I will act.
> (Ezekiel 17:22-24)

The history of Israel and all the nations is at the core of what God is doing in the world, and the prophets are intent on reminding the people and their leaders of God's intent for all the peoples of the earth.

The trees in the parables of Ezekial and Jesus turn everything in reality on its head. The poor of the earth, the scattered and unwanted birds of the air, like the woman bent double at the back of the worshippers in the synagogue, are the ones that come seeking shelter in the tree of the Lord, the gospel of good news for the poorest of the earth. The unlikely mustard seed, so tiny and insignificant, or the weed that grows unchecked in a garden or a vineyard, will become the tree of hope, will take over and seep into the nations of the world and become the kingdom of God's mercy for the least of the earth. There will be no stopping this tree of safety, of refuge, of sanctuary and shelter. What remains is to ask: have we as the Church, as those who follow Jesus – the gardener, the seeder, the one who prunes and seeks fruit – have we become that sheltering tree of hope in the world today?

The Wood of the Cross – The Tree of Life

There are so many other tree stories, but we will end this chapter with the wood of the cross, the Tree of Life, again an incongruous symbol that is paradoxical and unsettling – the parable of God's power and birthing in Jesus, the Crucified and Risen One.

I spent part of my childhood on the east coast of the United States, where dogwood trees could be found in every small copse and on the edges of fields that had not yet become urban or suburban developments. The dogwood tree lives in the shade of other trees, from which it sucks out the water and nutrients, and it bears no flowers for the first two or three years. Farmers who wanted to get rid of it would pour acid on its roots in the hope of jump-starting its growth, or they would simply cut it down, because it was regarded as a parasite that sapped the life of other trees and crops and destroyed everything around it. I was not aware of this as I roamed through the acres of green woods, though I did notice that there was always a space around the dogwood trees where nothing grew, and I would lie in this space under the shade of the branches.

There is a legend that the wood of the cross was the wood of a dogwood tree that had been cut down, useless. According to the legend, after Jesus was taken down from the cross, the wood was blood-soaked, and it was left standing upright on a hill outside of Jerusalem, as was the custom following crucifixions. But the crossbeam, the pole/bar of slavery, was cast aside in a dump. And when Jesus rose from the dead, both parts of the dead tree flowered in pinks and whites. At Easter, the blossoms appear through the blood of Christ on the cross. This is just a legend, but it affords us a way to ask questions. Do we stand upright in the face of persecution, rejection and terrible suffering? Do we stand with those who are the victims of injustice, violence and the aggression of nations? Are we willing to be the seed that falls into the ground and dies, so that we might rise with Jesus, the crucified and risen Lord? Are we trees of life, where all the bent-over people of the world may find shelter in our branches? Are we trees planted near the waters of life – the Scriptures giving fruit in every season – the fruits of justice and peace?

There will be more to say about trees, for they are found in the Book of Revelation and are part of the new heavens and the new earth, but, for now, we will leave the trees behind and end with a poem:

When I was younger I climbed trees
to hide, to go away from the ground
to visit birds and chattering squirrels.
Then way up at the top
I'd lean into the trunk
reeling like a bird drunk on berries
and stare wide-eyed in awe at air
rippling like skin right in front of me
and feel the tree swaying like a feather
in the wind, held with hard fingers of earth.

Dizzy, dancing, soul dissolving
I knew I'd found out some ancient wisdom
lost knowledge that was secret and necessary
for humans' survival. And I'd rock
frighteningly secure in that tree's old arms.
I'm homesick now for another tree
and that wisdom's hold.
Maybe age doesn't count.
Maybe fear of losing such a joy
can be given up in climbing.
Maybe it's time to tree sit
not to hide – but to find.
Ah – I climb. Ah – I climb.[3]

Notes

1. John Goltz, 'The Use and Misuse of Creation', graduate class.
2. Information available at http://news.independent.co.uk/environment/article 353803. ece, as 21 June 2006.
3. Written by the author on reading this quote from Thomas Merton: 'I am perhaps still on the side of the trees.' With thanks for some of these ideas to one of my students, John Goltz, who used this portion of Isaiah in his paper on creation.

Chapter Six

Jesus' Geography as told by Water

HARM NOT THE EARTH, NOR THE SEA, NOR THE TREES! We will now look at waters, rivers, seas, oceans, tears, some of those salty and sweet water places in the small geographical area that was Jesus' dwelling place on earth. It is about ninety miles from Nazareth to Jerusalem, and that was the length and breadth of Jesus' footprint on the ground and in its waters. His life is bounded by the Jordan river, the Dead Sea, the Sea of Galilee, springs and wells, as well as places lacking in water, like the desert, and places that know some water, such as gardens, fields and mountains. He describes himself as the 'living water, the gift of God' and he dies giving up his last bit of blood and water on the cross, while crying out that he thirsts (John 4 and 19).

We first meet John, who comes forth from the desert but who baptises with water, which will cleanse and wash out people's eyes and hearts; then we meet Jesus, when he comes to the Jordan river to be baptised by John (Mark 1). It is here in the river Jordan, as he stands with the water dripping off him, soaked and streaming water, that, Jesus Christ, the Son of God, is first introduced to us. It sets the tone for much that will follow.

> In those days, Jesus came from Nazareth in Galilee and was baptised by John in the Jordan. And just as he was coming up out of the water, he saw the heavens torn apart and the Spirit descending like a dove on him. And a voice came from heaven, 'You are my Son, the Beloved; with you I am well pleased'.
> (Mark 1:9-11)

This is Jesus' geography, placing him firmly on the earth and in the water! Incarnation happens solidly on ground, in water, and with Jesus looking up into the sky. Creation comes together in his body. This is the geography that Jesus knew intimately. With the mystery of the Incarnation, God dwells on earth and is flesh and blood and bone, as are we – being composed of about 85 per cent or more of water. The Son of God, the Son of Man, stands in the Jordan river, and from this moment forward, in this place, there is nothing that veils the face of God from human beings. This is our belief as Christians, baptised in water and the Spirit, who become the dwelling place of God upon the earth.

We, too, thrill to the words that are now addressed to us: 'You are my beloved, my child, and I take great delight in you!' Our lives in God, like Jesus' own life, begin in water – the waters of our mother's pain and birthing, and the waters of the Spirit that gave life to us in baptism.

Let us begin with a story, one that situates us on earth, in a place where the waters above and the waters below come together. It reveals how human beings both need water and abuse water. It also reveals why the earth is suffering from our greed and our lack of concern for our resources, especially water.

The story is called 'Enough is Enough' and it is from the Quinault tribe of the northwestern coast of what is now the United States and Canada.[1] Clarke explains that Clarence Pickernell, a Quinault-Chehalis-Cowlitz from Tahola, Washington, told it in 1951, having learned it from his great-grandmother.) This is the way I tell it.

Once upon a time – a long time ago – there was peace in the land. Everything, two-leggeds, four-leggeds, all the animals, the plants and the birds, lived in peace. There was always an abundance of food, water and shelter, so that all enjoyed sharing and celebrating with one another. It was a time of beginnings, a time of peace.

During this time, long ago, people lived on the flat plains that are now eastern Washington State. If you look at a map today, or travel to the area, you will see that there is a huge mountain range separating the eastern and the western lands and peoples. The western side is covered with dense forests and ocean, while the east consists of wind-swept plains and near-desert. But this is not how it was in the beginning.

In the beginning, the rain didn't come from above! It came from below, welling up from the earth. Everything drank from the ground: trees, plants, bushes, animals, even streams and rivers. This is how it was. Then one day, no one knows why, the waters dried up and no longer rose out of the ground. First everything turned brown and wilted, and then the waters in the streams and rivers evaporated. The salmon couldn't come upriver; the animals and people couldn't find water. Many of the animals and plants, flowers and trees died. The people lived in thirst and many of them died too.

It was decided that one of the warriors must go to the Ocean, the great sea, and beg for water. And so the chosen warrior stood before the Ocean and begged, telling the great waters of the pain of the people, the animals and the land itself. 'Everything is dying of thirst! Help us to live!' And Ocean had pity on the people and offered to send some of his children, his sons the Clouds and his daughters the Rain, to help them out. Clouds and Rain ran across the sky and hovered over the land, and with time things stirred and came back to life and began to flourish, and water returned to the rivers and lakes and streams.

The people decided that they couldn't let a similar situation happen again. So they dug a huge hole in the ground so that the Clouds and the Rain could fill it up and they'd never have to worry about water again. It took many, many moons before the water levels returned to normal. Meanwhile, Ocean began to miss his children, Clouds and Rain, and he sent messengers to the people asking that they be returned home to him. But the people refused, saying, 'We need more water. We must have more water.' The messenger argued with them: 'You have more than enough moisture now. Ocean has been so gracious and generous with you. It is time to let his children go back home. You have what you need. Let that be enough.' 'No,' the people said, over and over again. 'No, we want more.'

The messenger began to plead, telling them that Ocean was sad now, but could become very angry when treated badly. 'You must in justice let Ocean's children go home,' he reiterated. But they refused. Before leaving, the messenger said, 'Enough is Enough.' And he went home to Ocean without the children, Clouds and Rain. Ocean wept and then grew angry, and he spoke solemnly to the Great Spirit. 'Look upon the humans you have made,' he said. 'They grow greedy and they are never satisfied. They always want more. They want too much and they have kept the gifts of my children Clouds and Rain that I shared with them in their need. Do something so that they will know that their actions are evil.' And the Great Spirit answered Ocean's prayer.

The Great Spirit leaned down and hovered over the earth in the west, near the Ocean, and scooped a huge handful of earth and laid it carefully across the flat plains of the east. The Great Spirit continued to pick up handful after handful of earth and deposit it on the plains, so that a range of mountains rose up, the Cascade Range, separating the east from the west, the dry plains from the Ocean. But moving all that earth left a big hole in the ground, so the Great Spirit let Ocean flow into it – it is now known as Puget Sound.

On the other side of the mountains, the people held on to Ocean's children, Clouds and Rain, even after they saw what was happening. Clouds and Rain filled up the big hole that the people had dug; it is called Chelan Lake. People still use this lake to store water, but often its level is low, and there is little moisture or rain on the eastern plains. Clouds and Rain are so lonely for their father Ocean that they refuse to fall upon the land. And Ocean mourns his children, lamenting his loss. If you walk the beach, especially at night, you can hear Ocean's tears fall softly but continually, as they lap against the shore. Ocean and Clouds and Rain are still separated and the people still have to live without much water – but it didn't have to be this way. If only they had learned that enough is enough.

This story speaks about greed, wanting to be secure by one's own control, the effects of wanting too much, taking too much and forgetting the balance and the harmony of earth. It is a reminder to us of our attitude to water, the way in which we waste and pollute it, and deprive our brothers and sisters in the developing world of access to this essential and precious commodity.

In a recent statement by Archbishop Celestino Migliore, the Holy See's permanent observer to the United Nations, during a session of the UN Economic and Social Council's Commission on Sustainable Development, the issue of drinking water was brought up. This is a small portion of his statement:

> Within twenty years the reserves of water per person will be a third of what they were in 1950 and, by 2025, a third of the world's nations will have catastrophically low levels of water. Even today, 34,000 people die every day for lack of clean water: one and a half billion people do not have access to clean water, a figure which could rise to three billion by 2025. [This is half the world's population of circa 6.6 billion people.] This is already a humanitarian and environmental crisis, as well as a question of social justice.[2]

We are beginning to see the larger global picture, at least in terms of how it affects human beings worldwide, and to call it a question of justice that all people have drinking water. Yet, we are far from making sure that water is provided to all human beings, and we are even farther from seeing the connection between the degradation of the salt waters of the oceans and the provision of drinking water for survival. We still don't see the world as one organism. We may see ourselves as in the centre, but the reality is that we are not central, except perhaps in the damage we can do and how we hinder the continued existence of both the human race and the earth itself. (Note: One of the root meanings of the word 'satan' is 'hinderer'.)

Four-fifths of the world consists of undrinkable sea water. In fact, water covers 71 per cent of the surface of our planet. Our own bodies comprise more than 85 per cent water. The health of the oceans, the state of sweet waters, is bound to what is moving around inside our flesh. We tend to think of the oceans as barriers that separate us from other continents, or we see them as watery modes of conveyance and transportation for shipping, or as a source of seaweed, fish, oil (whales), or as a place in which to enjoy a vacation. Norwegian anthropologist and sailor, Thor Heyerdahl, has this to say about how we view the oceans:

> If we remember our schoolday lessons, we realise it acts as a filter, receiving dirty river water and returning it to our fields through evaporation, clouds, and rain. It is probably not unreasonable to assume that most people regard

the dominant space of the ocean on our planet as more of a disadvantage than an advantage. With less land covered by the ocean, there would be more fields to cultivate, more resources available, and more space for the growing population to expand. The fact, however, is that the proportion of land to ocean is either extremely well planned or a remarkably happy coincidence, since it is this composition which has made life possible, at least in the form we know it, just on this one planet. (Tal, 2006, pp. 30–1)

He goes on to deliver a precise and amazing biology lesson on how life developed in the oceans. With solar energy, life came on to land, and lung-breathing creatures came forth eventually (that's us, breathing air instead of water). It is the plant life in the sea that creates the oxygen we need to breathe. Heyerdahl reminds us that 'man represents the crown of a mighty family tree with all its roots in the ocean. We cannot overlook this biological background' (2006, p. 32).

The ocean is, so to speak, our umbilical cord to the planet, and we are bound biologically to a complex ecosystem that is as much connected to the ocean as it is to the air and the ground. The base of the system is found in the sea.

Thor Heyerdahl almost drowned as a child, but he loved the sea and he was one of the foremost spokespeople for the beleaguered seas of the earth. He was the builder, with friends, of the Kon-Tiki raft, an aboriginal balsa raft that sailed with a crew of five for one hundred and one days in 1947, from Peru to Polynesia; eight-thousand kilometres! He was an explorer who was interested in communication between diverse and far-flung cultures and he learned that we must pull together as human beings if we are going to make it as a community afloat on this planet. He was fond of saying:

Our planet is bigger than the reed bundles that have carried us across the seas, and yet small enough to run the same risks, unless those of us still alive open our eyes and minds to the desperate need for intelligent collaboration, to save ourselves and our common civilisation from what we are about to convert into a sinking ship. (2006, p. 28)

After his second trip in 1969 in another raft, the Ra, he learned of the devastation already taking place in the ocean. The major problem was oil slicks and chemical spills. In twenty years, the ocean had started to reveal that we treat it as a 'sewer', and it was polluted on a vast scale universally. Heyerdahl died in 2002, but his work is foundational and it has set the priorities for the ecology of the oceans, concentrating on pivotal areas like the Mediterranean, Baltic and Red Seas, which are small enough for studying the effects of dumping raw sewage, ballast from ships and pollution from corporations.

Did Jesus ever make it to the Mediterranean Sea and walk along its coast? We know he spent a lot of time walking by the Sea of Galilee and he walked to Jerusalem from Nazareth, so he had to pass by the Dead Sea – which is what most of the oceans are in danger of becoming, just two thousand years later. There have been millions of years of natural pollution. We humans are new at this venture, but, unfortunately, we are far too good at it, and we move much more quickly than nature in adding scum, oil, poisons and toxins to the oceans (and air), faster than nature can absorb it, filter it and process it so that it is not as lethal to humans, animals, fish, mammals, birds and the rest of the environment. Heyerdahl wrote:

> One might say that on the seventh day, when God rested, man took over as Creator. He began to redesign the world and mould it to his own liking. Century after century, he has worked without a blueprint to build a man-made world, each inventor throwing in an idea, each mason thrusting in a stone wherever a hand could reach. Only in very recent years have we begun to wonder what we are building. (2006, p. 30)

What we are making of earth might be a global disaster, harmful to all and certainly not progress, but rather a turn towards regression or catapulting the world backwards in time, in evolution and life. I am grateful to his writings for much of the technological information culled from his sources.

Only a fraction of life in the ocean, a thin layer at the top, needs to be polluted in order to destroy all life. Much marine life is concentrated near the surface, relying on the sun, and even more is concentrated near shores, the places where water and land and air converge. This layer is deeper in the tropics, about eighty to one hundred metres deep, but in the northern latitudes it's as thin as fifteen to twenty metres. Most of the pollution comes from the land and from human beings, by what we dump into the oceans and into rivers that flow towards the seas. We dump everything from nuclear waste and toxic chemicals like arsenic to biological and medical waste. Such waste may be in containers, but no containers last long in the sea. Toxic materials also seep down to the oceans from industrial pipes and as run-off from fertilisers and sewers. We adults need some basic biology and chemistry lessons to remember foundational processes. The ocean filters itself through the air! The clean air tries to rise, while all the toxins sink in the waters. We have dumped more than a billion tons of DDT alone into the oceans and ground, with a hundred million more tons each year – and this is just one pesticide. We pollute from below and then we pollute from above with the toxins released through smoke stacks, smog, emissions and smoke fumes.

And that brings us to oil, gasoline and fuel supplies, the energy of choice of the first world. We are no longer even outraged when we hear of oil spills. We have accepted the fact that they are a part of the process of transportation and distribution. Even the bombing of Lebanon's oil reserves in 2006, so that they would leak into the Mediterranean Sea, barely received a mention in the press accounts of the virtual destruction of an entire country in less than three weeks. Our pollution of the oceans is being done quickly. In the last sixty years, we have ignored the fact that whatever we put into the oceans and rivers and seas moves around the world in currents, depositing our waste as far away as the Antarctic and the Arctic, on coral reefs in the Caribbean and the South Pacific and in every tree and gulp of air that envelopes our planet. The trite saying 'What goes around, comes around' is literally true in this case, for it all comes back to us, in water, air and food, and in the climatic irregularities that are becoming the norm. Once these were called 'acts of God', but now they are clearly attributable to us.

Water into Wine

The story of the wedding feast at Cana, which appears only in John's gospel, chapter 2, might serve as an example of what we need to do with the polluted waters of the earth today. We need to learn the art and the miracle of turning polluted waters into pure waters, and waters that kill into waters of celebration that sustain all life. It is interesting to note that this story is followed immediately by the account of Jesus going up to Jerusalem and driving the money changers out of the Temple, as they were polluting the worship of God and the prayers of the people. The two stories are bound tightly together, though we are in the habit of never even noticing that they are in the same chapter, following one upon the other, and that Jesus has a habit of doing something with his disciples and speaking about it first, and then tackling it in the larger public arena.

> On the third day there was a wedding in Cana of Galilee, and the mother of Jesus was there. Jesus and his disciples had also been invited to the wedding. When the wine gave out, the mother of Jesus said to him, 'They have no wine.' And Jesus said to her, 'Woman, what concern is that to you and to me? My hour has not yet come.' His mother said to the servants, 'Do whatever he tells you.' Now standing there were six stone water jars for the Jewish rites of purification, each holding twenty or thirty gallons. Jesus said to them, 'Fill the jars with water.' And they filled them to the brim. He said to them, 'Now, draw some out, and take it to the chief steward.' So they took it. When the steward tasted the water that had become wine, and did not know where it came from (though the servants who had drawn the water knew), the steward called the bridegroom and said to him, 'Everyone serves the good wine first, and then the inferior

wine after the guests have become drunk. But you have kept the good wine until now.' Jesus did this, the first of his signs, in Cana of Galilee, and revealed his glory; and his disciples believed in him.

(John 2:1-11)

This story starts with a lead-in phrase that should alert us to the fact that this is not primarily about an actual wedding it is much more than that. It begins 'On the third day' – the opening for a resurrection account in the early church. This chapter is aligned with chapter 19 in John's gospel and the account of the crucifixion of Jesus. This is known as chiastic structure. Parellelism is a basic form in John's Gospel. The wedding feast is the ancient Jewish image for the coming of the Messiah and the presence of justice and peace in the world, so clearly that all will see this as a sign, a signal to the nations that God has visited the people. This story is John's way of announcing Jesus' public entry into ministry and the beginning of the kingdom of God in history. There are echoes of what he is doing in Isaiah:

Ho, all who are thirsty,
Come for water.
Even if you have no money;
Come, buy food and eat;
Wine and milk without cost.
Why do you spend money for what is not bread,
Your earnings for what does not satisfy?
Give heed to Me,
And you shall eat choice food
And enjoy the richest viands.
Incline your ear and come to Me;
Hearken, and you shall be revived.
And I will make with you an everlasting covenant,
The enduring loyalty promised to David.

(Isaiah 55:1-3)

This is the background of the wedding feast to which Jesus, his mother and his disciples have been invited. It is Jesus' presence that will announce that never again will there be a shortage, a lack in the necessities of an abundant life for all. The poor are singled out and encouraged to come, while all are chided for spending money and energy on things that aren't bread (the necessities of life) and then on things that provide no satisfaction at all. Yahweh God reminds us that if we 'incline our ears', then we will feast on the presence and the Word of God among us, as close to us as a bride and groom in the community of those who are invited to a wedding feast.

What follows is the more familiar segment of Isaiah, where the Word of Yahweh God in the prophet's mouth is like the rain and the snow that comes down from the heavens, to water the earth and to give both seed to those who sow, and bread to those who harvest – sustenance for living. This Word goes forth from the mouth of God, out into the heavens, the waters and the air, 'soaking the earth and making it bring forth vegetation' – a strong creation image – and 'it does not come back to Me unfulfilled, but performs what I purpose; achieves what I sent it to do' (Isaiah 55:9-11). Then follows the description of what happens after the eating/drinking, the feasting:

> Yea, you shall leave in joy and be led home secure.
> Before you, mount and hill shall shout aloud,
> And all the trees of the field shall clap their hands.
> Instead of the brier, a cypress shall rise.
> These shall stand as a testimony to the Lord,
> As an everlasting sign that shall not perish.
> Thus said the Lord:
> Observe what is right and do what is just;
> For soon My salvation shall come,
> And my deliverance be revealed.
> (Isaiah 55:12-13; 56:1)

This is the Lord's promise of glorious restoration, leading the people back out of exile in Babylon, back home, but the nature of the restoration will depend on the people's response, whether or not they listen to, heed and obey the Word of the Lord, as the earth and the seasons and nature obey.

The theological account of the wedding feast at Cana and the transformation of water into wine needs to be read and interpreted in light of the longing for the coming of justice and the care of the poor that Isaiah demands. The wedding celebration must have been in full swing for some time because the wine ran out. One of the tenets of John's gospel is that the old covenant, and the old rituals and sacrifices of the Temple, are no longer a blueprint for the worship of God. The new covenant will be in the life blood of Jesus, in his living and dying, in the ritual of the Eucharist, in the taking, the thinking, appears the breaking and the sharing of bread among all believers. In the new dispensation, the only sacrifice that God wants is mercy, forgiveness, reconciliation and communion. This is the new wine, made from the waters of the covenants of creation, of Noah, and the Exodus, the exile and the prophets.

The need of the community to continue with the celebration, and the averting of humiliation for the bride and groom, is brought to Jesus' attention by his mother, who is never named in the text (or in John's gospel at all). She is a symbol for the members of the church's body: everyone from those who are hosting the wedding to those in the backrooms, the servants who fill the water jars, to the steward who tastes the wine. At the foot of the cross in chapter 19, we will find the beloved community of John's gospel. There are four singled out for memory: the mother of Jesus, his mother's sister, Mary the wife of Clopas, Mary Magdalene, and the disciple whom Jesus loved. These form the initial community of the beloved disciple (never named either), and they constitute on the one hand those who stand at the foot of the cross as the silent witnesses to injustice – putting their bodies alongside those who are unjustly tortured – and on the other hand the servants at the wedding feast, who fill the jars with water and bring them out to the steward to check, to taste and then to share with others. These servants are the only ones who know where the wine has come from. They are the ones who obeyed and followed the injunction of the mother: 'Do whatever he tells you.' They are the ones who obey the Word of the Lord, and their obedience draws forth a 'miracle' – a marvellous thing to behold. Our obedience to the Word of the Lord, to do whatever God tells us to do in Jesus, will continually bring forth miracles that others need so that the kingdom of justice, mercy and peace can become a reality. Obedience brings forth abundance that is to be shared with all. Surprisingly, what has been saved for last is now the best wine yet.

What is the miracle? How did it happen? What does it mean that Jesus turned water into wine, relying on the servants to obey his instructions so that a minor disaster could be averted for the couple and their guests? Perhaps there are some surprising answers! First a quote from Augustine, who is said to have been baptised on Easter Eve 387:

> The miracle of our Lord, Jesus Christ, by which He made wine from water is certainly no wonder for those who know that God did it. For He, the very one who every year does this on vines, made wine on that day at the wedding in those six water jars, which He ordered to be filled with water. For just as what the attendants put into the water jars was turned into wine by the Lord's effort, so also what the clouds pour down is turned into wine by the effort of the same Lord. But that does not amaze us because it happens every year; by its regularity it has lost its wonderment. Yet it merits even greater reflection than that which was done in the water jars.
>
> For who is there who reflects upon the works of God, by which this whole world is governed and managed, and is not struck dumb and overwhelmed by miracles? (Miller, 1997, p. 122)

As noted by Augustine, we make a much bigger thing out of the changing of water into wine in the water jars than we do of the miracle of the earth and the numerous works of creation that are continuous upon the earth. We need to go back and look at how the world works, at the patterns and developing processes that have sustained the world for hundreds of millions of years, and relearn the interconnections between water, air, fire and earth and human beings. But in the learning this time, we need to take the seventh day of creation and make it a day of reflection, of contemplation, and of integrating what happens on the other six days into our minds, our hearts and our imaginations, so that we can imitate the God of Creation in our work, in our inventions, in our technological developments and in our discovery of the earth and the universe in which we live. Education must become the source for teaching everyone, young and old alike, how to use the earth to better serve all the people that dwell here with us. This education must not only be the responsibility of schools, but of corporations, community groups, parish projects and adult workshops. This is what is needed in spirituality, in prayer and in action, to promote clean energy resources, clean water, fresh food distribution, shared gardens and renewable lifestyles.

Some of us may find the degree of pollution of the world's water overwhelming, and wonder what we as individuals can do to turn it around. Perhaps this is what the scientists and community leaders, educators and medical personnel in Bolivia and Peru feel about pollution that is degrading Lake Titicaca, where a neon green scum floats on the water, with dangling, twisted underwater roots, infesting the fish and everything that grows along the Lake's shores. But locally everyone, every group, has their own shoreline, their own rivers and lakes and stream beds to work on, and each contrbutes to the improvement of the whole. The folk singer Pete Seeger lived most of his life on the Hudson River in NY and watched it go from a clear running river with fish and wildlife along its shores to a polluted river that was unsafe to swim in, so degraded that it was dangerous to eat the fish caught in it. He started doing concerts to pay for the clean up of the river, calling for the removal of toxic wastes dumped into the waters over decades and alerting people to the corporations that were the cause of the smell and the destruction of the water and all that inhabited it. His contribution was significant.

Do a little exploring and adventuring and, with others, find your waters, contemplate them, and then do study and research and the hard work of returning them to the 'good' of God's initial handiwork in creation.

This is where turning water into wine in jars starts: turning all the human-made technological substances that kill, maim, cause birth defects and disease, into useful commodities. It is called conversion technology. And at this stage of history, it is the underlying foundation for creating medicines and serving to decontaminate water, food and air resources. This, along with clean energy and the use of alternative fuels, eco-friendly cars, houses, buildings and transportation systems is essential. It's time for a back-to-the-basics approach in all these areas, so that there will be a world worth living in as we grow older and our children come of age.

We will close this chapter with a story from a man by the name of Alejandro Cruz Martinez, a poet and teacher who was also a community organiser, working with his people to regain lost water rights in his local area. He was killed in 1986 while meeting with his neighbours. He had taken the story from the oral history of the Zapotec Indians of Oaxaca, Mexico. His widow has given permission to adapt the story and to use it so that others will take to heart the immediate need of people everywhere for water and to heed the voices and the presence of those who speak the words of truth, the Word of God of the Earth and the Seas and the Air. The story is called 'The Woman Who Outshone the Sun'. (Note: Lucia means light.)

One day, Lucia Zentero arrived. Everyone in the village was astounded. No one knew where she came from, or who she was, or had ever seen anyone like her before. She was amazing! As she walked into the village, thousands of dancing butterflies flew alongside her. She wore wild colourful skirts and brightly coloured scarves, and she walked proudly, softly, with great dignity and surety. Her long raven-black hair streamed out behind her, held in the hands of the wind. And a loyal iguana walked at her side.

No one knew her origins or where she had walked from. She was a stranger, unseen before, and people had all sorts of things to say about her. Some said that nothing shone as brightly as Lucia Zentero, that she brought light wherever she walked, but there were others who were not so kind: they said that Lucia Zentero blocked out the light. They all had different feelings about someone who was so beautiful, so different, so unlike them and so strange.

Now there used to be a river that ran outside of the town, almost the same river that runs by there now. And people said that when Lucia Zentero went down to the river to bathe, that the river fell in love with her! The water would rise up from its bed and would flow through her shining black hair. When she had finished bathing, she would sit on the riverbank and comb out her long hair with a comb made from the wood of the mesquite tree. And when she combed her hair, all the water and the fishes and the otters would flow out of her hair and return to the riverbed. The elders of the village said that Lucia Zentero knew the ways of the earth and the waters, and that she should be honoured and treated with great respect. But there were others who were afraid of her and her powers because they did not understand her. They would not speak with her and they refused to return her greetings. They spied on her and talked about her. But Lucia did not return the meanness of the people. She walked with her head up high and her hair streaming out behind her. She would keep to herself, which angered some and made others fear her, saying that she had come to the village and the river to harm them. As their fear grew, so did their meanness, and eventually Lucia Zentero was driven out.

But before she left, she went back to the river one more time to bathe and to say goodbye to the waters that she so loved. When she had finished bathing, she rose up and left the river, but the river wouldn't leave her! When she started to run the comb through her wet hair, the water and the fishes and the otters and butterflies and dragonflies refused to return to the riverbed. And so Lucia Zentero left, and took the river and all its creatures with her!

The people were shocked. They never thought the river would leave them. What would they do without their water? Now all that was left was a dry bed, and a serpent of sand where the water had once been. Soon, things began to change for the worse. Where once there had been trees for shade, and bushes and flowers, weeds and herbs, and cool breezes from the water, and wild foods, now there was nothing but blowing sand and grit, with no water to drink and no fish to eat. The birds and the otters disappeared, and no rain came. The people now understood how much the river had meant to them, and they began to understand too why the river had loved Lucia Zentero: because she had so loved the river. The elders suggested that they should try to find Lucia and ask her forgiveness, and to give back their river, but some were still too afraid, and so the drought continued. Finally, they all agreed that they must look for her, but where had she gone? It was the children who thought that she might have gone to the iguana caves away from the village, up towards the mountains. So the whole village walked for days and finally found the caves, with the help of the children.

Lucia Zentero knew they were coming, but she didn't see them. She stood at the entrance to the cave with her back to them. This was her refuge from the people. For a long while, no one said a word, and then the children started to cry out, 'Lucia, we are sorry and have come to ask your forgiveness. Please have mercy on us and give us back our river.' Lucia Zentero turned and looked at the people, and saw their tired, worn and frightened faces, and she felt compassion for them. She spoke, saying, 'I will ask the river to go back to you. But just as the river gives water to all who are thirsty, no matter who they are, so you must learn to treat everyone with kindness, especially those who seem different from you.' The people stood and hung their heads, remembering how inhospitable and mean they had been, and they felt a great shame.

Lucia saw how truly sad and sorry they were, and so she returned to the village, bringing the river with her. As she sat and combed out her hair, the water streamed back into the dry bed, and then all the fish and the otters and the butterflies and the dragonflies returned to the waters. The people were ecstatic. They poured water over themselves, and splashed and jumped in it, playing and laughing and singing. Even the animals joined in, and some cried in gratitude, their tears mixing with the fresh water. With all the excitement and celebration, no one noticed that Lucia Zentero had disappeared again. There was silence and sadness, but then the elders spoke, telling the children that even though she was gone, she had not really left them; they might never see her again, but every time they looked at the river, the rain and the clouds, the otters and the fish, the butterflies, flowers and dragonflies, they would know that she was there with them, helping them to live with acceptance, and welcoming all who came, especially the stranger. She would be in the hearts of all those who loved the river and loved anyone who was thirsty. And as long as there were people who loved the river, the river would stay and love them, like it loved Lucia Zentero.

It is time to love a river, an ocean, a piece of shoreline, a trickle of fresh water from a mountainside, a well of living water. And it is time to love one another – all the strangers who, perhaps, are here to bring us appreciation and eyes to see what we have taken for granted or misused. If we drink of the Living Water and of the new wine of the Word of God made flesh in Jesus, then we must take special care of waters: springs in deserts, fresh mountain run-off, the snow, the rain, the beaches and the oceans – waters all. If Jesus walked along the shores of our waters today and breathed in our air, what would he say to us? Among his last words as he died were 'I thirst'. He thirsted for us, but he thirsted too for water, for integrity, for all that God had made and for all those who would come after us to know life ever more abundantly.

In the story of the woman at the well in Samaria (John 4), Jesus sought to give her, and us, Living Water – a Jewish term for the Word of God, the Torah. Anyone who would drink of the water that he would give would become living water themselves, a fountain in the desert, springing up to life that is everlasting, pure and true. Jesus tells the woman that he is sweet water for a weary, thirsty world. The world still thirsts for this water as surely and as deeply as it thirsts for clean fresh water to drink. This mystery of water – an essential component of our bodies, necessary to our daily survival, and on a deeper level the source of our knowledge of God – has been offered to us. We thirst! We thirst!

Notes

1. A version of it can be found in *Indian Legends of the Pacific Northwest* by Ella Elizabeth Clark (1953).

2. *Zenit* News Agency, 'The World Seen From Rome', 15 May 2006 (Zenit.org).

Chapter Seven

New Heaven and New Earth

The phrase 'a new heaven and a new earth' is vaguely familiar to most people, but most would be hard pressed to explain what it means. Is it a place? Is it a relationship or attitude, or even a feeling? Is it a reward or a veiled threat, with the intimation that not everyone will be there or ever know what it is? Is it only in the future, and so a concept or a hope or a dream? Is it a way of describing what already exists: the heavens and the earth created by God thousands of millions of years ago, but restored, refashioned, made new, similar to the phrase 'new creation'? Does it assume that the old heavens (sky, atmosphere) and the old earth (the planet, the ground of this world) will be no more, destroyed either by us or by a deity. For the Jewish and Christian God, what would the destruction and ruin of the old heavens and earth say about creation, that which in the beginning was called good? What would it imply about this God, whose history is one of faithfulness, forgiveness and mercy, which develops and grows in leaps and bounds beyond human beings and then waits for them to catch up? What would it mean for Resurrection, which radically alters and reseeds creation with the force of life that is the Spirit of God, the Body of God, the Word of God that will never die again?

It is necessary to put our many questions into words before we try to talk about 'a new heaven and a new earth' as they appear in the earlier testament in the Book of Isaiah and in the later testament, in the very last book of the Christian Bible, the Book of Revelation. Before examining these texts, we will consider two stories that speak of heaven and hell as interior states of being, of union and communion, and it is a place to start but not to end. The first is a Zen story.

Once upon a time, there was a famous samurai warrior. He was very sure of himself, of his prowess and his discipline. He returned to the monastery where he had trained and he approached the new master there and said, 'I have heard that you know the secret of heaven and hell! If this is so, then please instruct me immediately as to their nature, their difference and their pulls on human beings.' The monk looked up from what he was doing (weeding the garden) and saw the former student arrayed in his battle dress, his armour and sword. He responded by asking him, 'Who are you?' The man pulled himself up to his full height and answered, 'I am a samurai!' The old monk looked up at him and a smile began to form around the edges of his mouth. 'Oh, you're a samurai!' he said 'Don't make me laugh!' Then he started to laugh, chuckling deep, and returned to weeding the garden.

The warrior stood, but his shoulders sagged, the surety gone out of him, and he brooded. The monk ignored him. The warrior grew angry and enraged, and eventually he drew his sword and raised it over the monk's head. 'How dare you insult me?' He spat the words out! The monk calmly looked up at him and declared, 'Ah, here open the gates of hell!' The samurai froze, sword in mid-air. The monk's eyes arrested him, brought him up short, and in that moment he saw himself as he truly was – arrogant, aggressive, without discipline or self-control – and he lowered the sword and bowed his head. He put the sword away and stood there, judged and seen. The monk continued looking at him and said, 'Ah, here open the gates of heaven!' And this time he truly smiled!

This disarmingly simple story reveals the psychological nature of the concepts of heaven and hell, which are very individualistic and personal. The story is a reminder to us of some aspects of Christian spirituality which have degraded this earth and this life, pointing to the afterlife, another world called heaven, that was thought to be more important than this world, this life and this time of the present. Christian spirituality has too often highlighted individual concepts of religion that saw sexuality, marriage, this world, nature, science, technology and even knowledge as negative, or at least as not as good as their 'opposites', which were separated out as better and holier and more likely to offer salvation. Such attitudes betray a somewhat limited view of the Incarnation, whereby God became flesh and blood and dwelt on this earth, in a particular time, place, race and circumstance of history, and continues to dwell with us 'until the end of time' (Matthew 24). With Jesus, we are sent into the world to love all that has been created, and to live with the specificity and limitedness of being human beings, in a community, in time.

There is another story, this one from the Jewish tradition, which goes beyond personal or dualistic concepts of heaven and earth. It is from the Hasidic tradition of the late seventeenth and eighteenth centuries in Eastern Europe.

Once upon a time, there was a very holy rabbi. He loved the Torah and God and his people, who were very poor and persecuted in their country. He loved his country too, and he loved the others who were not Jews, but they did not make it easy to love them. He spent most of his days preparing his weekly Torah portion, studying and praying, and listening to the many needs of his people, financial, medical and spiritual. It was a hard life and he often doubted whether anything he did was useful. He knew the people looked up to him, so he tried hard to be faithful, to bring them hope and to encourage them with the Torah and the daily prayers and rituals.

One Sabbath afternoon he was in his study when suddenly the prophet Elijah appeared before him. He was terrified! He cried out in distress, but Elijah was quick to calm his fears, saying, 'The Holy One, blest be His Name, is pleased with you! And He has sent me to bring you a gift for your faithfulness and for all that you do for his suffering and struggling people!' The rabbi was stunned – a gift from the Holy One! 'What would you like?' Elijah asked. The rabbi stood there in shock, but he had wondered about Paradise – Gan-eden – so often, and he'd heard that they studied Torah in heaven on Sabbath afternoons – all the great leaders, patriarchs and matriarchs; if only he could have a visit to heaven, that would make all the difference to his difficult daily world. He didn't even speak the thought aloud, yet Elijah said, 'Fine, Paradise it is.' And he snapped his fingers and he and the rabbi stood at the gates of Paradise. They opened, and the rabbi and Elijah walked into a world that was lovely, beyond description, lush, like the garden of Eden was in the beginning perhaps. It smelled unbelievably fresh and it was filled with light. The rabbi wandered around in a daze, filled with an enormous sense of peace and well-being.

Elijah said nothing and let the rabbi just soak it all in. It took the rabbi a while but he began to realise that there were very few people in heaven! There were a few clusters of people here and there studying Torah, walking as friends, laughing, singing, making music, eating...but there really weren't many people in Paradise. The rabbi grew distressed as he walked around, and finally he turned to Elijah and asked, 'Where is everyone? After all these years, have only these few people made it to Paradise?' Elijah laughed and said, 'You, too, Rabbi. I would have thought you would have known!' 'Known what?' the rabbi asked. Elijah looked at him solemnly and said, 'The saints are not in Paradise! Paradise is in the saints! Most people realise that as soon as they get here, and then they go back to earth to live and bring hope and light to all the world. They bring Paradise back to earth with them.' Then Elijah snapped his fingers and the rabbi was back in his study, alone. It was late afternoon on the Sabbath and he stood there stunned.

He began to pray, rocking back and forth, his heart and his mind filled with so many feelings. Then he stopped and wondered to himself: had he ever really looked at anyone here on earth? Had he ever caught a glimpse of Paradise in people's eyes, in their faces? And then, more soberly, he asked himself: does anyone see Paradise in my face, in my eyes? In that moment, his life was changed for ever. He walked the streets of his village, looking intently into the faces of everyone, not just the Jews he knew who came to his services, but everyone: the beggars, the strangers, the visitors. He knew what to look for now and Paradise; Heaven is in the saints and Paradise is here on earth.

When he died, crowds came to his funeral, and everyone spoke of how he had brought light and hope and such joy with him, and that he always looked you right in the eyes and smiled, his face lighting up when he saw you – as though he saw something there that no one else did.

Heaven is here on earth. That is often thought, or at least hoped, to be the case. And is the reverse also true? Is earth to be found in heaven? Or is the earth, this place that God made and called 'good' over and over again, to become the new heaven and the new earth? This thought is imbedded in the early writings of Paul, when he speaks of the power of the Resurrection, the everlasting fullness of life which has now been seeded in every human being. Death is not the last word. There is always life, ever more abundant life, for human beings because of Jesus' life, death and resurrection. The earth is a part of this new creation, this new way of living. Jesus' body in the earth has sowed life everlasting into the very ground:

> I consider that the sufferings of this present time are not worth comparing with the glory about to be revealed to us. For the creation waits with eager longing for the revealing of the children of God; for the creation was subjected to futility, not of its own will but by the will of the one who subjected it, in hope, that the creation itself will be set free from its bondage to decay and will obtain the freedom of the glory of the children of God. We know that the whole creation has been groaning in labour pains until now; and not only the creation, but we ourselves, who have the first fruits of the Spirit, groan inwardly while we wait for adoption, the redemption of our bodies. For in hope we were saved. Now hope that is seen is not hope. For who hopes for what is seen? But if we hope for what we do not see, we wait for it with patience.
>
> (Romans 8:18-25)

This passage continues with Paul reminding his community in Rome that it is the Spirit that prays in us – that we don't even know how to pray. The Spirit of God, in a sense, prays in the earth, in all creation, teaching all that was made to be holy to be one. Paul reminds them that, in the midst of hard times, of waiting, 'all things work together for good for those who love God'. Perhaps all things also work together for the good of the earth, if we, who are the children of God, do the work of the Spirit. The gifts of the Spirit are not for us individually, but for the building up of the community. And what if we need to start looking at the gifts given to us to build up and recreate the whole world and all that is within it, including the soil, air, water, resources, plants, animals, everything, including human beings? If we are now to co-create with God the new heavens and the new earth, what is it to look like?

In the penultimate chapter of Deutero-Isaiah, the prophet Isaiah sings in exalted and exuberant language of what God will do. The initial promises of hope are found in Isaiah 40-48 (some of which we have looked at with regard to the land and the poor). But this 'new heaven' and 'new earth' goes well beyond anything before. Listen:

> For behold! I am creating
> A new heaven and a new earth;
> The former things shall not be remembered.
> They shall never come to mind.
> Be glad, then, and rejoice forever
> In what I am creating.
> For I shall create Jerusalem as a joy,
> And her people as a delight;
> And I will rejoice in Jerusalem
> And delight in her people.
> Never again shall be heard there
> The sounds of weeping and wailing.
> No more shall there be an infant or a greybeard
> Who does not live out his days.
> He who dies at a hundred years
> Shall be reckoned a youth,
> And he who fails to reach a hundred
> shall be reckoned accursed.
> (Isaiah 65:17-20)

There is more, but we must take a portion at a time. First, the phrase 'I am creating' is repeated twice. This is not something done and finished. It is continual, in the past, in the present and in the future; like the processes of the original creation of Genesis. And time begins again. What has been a horror is forgotten, and the effects of that horror are forgotten too: suffering, pain, loss, grief and death. Instead of a short hard life of pain and sorrow, there is long life, abundant life for all, and this long life has always been the symbol of faithfulness and knowledge of Yahweh God. One is given longevity to enjoy life and to relate to God. This is earth transformed, brought to birth, as it was hoped for in the beginning. Isaiah continues with a description of very 'earthly' pleasures and daily realities that are made new:

They shall build houses and dwell in them,
They shall plant vineyards and enjoy their fruit.
They shall not build for others to dwell in,
Or plant for others to enjoy.
For the days of My people shall be
As long as the days of a tree,
My chosen ones shall outline
The work of their hands.
They shall not toil to no purpose;
They shall not bear children 'for terror',
But they shall be a people blessed by the Lord,
And their offspring shall remain with them.
Before they pray, I will answer;
While they are still speaking, I will respond.
The wolf and the lamb shall graze together,
And the lion shall eat straw like the ox,
And the serpent's food shall be earth.
In all My sacred mount
Nothing evil or vile shall be done
— said the Lord.
          (Isaiah 65:21-25)

This is as specific and as down-to-earth as one can get. The positive affirmations of life declare that there will be no slavery, no occupation by foreign countries, no selling of one's children or one's land, or building and working for others, with nothing for themselves except endless toil and drudgery. No, the people of God will know God's intimacy, God's nearness, God's shade and protection. There will be no war, no killing, no need to beg for what one needs, for God will attend to them all before they are even uttered aloud or in one's heart. This is heaven on earth's ground, using earth's resources, shared amongst the whole people of God for all time.

In his closing chapters, Isaiah continues to speak about the new heaven and the new earth. He begins by declaring that this new birth will be without labour pangs, and an entire nation will be born within a day, and there will be endless cause for rejoicing:

Rejoice with Jerusalem and be glad for her,
All you who love her!
Join in the jubilation,
All you who mourned over her –
That you may suck from her breast

Consolation to the full,
That you may draw from her bosom
Glory to your delight.

For thus said the Lord:
I will extend to her
Prosperity like a stream,
The wealth of the nations
Like a wadi in flood;
And you shall drink of it.
You shall be carried on shoulders
And dandled upon knees.
As a mother comforts her son
So I will comfort you;
You shall find comfort in Jerusalem.
You shall see and your heart shall rejoice,
Your limbs shall flourish like grass.
The power of the Lord shall be revealed
On behalf of His servants;
But He shall rage against His foes.
(Isaiah 66:10-14)

There is to be prosperity, economic and social equality, and wealth distributed to all. The feel of the place will be one of comfort, of security, of being at home, in a family, dangled on knees and held in arms, nurtured and given life. This richness and well-being extends from the bodies of human beings and their relationships with one another and with Yahweh God, to the city and the ground and the buildings and the land – all creation sings of the goodness of God, given lavishly as gift.

What follows is a prayer/meditation/journey of the soul, written by Rabbi Zalman Schachter-Shalomi. It reveals that many in the Jewish community are seeking new ways to interpret the Torah in a universal and more inclusive hope.

Doorway: Earth as an Icon

Take a few quiet moments, if you will, and make the following mind-journey with me.

Imagine yourself soaring over the vast plaza of the Western Wall, the Jewish people's holiest site. Below you, small dark figures walk or stand near the wall and sway. You see the men's and women's sections. Maybe some day there will be a place where both can pray together.

Now rise higher until you can see all of the Old City below you. If you know the lay of the land, you can pick out the different quarters – Jewish, Christian, Moslem. How these neighbours have fought over the centuries! How much blood has been spilled!

Keep rising, higher and higher, until you're at the level of satellite photos. In the centre, still, is Israel. You can see the Moslem lands of North Africa, and the Middle East and the Christian-dominated countries of Europe.

Keep rising outward and upward in your mind until finally, like an astronaut, you can picture our entire planet below you, suspended blue and lovely in space. Spend some time just gazing down at her from your position out in space. She looks so serene from here. Think of the expression 'the Promised Land'. Could this take on new meaning?

Now remember the verse that we sing in taking out the Torah: 'Etz chayim hi la-machazikim bah. She is the Tree of Life to all who hold to her.' Think of all the citizens of Earth around the globe, held to her surface by gravity's embrace. Can this phrase, too, take on new meaning? (Schachter–Shalomi, with Segel, 2005, pp. 153–4)

Other leaders and members of the other faiths are also looking at the world and at their texts and rituals, their expressions of belief in new ways, to incorporate earth and heaven in them, now and for ever. Thich Nhat Hanh, a Vietnamese Buddhist who now lives in France, speaks of the Kingdom of Heaven. Can we read these words and wonder?

We do not have to die to enter the Kingdom of Heaven. In fact we have to be fully alive. When we breathe in and out and hug a beautiful tree, we are in Heaven. When we take one conscious breath, aware of our eyes, our heart, our liver, and our non-toothache, we are transported to Paradise right away. Peace is available. We only have to touch it. When we are truly alive, we can see that the tree is part of Heaven, and we are also part of Heaven. The whole universe is conspiring to reveal this to us, but we are so out of touch that we invest our resources in cutting down the trees. If we want to enter Heaven on Earth, we need only one conscious step and one conscious breath. When we touch peace, everything becomes real. We become ourselves, fully alive in the present moment, and the tree, our child, and everything else reveal themselves to us in their full splendour. The miracle is not to walk on thin air or water, but to walk on Earth.[1]

Throughout history, in creation, in word, in the prophets, in covenant and in the person of Jesus Christ, God has been trying to say the same thing over and over again: make heaven and earth what I, your God, made them to be – new heaven and new earth, heaven on earth, heaven within us – it is all the same. We are to imitate God and repair the world, restore earth, make it all whole and holy again, so that its inherent life becomes ever more abundant and available, shared with every human being in communion and passed on to the next generations. This is the way it was in the beginning, and the way it is supposed to be at the end. And we are in the middle, trying to make it a reality in our lives, in our time and place.

Is heaven a place? I hope so, I dearly hope so, and I hope and pray it is earth, this beloved, beautiful spinning planet we have been so blessed to live on. I'm not alone in this hope and belief. It is buried in so many people's stories worldwide. The story we will look at now is an Irish one, and it takes place in Innisfree, an island in a lake (fittingly, where heaven and earth and the waters all come together to make a place of loveliness). This is the way I heard it told on my first visit to Ireland more than fifteen years ago.

Once upon a time, there was a holy man who lived on the isle of Innisfree. He was in awe of everything – the waters, the weather, the wind, the small creatures he shared the land and sea and air with, the towering trees, the rocks, the very ground he walked on, and planted his vegetables in, and ate of the harvest from yearly. He was old, ancient – no one knew how old he was – he had just been there as long as anyone who knew him and visited the island could remember. But the day came for him to die, as we all do, and they took him outside his small hut and laid him down on his beloved ground, and they chanted music and prayers, and old songs that he loved, while they waited for him to go to his rest. In the last moment, he ran his hands over the earth and collected two fistfuls of his beloved island and held them tightly in his hands. And he died.

They buried him on a hill so that he would be at home with the air, the sea and the land, and they mourned the loss of his presence to them. He, however, found himself at the gates of Heaven, with Peter standing there, smiling broadly, and the gates open wide. 'Welcome home,' he was told, 'we have waited long for you.' He started to step in but Peter's hand stopped him. 'You cannot enter here with anything of old earth or heaven,' he said. 'You'll have to drop the dirt you've got clutched in your hands.' The old man stopped and blurted out, 'Never! I love it too dearly to let it go.' Peter begged and pleaded, but the man was adamant that he would never let go of the soil. And so the gates closed and there was silence. Every time someone new came and was welcomed in, Peter would look at the old man and mouth the words, 'Come in, let go of the dirt', but the old man would shake his head.

Ages went by, and Peter came out with Patrick and Bridget and Columba, all Irish saints, to plead with the man, 'Please come in, let go of the past. Let go of what you loved so dearly.' They tried to cajole him, but he wouldn't budge or let his dirt go. Again the ages went by.

The next time Peter came out, he came with Jesus. Now it was Jesus who comforted the old man. He touched his shoulder and his face, stroking it like a mother would stroke her child. And he said to him, 'Please, come in. I have missed you these long aeons. Remember the words of old – that something is prepared for you, mansions beyond your imagining; that eye has not seen and ear has not heard what is prepared for those who love.' But the man just stood there, nearly limp, his hands filled with the dirt he'd brought from the land that had held him all his life and taught him all that he knew of life and love, even of God. Jesus extended his hand to him, saying, 'Come, take my hand and we will go home together.' It was Jesus' eyes – filled with light – that transfigured him; he'd seen that light before sometimes when he would stand on the shore and look at the sun coming or leaving, and it would blind him for a moment, but it was so filled with peace, beckoning him – and he had taken it as hope. Now the man reached back and dropped the dirt from his hands, and he and Jesus walked in through the gates together, hand in hand. They turned a corner as soon as they got past the gates, and there, laid out before him, was his beloved Innisfree!

Is it just a quaint story? No, it is the story of people who know and treasure earth and are bound to it as closely as they are bound by family ties, and as closely as they are connected to the God who made it and gave it to them as heritage, for safe-keeping. It echoes very precisely with a piece found in Paul's writings (see Romans 8:18-25), that all creation waits with its siblings, human beings, for the fullness of life, of salvation, to become reality. Creation did not do anything to betray the Maker; it was human beings who broke faith with their Creator, but they are once again reconciled and united in Jesus' life, death and resurrection. Heaven and earth, too, are looking in hope to the fullness of freedom and life. Karl Rahner believed this as he wrote this sermon for Easter:

[Christ] rose not to show that he was leaving the tomb of the earth once and for all, but in order to demonstrate that precisely that tomb of the dead – the body and the earth – has finally changed into the glorious, immeasurable house of the living God and of the God-filled soul of the Son. He did not go forth from the dwelling place of earth by rising from the dead. For he still possesses, of course, definitively and transfigured, his body, which is a piece of the earth, a piece which still belongs to it as a part of its reality and destiny...Already from the heart of the world into which he descended in death, the new forces of a transfigured earth are at work. (Raffelt, 1993, p. 195)

The Book of Revelation

The phrase 'a new heaven and a new earth' is first found in Isaiah, as we have seen, and is last referenced in the Book of Revelation.

The Book of Revelation is a series of letters and then a collection of visions given to the churches of the early first century as hope, as lifelines, to help them to hang on to their faith and to remain faithful under terrible persecution. It is not so much about the end of the world as the end of the Roman world and the end of any world that is not a world of life, of true worship of God and justice and peace for all. It uses literature that was familiar to the Jewish people and other peoples of the Mediterranean world to declare that judgement would come, that justice would prevail and that those who were faithful, especially those who had suffered persecution, torture, martyrdom and death for not worshipping the idols of Rome, would be saved. Justice would come in a person, the Lamb of God, Jesus the Lord, crucified and risen from the dead, now as the Son of Man in all his glory, judging all nations with justice and drawing those who died with him, into the experience of blessedness, of life for ever.

The first three chapters are letters to the churches, both praising them for something they have done well, and chastising them for specific failures. Then in chapter 4:1, 'there in heaven a door stood open!', and the voices and the visions begin.

This book of John is not reality. It is a vision or a prospect of what the writer and those who read it fervently hope will happen, couched in apocalyptic language. It is written not as a description of future reality but as a present exhortation.

For the writer, Rome is the new Babylon, which once destroyed the city of Jerusalem and the Temple, enslaving the people and dragging them into exile. Now the Book of Revelation reveals the breach between Rome and its idols and arrogance, as they persecute the Christians, those faithful to the teachings of Jesus. A massive struggle is envisaged between Good and Evil, Light and Darkness – a battle between King Christ, the Lamb and King Satan – and the struggle is initiated by Rome and all the nations that follow in Rome's footsteps across history. The visions end with a perfect city, conjured from the writings of Ezekiel and other religions' notions of what constitutes a geometrically proportioned city. The rest of the book is a psychological and religious hope, expressed in ancient language that cannot be taken literally. If it is, it loses its power and significance and becomes banal and simplistic, even deadly, if it is thought to prefigure actual reality in history.

The one who sees the visions is told to 'come up here, and I will show you what must take place after this'. The visionary describes himself as 'being in the spirit' in heaven, and he begins to tell of the visions in a symbolic language that is unreal, ethereal, both violent and terrifying, and comforting

– depending on where you put yourself in the dreams. The first one deals with heavenly worship – much like the images of Isaiah chanting the same words: 'Holy, holy, holy, the Lord God the Almighty, who was and is and is to come.' It is exalted praise of God, who is seated on the throne. Then he sees another, who is seated off to the right hand of the One on the throne, holding a scroll with writing on both sides, sealed with seven seals. And one like a 'slaughtered Lamb' goes and takes the scroll, while all of heaven sings that this one is the only one worthy to open the scrolls. All of heaven, the elders, the angels and living creatures, 'myriads and thousands of thousands', sing:

'Worthy is the Lamb that was slaughtered
to receive power and wealth and wisdom and might
and honour and glory and blessing!'
Then I heard every creature in heaven and on earth and under the earth and in the sea, and all that is in them, singing
'To the one seated on the throne and to the Lamb
be blessing and honour and glory and might for ever and ever!'
and the four living creatures said 'Amen!' And the elders fell down and worshipped.
        (Revelation 5:11-14)

This is the backdrop for what follows – the Lamb opening the seven seals. As the first four seals are opened, four horses that are white, red, black and pale green appear, and when he opens the fifth seal he sees under the altar (the scene is modelled after a temple/court) 'the souls of those who had been slaughtered for the word of God, and for the testimony they had given', and they cry out to God, asking how long will it be before God avenges their deaths on the inhabitants of the earth. They are given white robes and told to wait a while longer, until others join them, who will also die.

It is important to note again that this is a persecuted church, being butchered by Rome, living in terror and fear, and hoping that Jesus will return soon. And he is not returning. They must wait a while longer, and there will be others that will die and join them under the altar. It might also be noted that their prayer is not like the prayer of Jesus: to love one's enemies and forgive. Like most people, they want judgement and vengeance on those who persecute and kill them. Then the sixth seal is opened and the earth and the heavens (sun, moon and stars) experience havoc, and all the leaders of the earth cringe and try to hide: they seem to know that it is judgement day. They cry out, 'Fall on us and hide us from the face of the one seated on the throne and from the wrath of the Lamb; for the great day of their wrath has come, and who is able to stand?'

It is in this next chapter that the charge to 'Harm not the earth' is found:

> After this I saw four angels standing at the four corners of the earth, holding back the four winds of the earth so that no wind could blow on earth or sea or against any tree. I saw another angel ascending from the rising of the sun, having the seal of the living God, and he called with a loud voice to the four angels who had been given power to damage the earth and the sea, saying, 'Do not damage the earth or the sea or the trees, until we have marked the servants of our God with a seal on their foreheads.'
>
> And I heard the number of those who were sealed, one hundred forty four thousand, sealed out of every tribe of the people of Israel.
>
> (Revelation 7:1-4)

After the sealing of the Israelites, the writer sees a great multitude that cannot be counted from 'every nation, from all tribes and peoples and languages, standing before the throne and before the Lamb, robed in white, with palm branches in their hands', and they too cry out the praises of the Lamb and the one seated on the throne. The chapter ends with the praise of God by those chosen from both heaven and earth.

> He said to me, 'These are they who have come out of the great ordeal; they have washed their robes and made them white in the blood of the Lamb. For this reason they are before the throne of God, and worship him day and night within his temple, and the one who is seated on the throne will shelter them. They will hunger no more, and thirst no more; the sun will not strike them, nor any scorching heat; for the Lamb at the centre of the throne will be their shepherd, and he will guide them to springs of the water of life, and God will wipe away every tear from their eyes.'
>
> (Revelation 7:14-17)

This is encouragement and hope for the people persecuted and martyred and waiting for the power of Rome to be judged by God so that they will know vindication. What follows in the next two chapters is the destruction of the heavens and the earth and the seas, and a very violent destruction of anyone who did evil, or did not repent, and continued to worship idols and to commit murder. It is a judgement scene devoid of mercy or forgiveness. It is a scene that could be enacted by any vicious nation against its enemies, complete with torture, fear and all manner of horrors, except that it has the power to destroy heaven and earth as well. But then, at the beginning of chapter 10, after all the devastation, comes a very interesting piece of the vision:

And I saw another mighty angel coming down from heaven, wrapped in a cloud, with a rainbow over his head; his face was like the sun, and his legs like pillars of fire. He held a little scroll open in his hand. Setting his right foot on the sea and his left foot on the land, he gave a great shout, like a lion roaring. And when he shouted, the seven thunders sounded. And when the seven thunders had sounded, I was about to write, but I heard a voice from heaven, saying, 'Seal up what the seven thunders have said, and do not write it down.' Then the angel whom I saw standing on the sea and the land raised his right hand to heaven and swore by him who lives forever and ever, who created heaven and what is in it, the earth and what is in it, and the sea and what is in it: 'There will be no more delay, but in the days when the seventh angel is to blow his trumpet, the mystery of God will be fulfilled, as he announced to his servants the prophets.'

Then the voice that I had heard from heaven spoke to me again, saying, 'Go, take the scroll that is open in the hand of the angel who is standing on the sea and on the land.' So I went to the angel and told him to give me the little scroll; and he said to me, 'Take it, and eat; it will be bitter to your stomach, but sweet as honey in your mouth.' So I took the little scroll from the hand of the angel and ate it; it was sweet as honey in my mouth, but when I had eaten it, my stomach was made bitter.

Then they said to me, 'You must prophesy again about many peoples and nations and languages and kings.'

(Revelation 10)

It seems that even after the blood-letting, killing and destruction, the earth and the sea are still intact! And this last scroll, repeatedly referred to as the little scroll, is sealed, and the writer must eat it – sweet like honey in his mouth, but bitter in his stomach – like much of the words of God given to prophets such as Jeremiah, Ezekiel and Isaiah. These first chapters are about judgement, but if they are taken literally and fundamentally, ignoring all the Word of Good News, the Word of Jesus forgiving as he dies on the cross, they present a distorted view of God that has nothing to do with hope, with the coming of justice, and a judgement that is different to any other on earth. There are another ten chapters of prophesies and visions, with an array of dragons and bizarre creatures and bloodshed and violence. The Lamb and the 144,000 who are saved return repeatedly.

Just as we would not take the 144,000 literally, we cannot distort the visions and make them mean what we would like them to say: the core of the book is that there is judgement and those who follow the Lamb must remain faithful. Justice will be done, in God's time and in God's way, and everything is known to the one who sits on the throne and to the Lamb. There is talk of time, a thousand years (long gone now), and then another judgement comes and there is a resurrection…and yet another release of evil and destruction. It is more a vision of what is going on in the world, rather than what is going on in heaven! Then the last chapter is the one of unending hope, of unending life and the vision of 'a new heaven and a new earth' yet again. Let us look at it in portions that are workable.

> Then I saw a new heaven and a new earth; for the first heaven and the first earth had passed away, and the sea was no more. And I saw the holy city, the new Jerusalem, coming down out of heaven from God, prepared as a bride adorned for her husband. And I heard a loud voice from the throne saying, 'See, the home of God is among mortals.
> he will dwell with them;
> they will be his peoples,
> and God himself will be with them;
> he will wipe every tear from their eyes.
> death will be no more;
> mourning and crying and pain will be no more,
> for the first things have passed away.'
> (Revelation 21:1-4)

This vision echoes, in some ways, Isaiah's vision of a new heaven and a new earth, even to the extension of all peoples being included in it. God dwells with the people (as has always been the case in every time and place, but especially in the covenant, the Temple, the city of Jerusalem), and there will be no death, no destruction or pain. It is the image of a God wiping away all the tears of the past, the losses and hurts, the death and the sorrow, of each and every individual. We are once again described as 'mortals'. The first earth and heaven have passed away, as perhaps those who have died have passed away, but they also know life with God in a dwelling place coming down out of heaven to the earth.

Like many of the symbols in the book, this new city, Jerusalem, coming down out of heaven like a bride, mixes images and metaphors that don't necessarily connect logically, though they are bound to the history of Yahweh and Israel. They are strong images of the prophets. These portions must be read backwards more than forwards for any depth of understanding and meaning.

> Like many symbols of Revelation, this image has no visual clarity at all, it being difficult to translate the beauty of a bride into a city, especially when both are entangled in the Tiffany confection of precious stones which immediately follows. Its power derives rather from its appeal to language, drawing together

all the verbal patterns of the prophets' use of the city/woman image: John's words incorporate, within his own discourse, marital images from Isaiah and Ezekiel and the wedding formula found in Jeremiah and Hosea. It is not his intention to give the reader a Technicolour picture of heaven, but to convey the understanding that these words, which God now speaks, include and conclude all the pleas and promises, all the lover's addresses, which He has made to 'Jerusalem' throughout time. God's words, from alpha to omega, are fulfilled and simultaneously present in this symbolic city. The city where the word abides is (anagogically) the heavenly Jerusalem; it is (morally) the converted soul; it is (allegorically) the Church; it is also John's apocalypse itself, which seeks to culminate the sacred history of God among men not only describing – and heralding – the last things, the end of the world of history, but also by weaving into his own vision the words in which that history was told. (Dougherty, 1980, pp. 121–2)

The vision continues in symbolic language of possibility, and once again the visions are couched in the future tenses.

> And the one who was seated on the throne said, 'See, I am making all things new.' Also he said, 'Write this, for these words are trustworthy and true.' Then he said to me, 'It is done! I am the Alpha and the Omega, the beginning and the end. To the thirsty I will give water as a gift from the spring of the water of life. Those who conquer will inherit these things, and I will be their God and they will be my children. But as for the cowardly, the faithless, the polluted, the murderers, the fornicators, the sorcerers, the idolaters and all liars, their place will be in the lake that burns with fire and sulfur, which is the second death.'
> (Revelation 21:5-8)

This revelation is, as always, more about God than about us, or even heaven or earth. This God is the Creator and Maker, the Keeper, and the end, fulfilment, meaning and hope of all creation and all human beings. It does not mean annihilation and death or the end as we think of it. God is not like us – we are to be like God in God's image. We cannot interpret the Scriptures so that God acts like us! That is an insult to the God of life. God will always provide water: the water of life, the Word, the Torah, the relationship that we thirst for, as well as water to live on. No matter what happens on earth and in the heavens, no matter what nations and leaders do, God is the God of life. There is judgement, but there is always life.

The rest of this chapter is a description in great detail of the new city of Jerusalem, based on the old city and the Temple, and how it was to be built, and the measurements and resources and materials to be used. It is intricate and ornate, but there is one huge difference or lack: there is no temple in the city:

> I saw no temple in the city, for its temple is the Lord God the Almighty and the Lamb. And the city has no need of sun or moon to shine on it, for the glory of God is its light, and its lamp is the Lamb. The nations will walk by its light and the kings of the earth will bring their glory into it. Its gates will never be shut by day – and there will be no night there. People will bring into it the glory and the honour of the nations. But nothing unclean will ever enter it, nor anyone who practises abomination or falsehood, but only those who are written in the Lamb's book of life.
>
> (Revelation 21:22-27)

Again, this is an image of what earth and its peoples could become. The beginning of John's gospel began with this Light. It is the Light that has already come into the world, and with it came the beginnings of the new heaven and the new earth. These verses must be read with the Prologue of John's gospel in mind. They announce the presence of God in the world in a new way – now, here in the Incarnation and, even more so, in the resurrection of Jesus, and in the giving of the Spirit of God to us for all time. The first few paragraphs of John's gospel say all that has been spun out in the twenty-two chapters of the Book of Revelation in poetry that will take until forever to unearth, uncover and dig out its meaning.

> In the beginning was the Word, and the Word was with God, and the Word was God. He was in the beginning with God. All things came into being through him, and without him not one thing came into being. What has come into being in him was life, and the life was the light of all people. The light shines in the darkness, and the darkness did not overcome it.
>
> He was in the world, and the world came into being through him; yet the world did not know him. He came to what was his own, and his own people did not accept him. But to all who received him, who believed in his name, he gave power to become children of God, who were born, not of blood or the will of the flesh or of the will of man, but of God.
>
> And the Word became flesh and lived among us, and we have seen his glory, the glory as of a father's only son full of grace and truth. ...From his fullness we have all received, grace upon grace...No one has ever seen God. It is God the only Son, who is close to the Father's heart, who has made him known.
>
> (John 1:1-5; 10-14; 16, 18)

Perhaps we need to look at the new heaven and the new earth in positive ways, keeping in mind that our God is the God of life, never the God of death. Out of all death, our God brings forth life, ever more abundant, ever new, ever changed. The symbol of the cross, the horror of the world: even these are the wisdom of God. Nothing is unredeemable. Is that what is meant by the small scroll? Is it God's wish that we will eat that scroll, those words, those stories, those hopes and dreams of our Creator? Perhaps in our eating, the taste will not be to our liking, but it will train our palate to the ways of God so that we will do as Jesus asked us and 'love one another as I have loved you', extending that love out to the earth and the seas and the trees and all creation. What if the will of God is that this heaven and this earth, this planet, is being redeemed, and we are a part of that redemption and remaking in the image of God?

The last story told in John's gospel is that of Jesus preparing breakfast on the beach, with fish and bread and an open fire, and inviting his disciples to come and eat. He asks them if they have caught anything, and, of course, they haven't caught a thing. He tells them where in the sea to find the fish once again, and it is the beloved disciple who cries out that it is the Lord! They pull the boats into shore, and Jesus tells them to bring some of the fish they've caught. The story is sometimes referred as the 'great catch' – a play on so many fish, but also a play on Jesus catching his disciples once again! They sit and have breakfast together. Where the heaven and the earth and the sea and human beings come together, on a shore, a beach, there is a fire and fish and bread and forgiveness. It is the starting-over-again place. It implies beginning in a totally new way: the way of the crucified and risen Lord, where all destruction, violence, horror and misuse of human beings and creation is taken up as a cross, as a burden to be carried and as work to transform, as we transform and convert our own lives. We are a forgiven people: Peter, all the disciples, all of us. We are not only forgiven for what we do to one another, we are forgiven for what we do to earth, to wood and all the rest of what has been created for good. It is time to start again, with the grace and power of the Spirit that is given, to 'prove the world wrong, about sin, about evil, about injustice and violence', including what we are doing to God's beloved creation.

What will it look like, this new heaven and new earth? There is an ancient story from Ladakh in the Himalayas that is sometimes called 'Happiness', but I've been told that a better name for the story is 'Peace on Earth' – another name for heaven perhaps. Here's the story.

Once upon a time, there was a king and a kingdom. It was not a great and mighty kingdom but it was beautiful, nestled in the foothills of the mountains and filled with lush forests. The people were happy, and they say that words like beggar or thief or criminal were never spoken, and that people didn't even fight or raise their voices. Everyone lived together happily. Word began to spread about this place to the neighbouring kingdoms, where there were more than enough problems and strife and even wars – and plenty of robbers and beggars as well. The king of the next country decided to send his ambassador to the king of this marvellous place to find out what was the source of such happiness, prosperity, good will and peace.

The man arrived with his delegation and gifts and he proceeded to go straight to the king to ask him what was the source of such happiness in his kingdom. The king took the gifts, and when he heard the question he didn't hesitate to answer: 'Why, of course, I am the source of the happiness of my kingdom! My country, my people's happiness comes from my wisdom and graciousness, my generosity, just as a valley's fruitfulness is sourced by its river.' With the king's answer there came a long stillness in the court, and it was not a peaceful stillness. First, the poor ambassador was distraught – he couldn't go back and give his king that answer! He'd lose his head, because if all that was true, then the opposite was true as well – all the evils and misfortunes and quarrelling in his own country were sourced in his king! No, this wouldn't do at all.

And the members of the king's court weren't happy with the answer either. The king's counsellors began to talk among themselves, saying, 'What does he think we do all day and night? This kingdom wouldn't last a day without us – our planning and works and the direction that we give them.' The king's treasurer was put out too; he murmured to someone nearby, 'Why, of all the stupid things to say! If I didn't take care of his finances and make sure that they were well invested, there would be lots of fighting, and very little prosperity in the land.' The generals of the army were also annoyed, saying, 'Without our forces, our courage, our presence on the borders, where would we all be? Under someone else's leadership, that's where!' And the priests and magicians complained, 'Has he forgotten us? We're the ones who tell him what to do, when to do it, what the signs of the heavens are saying, what is worth remembering, and we perform the rites.'

Well, for the very first time, everyone was annoyed and angry at the king. News of what had happened spread quickly around the kingdom, and everyone heard about the king's words and about the words of all the other leaders and members of the king's court. And then the people expressed their views: 'What about us? We're the reason this kingdom is the way it is! We do the work, and raise families, and school the children.' Suddenly the whole kingdom was up in arms and their happiness and peace was gone.

Everyone was miserable, including the king. It was a very awkward time in the court. Nobody said anything and everyone was thinking awful things about everyone else. Even the king knew he was in trouble. But what was he to do? Then a serving girl came in with tea and cookies. Usually servants know their place, and enter and exit without a word, as though they are invisible. But not this time – this girl had something to say too! She turned and faced them all and said, 'You know, sometimes when the high and mighty make mistakes, they should go to the Old Man of the Forest and ask for his wisdom.' Then she left.

They were all so surprised that they didn't even scold her. The king immediately made a decision – tomorrow morning at daybreak, they would all go to see the Old Man of the Forest. Now, nobody knew exactly who this old man was, or where he had come from, or even where exactly he lived, but everyone knew about him, and many of the ordinary folk had gone to the woods to talk to him. He was poor but generous and he always seemed to know exactly what to do or say. The people knew that he loved the forest, and even the stars and flowers and animals, because of the way he talked about them, fed them and protected them.

They met him on the edge of the forest. His eyes shone bright and his face was radiant. He listened to them all talking at once, and then said, 'Follow me.' And off they went, into the forest, deeper and deeper. Finally, after hours of stumbling and walking, they entered a clearing, and they couldn't believe their eyes. Before them was the strangest thing they'd ever seen.

First, there was this magnificent tree towering over them. It was covered with flowers and with fruits, most of which they didn't recognise, and the leaves were almost golden in the sunlight. But even more strange was the pyramid or whatever it was that stood in its shadow. On the bottom was an elephant, on top of that a monkey, then a rabbit, and then a bird at the very top, all happily eating the fruits of the tree and feeding one another. The king and his people were invited to sit and rest, and the animals came down and fed them fruits and talked to them.

Then the Old Man of the Forest spoke. 'You see this tree and all of us sharing and eating of the tree? Well, it wasn't always like this. In the beginning, when the tree first started producing all these fruits and flowers and its leaves turned golden, all these animals came to me and they were all angry. Each of them kept telling the others to leave the tree alone, saying, "It's not yours; it's mine." I asked each one of them why they thought it was theirs, and they started answering: the elephant said it was his because when there was no rain he was the one who got water from the stream and gave it to the tree so that it would live and grow; and the monkey said it belonged to her because she kept guard over it and protected it from deer and boar and animals so that it could grow when it was young; and the rabbit argued that he was the one who pulled the weeds from under it and made sure that it had a place to spread out, especially when it was very small; and then the bird said that she was the one who had brought the seed that fell into the ground and became the tree.

'As they argued about who the tree belonged to, they slowly became aware of what they sounded like, and they were all a bit embarrassed. They looked at the tree and noticed that it had become ragged and had lost a lot of flowers, leaves, fruits and berries, with all of them tearing at it. They were ashamed at what they saw and they decided immediately that they would help the tree. So each one stood on top of the other, with the bird at the very top, and the tree was delighted that they were all together as friends. The animals realised that they loved the tree more than anything and wouldn't know what to do without it. And the tree, with great joy, thrived and blossomed again, with ever new and different fruits, flowers and growth. It always smelled great and it kept giving of its fruit to everyone. In fact, the smell spread on the air and through the forest and out into the whole countryside. This tree is the source of the peace and the prosperity of the kingdom!'

When the king and his retinue heard this, they wondered what to do – if this was the source, then it was crucial that everyone know about it. They had seen it for themselves and now they knew the truth. Somehow, they would now have to let all the people see it. Immediately everyone had ideas: the merchants and counsellors suggested that a road would have to be built, and the generals said that they would protect the visitors, and the tree of course, and they would need people to provide food, shelter, water. More and more suggestions were made and they were all talking at once.

Then the Old Man of the Forest cleared his throat and said, 'Listen to yourselves. You'd have all these hordes of people coming to trample through the forest and then you'd build a fence around the tree, and then you'd hawk this and that – no.' The king answered, 'Well, I've seen it and now I believe that this tree is the source of all the well-being and goodness in the land, but if I hadn't seen it, I don't know if I'd believe it.' The old man suggested, 'Why don't you paint pictures of it, and then all those who travel the land – the peddlers and the storytellers – can tell people of it, and they could talk about it and try to imitate the elephant, the monkey, the rabbit and the bird, all friends, sharing the wealth and the food, the shade and shelter of the tree.' 'Done!' cried the king.

And so it was that for years pictures were made, and small trees and pyramids of the strange animals carved, and the story told over and over again. Peace returned, even growing in some places. But with time, people didn't travel so much, as peddlers and storytellers grew to be a rarity, and many forgot about the Old Man of the Forest, and about the clearing and the tree and the animals. And with the passage of time, the peace faltered.

Now, practically no one knows the story, and look at the world! But now you know the story and you must share the word so that people can return to protecting the tree, the tree of such delights, which brings life to everyone – but it can only be given through sharing, not possession.

This story is for children aged four and older, so it fits most of us. It, too, depicts the new heaven and new earth, and what it is we must make of this earth. We must seek to undo the harm we have done, stop the fighting, and begin to share the riches and the resources with all.

All our stories and all our theology must be rewritten and interpreted so that new visions and new dreams of a new heaven and a new earth can reinterpret the old ones in Isaiah, the gospels and the Book of Revelation, so that they tell the deeper truths about life, about the God of life, and are not slanted towards ultimate destruction of creation and one another, belying God the Maker and Saviour inspiriting all things. That small scroll—what is it? Perhaps it is God's scroll of mercy, a scroll of dreams, a scroll of 'Ah, this is very good, yes, so good, such a delight; this is the way it will be', and that scroll being opened depends on us, once again. We can learn; we can change; we can live in the image of God as we have been created to do.

To end this chapter, I offer a poem for wondering, for hope, for what can be:

> Jump rope. Slide in stride. Watch the cycle and when the opening
> presents itself as emptiness – JUMP, the art of knowing how to enter
> the beat, the pattern, the expectation. Exuberance of watching
> double ropes synchronised in opposite directions, weaving invisibly
> in air. You hear it more than you see it. Music of air slapping air,
> rope slapping ground, how to insert oneself as one note just in the right
> place and moment? And it's better when another and another joins
> at just their time and the rope gets crowded. High stepping, laughing,
> jumping, playing for life. Whenever the ropes tangle, we stop only
> as a pause to catch our breath. Let's do it again, cry out the children
> of the earth.

Written by the author, after reading that if everyone in the world jumped up and down at the same time, the earth would be jolted off its axis! What in the world can't we do together?

Note

1.   Touching Peace, Parallax Press, 1992 (a card).

Chapter Eight

The Eighth Day – Job and Yahweh God in Conversation

To begin this chapter, we will consider a portion of the Book of Job found in chapters 38 and 39 that is often referred to as a creation account.

Job has pleaded, begged and angrily demanded that God answer him and explain the misfortune that has happened to him. He gets his answer finally, after thirty-seven chapters! But he does not get what he was expecting. The answer does get to the heart of the matter, with the writer using a particular literary style known as 'onomasticon', a form of teaching that was often used in the Ancient Near East. This is how the teaching method is described:

> These were lists of names of things that had similar characteristics and were probably early attempts at classification of natural phenomena. They demonstrate the universal human desire to understand the universe and have survived as a pre-scientific effort to preserve this understanding…lists of cosmological, meteorological or other natural phenomena were not unique in the ancient world…
>
> The manner in which this literary form is used in the Book of Job and the very reason that it is used at all are very significant. In addressing Job, Yahweh elaborates upon each item in the scientific list, noting the unique characteristics of each marvel and challenging Job's knowledge of and power over it. Assuming the role of the teacher, Yahweh utilises the didactic method of interrogation. Because the situation is polemical rather than merely instructional, the rhetorical questions set to Job are ironic in nature. Job is forced to acknowledge his limitations. This indirect procedure leads him to new anthropological insights and a different theological position. (Bergant, 1980, p. 180)

This is the pattern of these last chapters of the book – interrogation-declaration-interrogation – and then Job replies each time. And it is a fitting end for our own book. Hopefully, the intense and focused look at some of the vastness of the universe, and the earth's intricacies, as well as its complex interstices, will push us to look at who we are and make us re-evaluate how we have perceived the earth and God. The exegesis and reflections on the Scriptures from the Jewish and the Christian points of view, and from other religions, will make us think twice about whether or not we know and are sure of who God is and what God wants of us in relation to Creation, and call us to bend and bow our heads and be humbled by the awesomeness of God and what has been shared with us, as both gift and responsibility.

Job has been questioning God's plans, God's intentions, God's justice and God's very existence in the world, of history, of creation and in Job's own life. This first speech of God comes out of the heavens and is directed right at Job. The words are stunning, especially if we take them as directed at us today:

> Who is this who darkens counsel,
> Speaking without knowledge?
> Gird your loins like a man;
> I will ask and you will inform Me.
>
> Where were you when I laid the earth's foundations?
> Speak if you have understanding.
> Do you know who fixed its dimensions
> Or who measured it with a line?
> Onto what were its bases sunk?
> Who set its cornerstone
> When the morning stars sang together
> And all the divine beings shouted for joy?
>
> Who closed the sea behind doors
> When it gushed forth out of the womb,
> When I clothed it in clouds,
> Swaddled it in dense clouds,
> When I made breakers My limit for it,
> And set up its bar and doors,
> And said, 'You may come so far and no farther;
> Here your surging waves will stop'?
> Have you ever commanded the day to break,
> Assigned the dawn its place,
> So that it seizes the corners of the earth
> And shakes the wicked out of it?
> It changes the clay under the seal
> Till [its hues] are fixed like those of a garment.
> Their light is withheld from the wicked,
> And the upraised arm is broken.
>
> (Job 38:2-15)

There is order in the universe. It is carefully set in motion. It follows rules. It obeys! Immense power is controlled and held in check and submits to its Creator. The whole world is filled with God's limits and flow, God's design and justice.

Through Job, we are questioned about our knowledge and our use of the world. We are asked about our limited experiences with the world and creation. The questions are precise, battering at Job's and our minds and hearts:

> Have you penetrated to the sources of the sea,
> Or walked in the recesses of the deep?
> Have the gates of death been disclosed to you?
> Have you seen the gates of deep darkness?
> Have you surveyed the expanses of the earth?
> If you know of these – tell Me.
>
> Which path leads to where light dwells,
> And where is the place of darkness,
> That you may take it to its domain
> And know the way to its home?
> Surely you know, for you were born then,
> And the number of your years is many!
>
> Have you penetrated the vaults of snow,
> Seen the vaults of hail,
> Which I have put aside for a time of adversity,
> For a day of war and battle?
> By what path is the west wind dispersed,
> The east wind scattered over the earth?
> Who cut a channel for the torrents
> And a path for the thunderstorms
> To rain down on uninhabited land,
> On the wilderness where no man is,
> To saturate the desolate wasteland,
> And make the crop of grass sprout forth?
> Does the rain have a father?
> Who begot the dewdrops?
> From whose belly came forth the ice?
> Who gave birth to the frost of heaven?
> Water congeals like stone,
> And the surface of the deep compacts.
> (Job 38:16-30)

God gets more and more personal in describing what all these things are and how they exist, live and move and have their being, and how closely aligned God is with all of them. God is father, mother and creator, keeper and sustainer. God knows everything that is happening with all things, everywhere, on the earth, in the seas and in the heavens, and in human beings' actions and hearts, with the just and the evil and the violent of the earth. There is so much that we are unaware of, and yet Yahweh God is conscious of it, watching it, nurturing it, giving it what it needs, or shifting the forces of the universe.

I remember the first time I climbed in and saw Crater Lake in the western part of the United States. It shocked me with its beauty, its isolation and its depth, its shifting mirror of colour reflected from the clouds and weather, and its just having been there for millions of years. It is only in the last hundred or so years that any number of people have seen it or even know it is there! It was overwhelming to realise that it had existed for so long, unbeknown to most of the human race, its beauty unseen except by a privileged few, and God. How many places in the world are like that: for God's eyes only for most of their existence? And the same goes for most human beings. There are about 6.6 billion people in the world today. Who knows their beauty and understands them, apart from the handful of people who are their family, their friends and their neighbours, who are privileged to know them, and to appreciate and love them?

Soon, Yahweh's questions move out into the universe, into the stars and the planets and the unknowns:

> Can you tie cords to Pleiades
> Or undo the reins of Orion?
> Can you lead out Mazzaroth in its season,
> Conduct the Bear with her sons?
> Do you know the laws of heaven
> Or impose its authority on earth?
> Can you send up an order to the clouds
> For an abundance of water to cover you?
> Can you dispatch the lightning on a mission
> And have it answer you, 'I am ready'?
> Who put wisdom in the hidden parts?
> Who gave understanding to the mind?
> Who is wise enough to give an account of the heavens?
> Who can tilt the bottles of the sky?
> Whereupon the earth melts into a mass,
> And its clods stick together.
>   (Job 38:31-39)

This is wisdom. This is knowledge. This is a glimpse into God and a mirror reflecting back to us, on us. We have to start learning to see, to contemplate, to study and to absorb what is all around us, daily, nightly, seasonally, yearly, over all the decades in our small lives.

Now the engineer, the astrophysicist, the astronomer, the geologist and mariner turns to the animals. There are ones that elude human control and we don't know what to do with them. They are strange, and sometimes we are revolted by them or afraid of them, but each has its significance. Each says something about its maker. Each was given its own level of freedom, and God takes delight in all, whether we appreciate this or not. Animals were not all made specifically for us to domesticate them or eat them or profit from them.

> Can you hunt prey for the lion,
> And satisfy the appetite of the king of beasts?
> They crouch in their dens,
> Lie in ambush in their lairs.
> Who provides food for the raven
> When his young cry out to God
> And wander about without food?

> 39
> Do you know the season when the mountain-goats give birth?
> Can you mark the time when the hinds calve?
> Can you count the months they must complete?
> Do you know the season they give birth,
> When they crouch to bring forth their offspring,
> To deliver their young?
> Their young are healthy; they grow up in the open,
> They leave and return no more.
> Who sets the wild ass free?
> Who loosens the bonds of the onager,
> Whose home I have made the wilderness,
> The salt land his dwelling place?
> He scoffs at the tumult of the city,
> Does not hear the shouts of the driver.
> He roams the hills of his pasture;
> He searches the hills for any green thing.

> Would the wild ox agree to serve you?
> Would he spend the night at your crib?
> Can you hold the wild ox by ropes to the furrow?

Would he plow up the valleys behind you?
Would you rely on his great strength
And leave your toil to him?
Would you trust him to bring in the seed
And gather it from your threshing floor?
(Job 38:39-41 and Job 39:1-12)

The animals and birds have their own lives. They live bound closely to seasons and time, and to geographical places, and we know very little about them really. Carl Sagan once said in a lecture, 'It is of interest to note that while some dolphins are reported to have learned English – up to fifty words used in correct context – no human being has been reported to have learned dolphinese!' The truth of this statement and the ramifications of it stuck with me. Amazing!

Yet we are ingenious at killing and at extinction. There are ten animals that are endangered in the United States alone – some well known, others less so – and they go on and off the endangered species lists. They are the bald eagle – the symbol of the country; the Canadian lynx – solitary and shy, it lives in snow and evergreen forests; the Chinook salmon – a powerful swimmer, its connection to its ecosystem is vast, and more is being learned every day about its connection to bears, rivers, tree bark, birds and insects; the Florida panther – which lives in the Everglades and is the symbol of an Indian tribe – less than twenty-nine of them remain; the Grey Wolf – which used to roam in practically the entire country but now mostly only survives in Yellowstone National Park, though efforts are underway to integrate it back into a few states; the grizzly bear – huge and fast moving, and a symbol of protecting forests from fires; the Karner Blue butterfly – about the size of a postage stamp, with dark blue and silvery wings with black edges, exquisite in its beauty and so easily missed or just unseen or unknown; the alligator – with its great jaws and huge body, which can swim silently and attack quickly; the Peregrine falcon – soaring and riding wind currents; and lastly, the whooping crane – a huge bird that can lift off with grace. These are all in danger from us! Do you know which species of your country is in similar peril?

God continues to describe a menagerie of creatures that do not seem to exist for any good reason and those that seem dim-witted or strange, and then ends with an incredible description of the horse, the hawk and the eagle. They are psalms of praise pointed out to Job: 'See them, notice them, they are mine!'

The wing of the ostrich beats joyously;
Are her pinions and plumage like the stork's?
She leaves her eggs on the ground,
Letting them warm in the dirt,
Forgetting they may be crushed underfoot,

Or trampled by a wild beast.
Her young are cruelly abandoned as if they were not hers;
Her labour is in vain for lack of concern.
For God deprived her of wisdom,
Gave her no share of understanding,
Else she would soar on high,
Scoffing at the horse and its rider.

Do you give the horse strength?
Do you clothe his neck with a mane?
Do you make him quiver like locusts,
His majestic snorting [spreading] terror?
He paws with force, he runs with vigour,
Charging into battle.
He scoffs at fear; he cannot be frightened;
He does not recoil from the sword.
A quiverful of arrows whizzes by him,
And the flashing spear and the javelin.
Trembling with excitement, he swallows the land;
He does not turn aside at the blast of the trumpet.
As the trumpet sounds, he says, 'Aha!'
From afar he smells the battle,
The roaring and the shouting of the officers.

(Job 39:13-25)

The amount of information is staggering. These creatures are not subject to us – even the horse that can be reined in and ridden for battle is, at its roots, wild, and its power is from God. We judge the animals and birds, like the ostrich, by our standards and are ignorant of their insertion into a biosphere, a place in the world where all is connected and plays into everything else; to disturb one thing is to upset the balance and cause havoc and destruction to many life-forms. Most often, we are totally unaware of how the animals live with one another, co-dependent for survival, for we have forgotten that connection between ourselves and the created world of air, land, sea and creatures.

These dramatic words from Yahweh may seem like a lot of flash and dazzle, but they encompass a knowledge and wisdom that we humans have a tendency to disregard. As Yahweh describes all these forces and creations, there is no mention of violence from God, of destruction or misuse, of fear and enmity. We are all together, with the same God as our Creator. The Creator cares for everything, down to the details of food for ravens and lions and a safe place to deliver young for goats and birds. There is a gentle encompassing solicitude for everything that

God has imagined and created and intends to survive for ever. There is no height or depth, no corner of the universe, no cavern nor breath of wind, no microbe nor magnificent beast that God does not know and care for, and there is no human being and no event or moment of history that God is unaware of. God is, and God is everywhere. God is protective and yet stands back and lets the world and all that is in it live and move and develop. Because of our freedom, there is good and evil, there is misfortune and grace, there is prosperity and ruin. God does not do these things, but we effect them in tandem with the forces of the universe when we act personally and in history.

By now, Job and we know some more about God, but there is limitlessness left to know, and the beginning of wisdom is to realise this lack on our part and our need to have God's revelation.

Now it is time for Job to respond to God's questions and God's revelation of wisdom. Job has encountered the living, vibrant God, and it will mark him, as it is intended to mark us and to affect all that we do and how we respond in the world. This is one of the effects of true worship: conversion to the will and wisdom of God, if only in minuscule doses and decisions.

Job said in reply to the Lord:

'I know that You can do everything,
That nothing you propose is impossible for You.
"Who is this who obscure counsel without knowledge?"
Indeed, I spoke without understanding
Of things beyond me, which I did not know.
"Hear now, and I will speak;
I will ask, and You will inform me."
I had heard You with my ears,
But now I see You with my eyes;
Therefore, I recant and relent,
Being but dust and ashes.'
        (Job 42:1-6)

Job is beginning to learn and beginning to change and beginning to take notice of the wisdom of God all around him. We, too, must ask ourselves now: do we know our place in the world? Job surrendered to God. He didn't know or understand everything about God but he surrendered in trust to the God of life, the God that protects and cares.

Job, as small and as insignificant as he is, is an encouragement to us all. God listens and hears and bends to him and to each of us who are lovingly made in God's image. We have a unique dignity before God, which we must not forget, but we cannot take it for granted that it gives us a right of entitlement to everything on earth, including the earth itself. God answers us and will stand up for those on the side of truth, in God's ways and in God's time, but we must continue to struggle and seek for life and hope in spite of what friends, religions and other institutions may say is 'the way it is'. Job's lamentations now are transformed into mystery, into a sense of hope and a sense that there is more to know of God, and that he must be careful not to let pride or self-righteousness or false religiosity trip him into thinking that he knows the wisdom of God. Job goes back to living – living with hope.

> During the darkest periods of history, quite often a small number of men and women, scattered throughout the world, have been able to reverse the course of historical evolutions. This was only possible because they hoped beyond all hope. What had been bound for disintegration then entered into the current of a new dynamism.[1]

Job learned, and all of us who believe in God, in Jesus, know that what is at the heart of the world is love. It is an unbounded love, a love that has created all things, each in its own magnificent way, a love that has been set in motion from the beginning and is sustained. It is a love that is given irrevocably and freely. Its only demand is reciprocation and mutuality. Our individual experiences aren't enough to teach us about this God who is utterly transcendent – the vastness of the universe beyond us, and all around us, should remind us of that. But God is utterly immanent too, in Jesus who dwells with us here, for all time. Job's story tells us that we are not lost. We are not out here on our own. We are not to despair. God is with us. There is a marvellous prayer I was given in Bolivia, written by a man named Luis Espinal, who was murdered for giving the poor hope. It is a place to begin, always, again:

> Train us, Lord, to fling ourselves upon the impossible, for behind the impossible is your grace and your presence; we cannot fall into emptiness. The future is an enigma, our road is covered by mist, but we want to go on giving ourselves, because you continue hoping amid the night and weeping tears through a thousand human eyes.[2]

So now, today, what must we do? First, we must all learn to reverence the earth and to let the knowledge that we are all one seep deep into our bones and consciousness. The mystics and great men and women of the past have always had strong streaks of this in their spirituality. The Dominican master, Meister Eckhart (1260–1328), a monk and scholar and great preacher, wrote pieces of poetry that are stunning. This piece is called 'When I Was The Forest':

When I was the stream, when I
was the
forest, when I was still in the
field,
when I was every hoof, foot,
fin and wing, when I
was the sky
itself.

No one ever asked me did I have
a purpose, no one ever
wondered was there anything I
might need,
for there was nothing
I could not
love.
It was when I left all we once
were that
the agony began, the fear and
questions came,
and I wept, I wept. And tears
I had never known
before.

So I returned to the river, I
returned to
the mountains. I asked for their
hand in marriage again,
I begged – I begged to wed
every object
and creature,
and when they accepted,
God was ever present in my arms,
and he did not say,
'Where have you
been?'

For then I knew my soul – every
soul –
has always held
him.[3]

Don Sutherland says that when we lack reverence for the earth, we take no responsibility for it, and the decisions we make are all in the name of 'progress'. But he says that there are some signs of hope. He speaks of a non-profit institute, called Redefining Progress, that has developed an indice called Genuine Progress Indicator (GPI), measuring progress in a far different way than the usual indice of the Gross National Product (GNP). He describes it thus:

> The GPI subtracts items that diminish our quality of life such as environmental pollution, crime, noise, family breakdown, traffic congestion and loss of leisure time. The GPI adds value for things such as housework and parenting, volunteer work and wilderness sanctuaries. The result is a measurement of gross production adjusted for quality of life. The past fifty years show a continuing growth in gross production along with a continuing decline in genuine progress (Robbins, 398).

> Had we understood and shared Eckhart's view we would have adopted the GPI hundreds of years ago. Our deep reverence for the earth would have held us back from our rampage of destruction resulting in the almost total loss of the cod fishery, the Brazilian rainforests, the prairie grasslands, the Burrowing Owl, to name but a few of the earth's treasures.[4]

The Voice of Nature

Besides the individuals who have known this wisdom and sought to share it and live by its principles, there have been peoples and tribes that have learned of this reverence, this net cast over all of creation. When I first moved to New Mexico decades ago, the old woman whose house I rented told me all about spiders (which, along with snakes, I've never been all that drawn to). She had a small, hand-lettered sign tacked on the kitchen wall, which read: 'Don't worry, God, I'm not a very good housekeeper.' I wondered what in the world it meant. It seems that the native peoples here and in many places believe that God is a Spider that weaves a web that holds the world together, and it is a blessing for a spider to weave a web in your house! The story is told that when the conquerors arrived in North and South America, they brought globes with them – spheres with the known land areas/continents and waters on them, and lines of latitude and longitude encircling them. When the Indians saw these, they exclaimed, 'You know the Spider!' But, of course, they did not know the Spider – it was simply science. The Indians shook their heads and wondered about these people who had come across the oceans with their great boats and strength, but not much knowledge. I have grown to appreciate spiders, but the sign in my house reads 'In the bed, you're dead!' (after having been bitten on the face a few times!), though everywhere else they are allowed to live with me.

This voice of nature, this teaching of the world, is found throughout the continents, among many peoples. The Australian Aborigines talk of their Dreamtime and of the Great Ancestral Being, of how it was made, and how the world was given laws and gifts, to enable people to govern their own tribal lives, in everything from coming-of-age rituals, to where to find water, to what to eat or not eat, and what to use for healing. They believe that their Creator, their Ancestral Being, speaks with them in and through everything.

They tell the story of what happened when they were not faithful to their belief. It is from Southern Australia.

In the beginning, the voice of the Great Ancestor would speak every day from the great gum tree, and the entire tribe would gather around to listen to it. But as time went by, and the days became years, many grew tired of coming to the tree to listen – they would sleep in, or had work to do, or would go off somewhere else to visit someone. One by one, they all turned their backs on the tree, and on the voice that brought them wisdom, and they turned instead to their own interests and their own projects. The tree stopped speaking, and a great thundering silence began to settle into and over everything. The sea no longer made a sound. The wind was stilled. Nothing moved or seemed even to breathe anymore, and nothing spoke, not a bird or a beast. It was so quiet that it was terrifying, and everything seemed to be dying all around them.

The situation grew worse. The children stopped crying and laughing, the women and men stopped singing as they worked, the old ones no longer chanted or hummed, and the drums and instruments would not make notes. Everyone grew lonely and afraid. It was so quiet, so deathly still. Then they began, one by one, and then in small groups, to gather around the tree again. It was still silent. Soon everyone was coming back to the tree and praying silently and screaming in their hearts for the voice, for their Ancestor, to return and speak to them once more. They were ashamed and miserable, and afraid for their children – there were no stories, nothing to protect them, no one to give advice on watering holes or where the fish were, how to read the signs of danger/poison or harm.

Finally, the voice spoke again. It began by telling them that it was the last time they would hear it, because they had not listened to or obeyed or honoured it and its wisdom. But so that they would not be alone, the voice said that it would give them all a sign: they were to watch the tree and then to listen and see what happened, and learn from what they saw. Then the silence returned, but it was a different kind of stillness. And then there was lightning, and the tree split open from top to bottom, and a tongue of light came down from the skies and went inside the trunk – and then the tree closed up again!

From this, the people learned that the voice of their Great Ancestor would always be speaking – that it dwells with them and lives inside everything: in every tree and bird, rock and grain of sand, in every human being and every drop of water in the sea, in all types of weather. The voice would speak always for those who were open to hearing and to honouring its wisdom, and to obeying its directives. It has been so until now.

The Most Beautiful Song

Just as there is the choice of whether to listen to the voice and learn the language of the earth and heed its wisdom, there is also the choice not to hear, and to try to still the voice and to keep things the way we have made them. There is another story, this time from the Pgymy tribe in Africa, called 'The Most Beautiful Song'. It is haunting and sad, simple yet devastating.

Once upon a time, a young boy was walking in the forest that he loved, when he heard the most beautiful song ever. He followed it for hours, hoping to catch a glimpse of the singer. Eventually, he found a bird – a very ordinary looking bird. The bird allowed him to take it on his arm, and he brought it back to the camp, where he fed it and listened to its song. The bird ate from his hand and sang! Then it flew back, deep into the forest.

The next day the boy went looking for the bird again, and he spent the whole day following it and listening to its song. Then the boy brought the bird back to camp again and fed it. The bird rested and sang, and then flew back into the forest.

The boy's father was angry. He had let the boy feed the bird, but only from the boy's own supply of food, not from his supply or that of the others, and he was angry that the boy did nothing except chase after the bird all day. Again, on the third day, the boy brought the bird back and fed it. But this time the boy's father grasped hold of the bird before it could sing and he sent his son off on an errand. As soon as the boy had gone, the father killed the bird. Suddenly, there was a deep, sad silence throughout the whole forest and in the air, as though even the wind was mourning and had lost something vital. The man had killed the bird, and with it the song, and in doing so he had killed himself. He dropped down, dead. Dead for ever.

The story is indeed frightening. It is as though the concept of extinction was known and it was considered a horror aeons ago among those we call primitive societies. What are we doing to our world and creation? What are we killing? And what are we killing within us?

The opposite reality is also true: there is life. All around us there is a world of song, music, sound, silence and movement for us to listen to and read, to take heart from and to learn from, so as to enrich our lives. In literature, creation has often been compared to common realities. The Russian writer Dostoevski had much to say. The following description comes from a private paper, 'Religion and Science: The Seed Principles' by Jose de Vinck (2005, p. 5).

Creation is often compared to a game or a dance – both spontaneous and gratuitous activities indulged in for the sole pleasure of the performance. Creation is also compared to a garden, with the recurrent symbolism of the seed.

Dostoevski expresses his thoughts through the ascetical and saintly character of Father Zossima: 'Much on earth is hidden from us, but to make up for that, we have been given a precious mystic sense of our living bond with the other world, with the higher heavenly world, and the roots of our thoughts and feelings are not here, but in the other world. That is why the philosophers say we cannot understand the reality of the things on earth.'

He continues: 'God took seeds from different worlds and sowed them on this earth, and his garden grew up and everything came up that could come up. But what grows lives and is alive only through the feeling of its contact with other mysterious worlds. If that feeling grows weak or is destroyed in you, the heavenly growth will die away in you. Then you will be indifferent to life and even grow to hate it.'

It is as my Nana used to say at certain times of the day as the light shifted, coming into the world or leaving at dusk: 'Ah, there are other worlds – but they are hidden in this one – look!' And I've been looking, obeying that command ever since! This principle of expression, this source of wisdom, is ancient. The following is from the Jewish tradition, and it so strange and true:

For before the celestial world – known as the 377 compartments of the Holy One, blessed be He – was revealed; and before mist, electrum, curtain, throne, angel, seraph, wheel, animal, star, constellation, and firmament – the rectangle from which water springs – were made; and before the water, springs, lakes, rivers, and streams were created; and before the creation of animals, beasts, fowl, fish, creeping things, insects, reptiles, man, demons, spectres, night demons, spirits, and all kinds of ethers – before all these things there was an ether, an essence from which sprang a primordial light refined from myriads of luminaries; a light, which since it is the essence, is also called the Holy Spirit.[5]

There is a tradition in theology that says that the world, the universe and all that has been created by God and by human beings is a sacrament of the Spirit. It is all revelatory, all expressive of knowledge and wisdom, but we must learn to read its content, its direction and flow, and to interpret it through the lens of light, through the filter of life, life ever more abundant for everyone and everything, because it is the Spirit of Jesus the Risen Lord, which seeks, among us still, to give glory and praise to God in all things.

The following is from a paper by David S. Toolan, SJ, a working paper written for the US Catholic Conference's environmental justice programme that appeared in *America Magazine* of 24 February 1996. It is a very scientific and yet has a mystical way of looking at creation, physics and chaos theory as revealing how strange and fascinating all of creation, every organism, is; that it is all about poetry as well.

Nature's story from the bottom up, then, is only partly grasped as one of determinism. Redundancy there is, but it is only half the picture. The other, complementary half is a story of turbulence or fluctuation that begets continual metamorphosis. Matter does as human beings do. It is not passive but active; it repeatedly takes the raw material of random noise and converts it into something else, another story of greater complexity and increasing stability. It is thus rich in promise. At one level or another, what Catholics call transubstantiation has been going on since the very beginning.

...How do living organisms appear within the above perspective? First, an organism is an information and thermodynamic system, receiving, storing and giving off both energy and information in all its forms, from the light of the sun to the flow of food, oxygen and heat passing through it. Second, it is not at equilibrium, since stability spells death. It is an eddy, a balancing at the edge of chaos, struggling upriver against the entropic flood. As the French philosopher of science Michel Serres puts it, 'the organism is a barrier of braided links that leaks like a wicker basket but can still function as a dam. Better yet, it is a quasi-stable turbulence that a flow produces, the eddy closed in on itself for an instant which finds its balance in the middle of the current and appears to move upstream...' (pp. 8–14)

Science sings too! And it is all one song, one uni-verse. There is a script in our origins, and each thing expresses it in its own inimitable way, from the stars to grass and air, to micro and macro organisms, including us! We live in constant flux, and in relation to everything else, aware and unaware – to the stars and weather, to others in and out of relationships, to global structures and people half a world away, to every corner of the environment.

As he writes about us as human beings, David S. Toolan says:

Like the sun and the moon, we are disturbances in the field, vortices in turbulent nature. We are probably the most recycled beings in the universe, even while we live dissolving and re-enfleshing. We regrow our entire physical body as we do our hair and nails. Nothing in our genes was present a year ago. The tissue of our stomach renews itself weekly; the skin is shed monthly and the liver regenerated every six weeks. At every moment a portion of the body's 10 (to the 28th) atoms is returning to the world outside, and 98% of them are replaced annually. Each time we breathe, we take in a quadrillion of atoms breathed by the rest of humanity within the last two weeks and more than a million atoms breathed personally by each person on earth...Star time and earth time speak through us; we are their soul, sound and tongue – the universe's strangest attractors.

This a most intriguing way of looking at ourselves. We are in a constant state of flux and change. Transformation is embedded in our genes, and we are here in a world that is constantly becoming in order to make conscious change, to direct it and make it holy. This inherent order, this drive towards transformation and growth, this oneness of the universe and its processes and organisms, this beauty that is beyond what poetry can describe (lots of languages are needed – scientific, mystical, theological, moral, biological, physical, musical, artistic, prayerful, mathematical, palaeontological, poetical), all are intimate with the Creator. There is no conflict between science and religion – there are only differing languages, processes and ways of framing the questions and the answers that are 'found' or discovered. There is no conflict between religions unless it is deliberately provoked by human beings.

There is another old story called 'The Agreement'.[6]

Once upon a time, long before there were any people living in this valley in northwestern Canada and the United States, there were bears...lots of them. And there were salmon...lots of them. There was the river from/to the sea that was the salmons' highway home, and it stretched up into the country of the bears. The bears loved the salmon and depended on them for their food. Now the bears and the salmon had an agreement: the bears would only take what they needed to eat, so that the salmon could make their way up river to spawn, and so survive, and there would be another season and more salmon. This is the way it was – in fact, this is the way it was with just about everything. There were agreements, and that's the way things lived and thrived and survived from season to season and from year to year.

Though the bears had made an agreement with the salmon, neither the bears nor the salmon had made an agreement with the river. Every year, the salmon came in from the deep ocean and tore up the river in their thousands, hundreds of thousands, fighting the currents, heading exhausted to their spawning grounds, to their home, to their death. One year, though, when the salmon arrived in, the river pulled back and the salmon were left panting and gasping on the beach until the tide came in. They tried again and again and again. It was autumn and it was necessary for the salmon to get upriver before it was too late. Eventually, there were words, a lot of them, between the river and the salmon. But there was no agreement. Finally, the river decided to let the salmon come in and up river. The river was packed with the salmon struggling upstream. Then the salmon arrived in the country of the bears, who were hungry and waiting impatiently for them.

Suddenly the river went wild. It went backwards in one direction and forwards in another, with boulders and rocks all over, and spumes of white water and the banks all rocky. The bears were terrified and hid behind the trees. The salmon didn't know what to do. Then the river stopped and all was quiet. Nothing moved or said anything. Then the river spoke, saying that it needed an agreement, just like the one that existed between the bears and the salmon. It was tired of being ignored and taken for granted, and only noticed when it was thought to be useful.

So the salmon and the river talked for days. The salmon explained who they were and where they came from, and what it was like to fight their way upriver to home, to spawn and die. And the bears talked about who they were; about their long sleep and how hungry they were, and how they needed to feed their young cubs; they said that the salmon were delicious and nutritious and they couldn't live without them. Then the river talked about where it came from, and how it went down to the sea and how it knew the seasons, and the birds and the otters; it told of how it had agreements with the wind and the rain and all the different kinds of fish that lived in it or used it to travel home. They talked about what they needed and what they'd give in exchange. They talked and they listened for a long time. And then, quite unexpectedly, the river said something no one had ever said before, or ever heard before. The river said it loved the salmon and it waited for their coming every year. Those words changed everything. This was truth. This was trust. This was the basis of a strong and powerful agreement, and everyone was very pleased. So they each went their own way, connected now to each other.

You think this is a story, but it's not – it's reality. It's the way things are and have been since the beginning. Life is all about agreements. You can't just take what you want and ignore others. You can't just live independent of others. Everyone has agreements – everyone, that is, except humans. What season of the year is it now? Go outside and listen, watch, feel – you will get a sense of all the agreements, between birds and winter, when to stay and when to go / return. You will feel them on your skin and breathe them in and out. It is said among the old ones and those who know the language of the trees that it is only humans who do not honour the agreements; they don't even think to make them anymore. They take everything for granted and they are so greedy and destructive. They do not even honour the common courtesies anymore, and so they keep breaking the heart of the Great Spirit. Can you hear the Great Spirit crying, moaning and aching across the world and through the skies?

When I have told this story among native peoples, and on different continents, the elders have approached me and told me that this is not the name of the story. The name of the story is 'Covenants'. They are agreements that are entered into before the Creator, who will demand an accounting of every creature's faithfulness. According to their story, the animals, birds and earth want to be witnesses when the Creator brings humans before the Great Spirit to give an account of what they have done and been for the earth. They want to be there to listen and to see justice done – finally.

I love the story because it can be changed to incorporate local geography, trees, species, favourite places and new awareness wherever it is told. At the same time, it frightens me because we humans live with so few covenants / agreements, and the ones we do have, we break, or many refuse to abide by: the Kyoto Agreement, treaties to do with landmines, child soldiers, nuclear weapons, biological weapons / warfare, destruction of civilian infrastructures or bombing of populations, polluting the waters, the air and the food chain. When will we ever get back to the common courtesies with one another?

New Covenants, New Agreements, New Commandments

There are places to start immediately. In August of 2006, the European University of Rome sponsored a congress on Ethics and the Environment and came up with a list of ten commandments for the environment. They are available on *Zenit*, under the title 'A Christian View of Man and Nature: Ten Commandments for the Environment', but they are couched in anthropological terms and priorities that are not necessarily helpful in their entirety. They should have begun with the last one.

This is the tenth commandment:

10) A spiritual response must be given to environmental questions, inspired by the conviction that creation is a gift that God has placed in the hands of mankind, to be used responsibly and with loving care. People's fundamental orientation towards the created world should be one of gratitude and thankfulness. The world, in fact, leads people back to the mystery of God who has created it and continues to sustain it. If God is forgotten, nature is emptied of its deepest meaning and left impoverished.

If, instead, nature is rediscovered in its role as something created, mankind can establish with it a relationship that takes into account its symbolic and mystical dimensions. This would open for mankind a path toward God, creator of the heavens and the earth.[7]

The language itself is archaic (we have to drop the word mankind from our vocabularies, especially in public documents) and we must stop using the language of production, economics, profit and development, and financial and political interests. Theology must also start at some new points of reference, in science, in poetry, in astronomy, in biology, in new discoveries, in mystical language, and stop separating human beings out as above/superior to all else. These notions and expressions, however they were originally intended, have got us to the state of crisis that the world and all human beings, but especially the poorest, are now mired in, and it is progressing at a furious pace downwards in a spiral of violence and deterioration. We need to begin to work with and dialogue with other religions and their rich traditions, and develop languages that will more universally help us to find solutions and change our directions immediately, together. This is from the Chinese tradition of the sixth century BC:

> In this world there is nothing softer
> or thinner than water.
> But to compel the hard and the unyielding,
> it has no equal.
> That the weak overcomes the strong,
> that the hard gives way to the gentle –
> this everyone knows,
> yet no one acts accordingly.[8]

There are so many places to begin, so much that individuals and communities, churches, institutions and governments can do. One organisation called the Syracuse Cultural Workers, based in Syracuse, New York, has been involved in organising and education for years. Its literature and calendars etc. bear the words: 'SCW products are feminist, multicultural, lesbian/gay allied, racially inclusive and honour elders and children.'[9] Members of the SCW community wrote the two pieces that follow.

How to Build Community

Turn off your TV.
Leave your house.
Know your neighbours.
Greet people.
Look up when you're walking.
Sit on your step.
Plant flowers.
Use your library.
Play together.
Buy from local merchants.
Share what you have.
Help a lost dog.
Take children to the park.
Honour elders.
Support neighbourhood schools.
Fix it even if you didn't break it.
Have pot lucks.
Garden together.
Pick up litter.
Read stories aloud.
Dance in the street.
Talk to the mail carrier.
Listen to the birds.
Put up a swing.
Help carry something heavy.
Barter for your goods.
Start a tradition.
Ask a question.
Hire young people for odd jobs.
Organise a block party.
Bake extra and share.
Ask for help when you need it.
Open your shades.
Sing together.
Share your skills.
Take back the night.
Turn up the music.
Turn down the music.
Listen before you react to anger.

Mediate a conflict.

Seek to understand.

Learn from new and uncomfortable angles.

Know that no one is silent though many are not heard – work to change this.

How to Build a Global Community

Think of no one as 'them'.

Don't confuse your comfort with your safety – talk to strangers.

Imagine other cultures through their poetry and novels.

Listen to music you don't understand; dance to it.

Act locally.

Notice the workings of power and privilege in your culture.

Question consumption.

Know how your lettuce and coffee are grown; wake up and smell the exploitation.

Look for Fair Trade and Union labels.

Help build economies from the bottom up.

Acquire for needs.

Learn a second (or third) language.

Visit people, places and cultures – not tourist attractions.

Play games from other cultures.

Watch films with subtitles.

Know your heritage.

Honour everyone's holidays.

Look at the moon and imagine someone else, somewhere else, looking at it too.

Read the UN's Universal Declaration of Human Rights.

Understand the global economy in terms of people, land and water.

Know where your bank banks.

Never believe you have a right to anyone else's resources.

Refuse to wear corporate logos: defy corporate domination.

Question military/corporate connections.

Don't confuse money with wealth or time with money.

Have a pen/email pal.

Honour indigenous cultures.

Judge governance by how well it meets all people's needs.

Eat adventurously.

Enjoy vegetables, beans and grains in your diet.

Choose curiosity over certainty.

Know where your water comes from and where your wastes go.
Pledge allegiance to the earth: question nationalism.
This South, Central and North – there are many Americas.
Assume that many others share your dreams.
Know that no one is silent though many are not heard – work to change this.

Many of the suggestions are universal, while some are specific to the United States. Make them fit your own country, your own traditions, and then make them for your own church/parish/school on a religious basis. Then give them as gifts for Epiphany – the feast, along with Easter, of Light.

We all need to begin with the globalisation of compassion and an ecology of heart that is profound, that encompasses every choice, every priority and every dream we have, individually and together, as members of the Church and of other groups. We need to belong to groups that are international and global, besides the 'one, holy, catholic and apostolic church'. Every Catholic should know the basics of all the other religions of the world, and be able to have a conversation on what we can learn from them and what we can share with them in a mutual dialogue that honours everyone. All must be taught not to harm anyone, for any reason, and that to resort to or use violence only escalates the problem and the level of harm that already exists. And perhaps in this way we will learn to extend that imperative to the earth, the trees, the seas and all creatures. Our world is under siege, and we must learn to live with that reality and not forget it for an instant, because what happens to the earth, the trees, the water, the air, will happen, and is already happening, to our bodies, our minds/hearts and souls.

When I was in high school I discovered this line from Albert Camus: 'A man's [or a woman's] great work is nothing but this slow trek to rediscover, through the detours of art, those two or three great and simple images in whose presence his [her] heart first opened.' This world is home – the only home any of us have ever known. A few have looked upon it with awe from space, and even fewer have walked on the moon – and found earth a far better place. Perhaps it is the only home we will ever know, for always. When the Holy One comes in judgement and glory and it is time for us to offer back to our God what has been so graciously and freely shared with us, what kind of state will this weary world be in? Will God weep for all that was lost? Will God call us to stand up as we are questioned, and God is revealed as once happened between Job and God?

With belief in the Incarnation and the Resurrection, nothing is impossible; in fact, things that were once thought impossible are highly likely to happen. It is time to start thinking about and praying for the impossible – for an abrupt turn around in our attitudes and actions in regard to the earth, other human beings and all creation, especially those creatures and places that are threatened with extinction – the many animals, plants, birds, fish and, indeed, places in the world that are being wiped out/annihilated and lost to the world for ever.

Wangari Maathai, the recipient of the Nobel Peace Prize in 2004 and the founder of the Green Belt Movement, spoke, in accepting her prize, of why the Movement did the things it did:

> Through the Green Belt Movement, thousands of ordinary citizens were mobilised and empowered to take action and effect change. They learned to overcome fear and a sense of helplessness, and moved to defend democratic rights. In time, the tree also became a symbol for peace and conflict resolution, especially during ethnic conflicts in Kenya when the Green Belt Movement used peace trees to reconcile disputing communities. During the ongoing rewriting of the Kenyan constitution, similar trees were planted in many parts of the country to promote a culture of peace. Using trees as a symbol of peace is in keeping with a widespread African tradition…
>
> Such practices are part of an extensive cultural heritage, which contributes both to the conservation of habitats, and to cultures of peace. With the destruction of these cultures and the introduction of new values, local biodiversity is no longer valued or protected, and, as a result, it is quickly degraded and disappears. For this reason, the Green Belt Movement explores the concept of cultural biodiversity, especially with respect to indigenous seeds and medicinal plants.
>
> As we progressively understood the causes of environmental degradation, we saw the need for good governance. Indeed, the state of any country's environment is a reflection of the kind of governance in place, and without good governance there can be no peace. Many countries which have poor governance systems are also likely to have conflicts and poor laws protecting the environment. (Tal, 2006, p. 257)

Wangari Maathai put many pieces of her world together – the earth, the trees, the people, the ancient traditions of culture, of place and religion – and combined them with the events of a violent history, of politics, tribalism, economics and environmental degradation. She has managed to draw together private hopes, community needs and public realities into a net that is redeeming for all. This is the model that we must use in every country, in every place, so that creation and all of us have a chance at survival, and we might have something worthwhile and wondrous to give to those who come after us. She summed up what she had done, what is being done by millions in her country, and what so many countries still have not begun:

As I conclude, I reflect upon my childhood experience when I would visit a stream next to our home to fetch water for my mother. I would drink water straight from the stream. Playing among the arrowroot leaves, I tried in vain to pick up the strands of frogs' eggs, believing they were beads. But every time I put my little finger under them, they would break. Later, I saw thousands of tadpoles: black, energetic, and wriggling through the clear water against the background of the brown earth. This is the world I inherited from my parents.

Today, over fifty years later, the stream has dried up, women walk long distances for water – which is not always clean – and children will never know what they have lost. The challenge is to restore the home of the tadpoles and give back to our children a world of beauty and wonder. (Tal, 2006, p. 259)

Notes

1. Brother Roger Schutz, Founder of Taizé (the cover of Pax Christi USA Annual Report 2005).
2. 'Gastar la vida' in *Oraciones a Quermarropa* (Lima: CEP, 1982), p. 69.
3. This peom was quoted in a column entitled 'Oneness with God, living things essential' in the *Prairie Messenger* written by Don Sutherland, who writes about ecology and justice issues. It is from a book called *Love Poems from God*, Penguin Books Australia, 2002.
4. *The Prairie Messenger*, Western Canada's Catholic Newspaper.
5. Rabbi Hama, trans. Ronald C. Kiener.
6. This story was originally found in a talk Barney Lopez gave. This is the way the author tells it.
7. *Zenit*, 23 August 2006.
8. Lao-Tzu, Sixth Century BC, Exley, 2000.
9. They have two pieces of material that are available in poster, notecard and bookmark form. Their address is Box 6367, Syracuse, NY 13217, USA. www.syrculturalworkers.com and scw@syrculturalworkers.com.

The Last Words

They say: This is the Way the World Will End

Almost a decade or more ago, when I finished a workshop in Oklahoma city, an elderly Cherokee woman approached me and told me a story. It was short but powerful and it had been in the tradition for longer than she knew. She had heard it from her great great grandmother, who was one of those driven out on the long forced march, now called The Trail of Tears, as they journeyed from North Carolina and pushed mercilessly along half a continent to settle in a place that was so different than anywhere they had ever seen before. From the remnant that survived, they once again became the Cherokee Nation. This is the tale that she told me that afternoon, standing behind a curtain away from others' eyes, acting it out as she spoke.

> Once upon a time, long, long ago when the round earth was first built, it spun and moved in a great arch. What held it stable in place on its axis was a tree that ran right through its centre – the tree of life. The roots of that tree were planted deep and firm in another land – the land of the Great Spirit. Now, what many people don't know, even to this day, is that the Great Spirit, the Maker of all things, is a Beaver! This Beaver lives at the base of the tree of life. It loves the tree. It leans against it and sleeps curled up beside it. It talks to the tree and tells it about all that is happening on the earth – about everything from the new births, the antics of the children and the weather, the movements of nations, wars and fights, new marriages and growth, as well as tales of individuals who stand out because they are really human – they love life and love all that the Creator has made.
>
> When the Great Beaver watches and listens, and senses what is happening on earth, and what is in the hearts of all the people, the Great Beaver is saddened, or joyful, or pensive, and sometimes worries a great deal – What are they thinking? What are they doing? Why do they do that? And the more the people of the earth do evil, harm one another, harm the earth, destroy creation, kill when it is not necessary, forgetting that they are all one tribe, one people on the one earth, the Great Beaver gets upset. And when the Great Beaver gets upset, it gnaws on the tree! It chews on the bark and eats through to the wood, chewing and gnashing its teeth in worry, in

desperation and in loneliness. What are they doing? What is going to happen to all that has been made? And the tree begins to list and wobble in the ground, and the earth begins to shift on its axis. There are earthquakes, hurricanes, tornadoes, wind storms, flooding, and all sorts of odd things begin to happen because the tree begins to list to one side and fall over.

But then the Great Beaver looks and looks to see something of life – another child born; friendships that endure, crops being planted and the earth honoured in the old ways; gratitude for rains; care for the old; respect for the sacred places of earth and water, and for the creatures that have endured for so many generations. And the Great Beaver loves it best when the people dance! They stand on the earth, their Mother, and they shuffle, their feet never leaving the ground; they tickle Mother with their feet, their shoulders and backs straight and their heads high, tossing their hair and feathers into the air, and tilting their faces towards their Maker, the sky. Great Beaver starts to shuffle too, and stops gnawing on the tree of life. The tree has a chance to regenerate, like the people and the earth that it holds securely in place, while the Great Beaver laughs and is delighted.

So you see, when we kill, maim, harm the earth, cause extinction, misuse the resources, the animals, birds, fish, and the very ground and waters and air of earth, the Great Beaver gnaws and chews at the base of the tree. When humans forget that they are the brothers and sisters of all that has been made, and that the Great Spirit is their Creator and has given them their mother and father, earth and sky to nurture them; when humans take what is not theirs and use it for destruction, for ruin and for harm, then the Great Beaver grows sad and chews and gnaws on the tree. And this is the way the world will end.

They say that in the past generation the Great Beaver has been upset so often that he has been chewing on the tree a lot, gnawing it down to a thin reed of a tree, and that the tree is lurching and swaying in the wind like a willow branch sweeping and dipping towards the ground. We must stop what we are doing and undo the harm. We must care for the earth and the animals, the fish and the waters, the birds and the air, even the places deep underground where the fires glow and burn. We must care for one another and learn the old ways of healing, of making family/kin of all our enemies and of eating together. And we must dance! The Great Beaver loves to watch us dance. Remember, when we dance, the Great Beaver stops gnawing at the tree and it has a chance to come back to strength and life. The Great Beaver takes delight in all that is made, especially in those made in the image and likeness of the Creator, those who know they reveal and reflect the Great Spirit – humans, the two-leggeds of the earth. Dance, or this is the way the world will end – or so they say.

Let us Pray

God, you who are our Creator, our Maker and Keeper, who has brought us into Light, drawing forth our souls into life by your word and design, by your desire to share your life with each and with all of us, come to our rescue.

We have so shattered the symmetry and beauty of your creation. We have brought so many species to extinction. We have betrayed your confidence and trust in us. We have dominated and destroyed rather than taken delight in and shared your dominion over the world and all its myriad wonders.

Father of Jesus, Lord of Light and Spirit of the World, help us to undo what we have done, to plant seeds of hope, learn genesis, protect what is endangered, stop extinction and repair the world, and care for all its inhabitants. Let us learn to tickle our mother the earth, shuffling lightly on her, and honour the air and skies of our father, taking hold of all our brothers and sisters, four-legged, winged, in swarms, finned and teeming in the seas.

May we make covenant with everything on earth, under the earth and above in the heavens, and with the angels and spirits of the skies and the deep, to restore the world and reclaim what you have graciously shared with us. May we live in your image and likeness, serving as the sun, moon and stars serve the rest of the universe, giving freedom and free rein to the process of life, of regeneration, of abundance for all.

May we learn to sub-due, giving what is right and just to every living creature, and learn to see, to name, to call forth, to contemplate and keep the goodness of all that is made alive and thriving, for ourselves and for those to follow us down to the seventh generation. As we pass on our faith and belief in you, may we be sure to pass on the earth and all its contents so that your first book of revelation might be savoured and taken delight in by all who come after us.

God, do not let us harm earth irreparably. May we remember that your first gesture was to bring forth Light and to breathe upon the stuff of the world – water, chaos and darkness – to begin the story of 'once upon a time…' Let us continue to tell the story and to make it come true – relying on your Grace and the abiding presence of your Word. May we learn the joy of obedience and take delight in your command to 'Increase, have dominion over and master the earth'…in a word, to love it as you have loved us and all that you have made for the children of God, especially those poor and lacking and in need, all the children of the world, the children of the universe.

May we sing and draw forth the music of the spheres, the harmony of the species and the rounds of all the levels of creation – atmosphere, skies, ground, waters and the core of the earth itself – in fire and solidity. Out of the chaos and mess that we have made of what you once formed in choruses of chant and response, let us learn the song of glory, the song of gratefulness and the song of growth that exudes joy and life ever more abundant for all, human and created.

God, when the time comes for us to offer back to you this grand gift of the world that you made and gave to us, may it be one of such surpassing loveliness that your breath will be taken away and you will be stunned into sheer delight that your creatures followed in your footsteps and imitated you beyond even the hope seeded in our beginnings. May your Grace, your Word and your Spirit prevail. Let it begin again: The earth is the Lord's and the heavens and all that dwell therein! We are the Lord's. Let there be Light! Amen. Amen. Alleluia.

Bibliography

Aguilar, Jose Victor and Diez, Miguel Cavada (trans.), *Free Trade: Free Rein for Transnational Corporations*, Kathy Ogle, EPICA, Washington DC, 2003, epicabooks@epica.org in Spanish publicacionesmaiz@hotmail.com.

Aguilar, Jose Victor and Diez, Miguel Cavada (trans.), *Ten Plagues of Globalization*, Kathy Ogle, EPICA, Washington DC, 2002.

Arthus-Bertrand, Yann, *Earth from Above*, with essays by various international writers, Harry N. Abrams Inc. Pub. NY, 2002.

Ayers, William, Hunt, Jean Ann and Quinn, Therese (eds), *Teaching for Social Justice*, The New Press, NY, 1998.

Balasuriya, Tissa, *Planetary Theology*, Orbis, Maryknoll, NY, 1984.

Bauman, Zygmunt, *Globalization: The Human Consequences*, Columbia University Press, NY, 1998.

Bell, David, *Wooly Animals: A Book of Beastly Tales*, Cistercian Studies Series No. 128, Cistercian Pub., Kalamazoo, MI 1992 (from Genesis to the Middle Ages).

Bello, Walden, *Deglobalization: Ideas for a New World Economy*, Global Issues Series, Zed Books, NY, 2002. (Twelve other books available in this series on aid, development, economies, farming, global warming, agriculture, etc.)

Bemis, Mary and Recio, Belinda (eds), *Nature through her Eyes: Art and Literature by Women*, The Nature Company, Berkeley, CA, 1994.

Bergant, Dianne, *Job, Ecclesiastes, Old Testament Message: A Biblical-Theological Commentary*, Vol. 18, Michael Glazier, Inc. Wilmington, Delaware, 1982.

Bergant, Dianne, *The Earth is the Lord's: The Bible, Ecology, and Worship*, (American Essays in Liturgy) Liturgical Press, Collegeville, MN, 1998.

Bernstein, Ellen, *Ecology and the Jewish Spirit: Where Nature and the Sacred Meet*, Jewish Lights Publishing, Woodstock, Vermont, 2000.

Bernstein, Ellen, *The of Creation: A Biblical Ecology*, Pilgrim Press, Cleveland, 2005.

Berrigan, Daniel, *Job and Death No Dominion*, Sheed and Ward, Franklin, WIS, 2000.

Berry, Thomas, *The Great Work: Our Way into the Future*, Bell Tower, NY, 1999.

Boff, Leonard, *The Cry of the Earth, the Cry of the Poor*, Orbis, Maryknoll, NY, 1997.

Boff, Leonardo and Elizondo, Virgil, *Ecology And Poverty*, Concilium, SCM Press/London, Orbis Books, Maryknoll, NY, 1995/5.

Borges, Phil (photographs), *Enduring Spirit*, intro. Isabel Allende for Amnesty International, Rizzoli, NY, 1998.

Boyer, Marie-France, *Tree-Talk, Memories, Myths and Timeless Customs*, Thames and Hudson, London, 1996.

Brian Swimme with Thomas Berry, *The Universe Story*, Harper Collins, San Francisco, 1992.

Brubaker, Pamela K., *Globalization at what Price? Economic Change and Daily Life*, Pilgrim Press, Cleveland, Ohio, 2001.

Bruchac, Joseph, *Our Stories Remember: American Indian History, Culture and Values through Storytelling*, Fulcrum Pub, Golden, Co, 2003.

Bruchac, Joseph, *Roots of Survival: Native American Storytelling and the Sacred*, Fulcrum Pub., Golden Co, 1996 and anything by this man, such as *Native Plant Stories, Native Animal Stories, Native American Stories* and the series *Keepers of Life* that he wrote with Michael

J. Caduto. (Plants, animals, earth, gardening come with teaching guides and some are available as audio books.)

Brueggemann, Walter, *The Land: Overtures to Biblical Theology*, Fortress Press, Philadelphia, PA, 1977.

Brueggemann, Walter, *The Prophetic Imagination*, Fortress Press, Minneapolis, MN, 1978.

Brueggemann, Walter, *Using God's Resources Wisely: Isaiah and Urban Possibility*, Westminster/John Knox, Lousiville, KY, 1993.

Buber, Martin, *The Prophetic Faith*, Collier/Macmillian, NY, 1949.

Butler, Tom (ed.), *Wild Earth: Wild Ideas for a World out of Balance*, Milkweed Pub., Minneapolis, MN, 2002.

Caduto, Michael J., *Earth Tales From Around The World*, Fulcrum Pub., Golden Co, 1997.

Campbell, Jeremy, *The Many Faces of God: Science's 400-Year Quest for Images of the Divine*, W.W. Norton & Company, NY, 2006.

Capra, Fritjof, *The Hidden Connections: Integrating the Biological, Cognitive and Social Dimensions of Life into a Science of Sustainability*, Doubleday, NY, 2002.

Capra, Fritjof, *The Web of Life*, Anchor Books, Random House, NY, 1996.

Carrier, Herve, SJ, *The Social Doctrine of the Church Revisited: A Guide for Study*, Pontifical Council for Justice and Peace, Vatican City, Rome, 1990.

Clark, Ella Elizabeth, *Indian Legends o the Pacific Northwest*, University of California Press, Berkeley, 1953.

Cleary, William, *How the Wild Things Pray*, Forest of Peace Pub, Leavenworth, KS, 1999.

Clifton, Carr (photographs) and Turner, Tom (text), *Wild By Law: The Sierra Club Legal Defense Fund and the Places it Has Saved*, Sierra Club Books, San Francisco, 1990.

Coleman, John and Ryan, Wm. (eds), *Globalization and Catholic Social Thought: Present Crisis, Future Hope*, Novalis, Toronto, Canada, 2006.

Comblin, Jose, *Cry of the Oppressed, Cry of Jesus: Meditations on Scripture and Contemporary Struggle*, Orbis, Maryknoll, NY, 1988.

Conference of Religious Ireland (CORI), *Human Dignity and Spirituality in a Globalised World*, No. 2, Spirituality for Social Engagement: Conference of the Justice Commission of the Conference of Religious of Ireland, Dominican Pub., Dublin, 2006.

Cotter, David W., *Berit Olam: Studies in Hebrew Narrative and Poetry*, Liturgical Press, Collegeville, MN, 2003.

Crossan, John Dominic, *The Dark Interval: Towards a Theology of Story*, Argus Communications, Niles, IL, 1975.

Curtis, Edward (photographs), *Songs of the Earth: A Timeless Collection of Native American Wisdom*, Courage Books, Running Press, Philadelpia, PA, 2003.

Dalai Lama, His Holiness the, *The Universe in a Single Atom: The Convergence of Science and Spirituality*, Morgan Road Books, NY, 2005.

Dalai Lama, *The Universe in a Single Atom: The Convergence of Science and Spirituality*, Morgan Road Books, NY, 2005.

David, Jennifer, *Story Keepers: Conversations with Aboriginal Writers*, Ningwakwe Learning Press, Owen Sound, Ontario, Canada, 2004.

de Chardin, Teilhard, (any book by him but especially) *The Human Phenomenon*, trans. de Chardin, Teilhard, *The Divine Milieu*, Harper and Row, NY, 1960.

de Chardin, Teilhard, *Man's Place In Nature*, Harper and Row, NY, 1966.

de Chardin, Teilhard, *Human Energy*, Harcourt Brace Jovanovich, NY, 1971.

de Chardin, Teilhard, *The Heart of the Matter*, Harcourt, Brace, Jovanovich, NY, 1979.

DeBerri, Edward P., Hug, James, with Henriot, Peter and Schultheis, Michael, *Catholic Sarah Appleton-Weber, Sussex Academic Press, Brighton, 1999.

Social Teaching: Our Best Kept Secret, Orbis Books, NY and Center of Concern, Washington DC, 1985 (4th edition revised/expanded).

DeGrasse Tyson, Neil and Goldsmith, Donald, *Origins: Fourteen Billion Years of Cosmic Evolution* (the Nova special on PBS), W.W. Norton & Co., NY, 2004.

Dempsey, Carol J. and Pazdan, Mary Margaret (eds), *Earth, Wind And Fire: Biblical and Theological Perspectives on Creation*, Liturgical Press, Collegeville, MN, 2004.

Dillard, Annie, *Pilgrim at Tinker Creek*, Harper's Magazine Press, NY, 1974.

Doolittle, Bev, *The Art of Bev Doolittle*, Texts and Poems by Elise Maclay, Bantam Books, NY, 1990 (symbols/art within paintings).

Dougherty, James, *The Fivesquare City: The City in the Religious Imagination*, University of Notre Dame Press, Notre Dame, Ind., 1980.

Echlin, Edeard P., *The Cosmic Circle: Jesus and Ecology*, Columba Press, Dublin, 2004.

Ehrlich, Gretel, *The Solace of Open Spaces*, Penguin Books Ltd, 1986 (and practically anything else written by her).

Ehrlich, Gretel, *Islands, the Universe, Home*, Penguin Books, NY, 1991.

Ehrlich, Gretel, *John Muir: Nature's Visionary*, National Geographic, Washington DC, 2000.

Ehrlich, Gretel, *The Future of Ice: A Journey Into Cold*, Panethon Books, NY, 2004.

Eisenberg Sasso, Sandy, *A Prayer for the Earth: The Story of Naamah, Noah's Wife*, Jewish Lights Publishing, NY, 1996.

Elder, John and Wong, Hertha (eds), *Family of Earth and Sky, Indigenous Tales of Nature from Around the World*, Beacon Press, Boston, MA, 1994.

Elper, Ora Wiskind and Handelman, Susan (eds), *Torah of the Mothers: Contemporary Jewish Women Read Classical Jewish Texts*, Urim Publications, Jerusalem/NY, 2006.

Emoto, Masaru, *The Hidden Messages in Water*, Beyond Words Pub., Hillsboro, Oregon, 2004. (See also *The Secret Life of Water* and *The True Power of Water*.)

Exley, Helen, *And Wisdom Comes Quietly*, Spencer, MA, and Watford, Herts, UK, 2000.

Fabel, Arthur and St John, Donald (eds), *Teilhard in the 21st Century: The Emerging Spirit of the Earth*, Orbis, Maryknoll, NY, 2003.

Friesen, John, *Aboriginal Spirituality and Biblical Theology: Closer than you Think*, University of Calgary, Alberta, 2000.

Gattuso, John (ed.), *A Circle of Nations: Voices And Visions of American Indians* (Native American Writers and Photographers), Beyond Words Pub., Hillsboro, Oregon, 1993.

Gebara, Ivone, *Longing for Running Water: Ecofeminism and Liberation*, Fortress Press, Minneapolis, MN, 1999.

Gebara, Ivone, *Out of the Depts: Womens' Experience of Evil and Salvation*, Fortress Press, Minneapolis, MN, 2002.

Girard, Marc, *The Poor Sacrament of God: Biblical and Theolgical Meditation*, Mediaspaul, Quebec, Canada, 1994.

Glancy, Diane, *The Man who Heard the Land*, Minnesota Historical Society, St Paul, MN, 2001.

Goodenough, Ursula, *The Sacred Depths of Nature*, Oxford University Press, NY, 1998.

Gottlieb, Roger (ed.), *This Sacred Earth: Religion, Nature, Environment*, Routledge, NY, 1996.

Guard Monroe, Jean and Williamson, Ray A., *They Dance in the Sky: Native American Star Myths*, Houghton Mifflin Co, Boston, MA, 1987.

Gunn Allen, Paula (ed.), *Spider Woman's Granddaughters: Traditional Tales and Contemporary Writing by Native American Women*, Beacon Press, Boston, MA, 1980.

Gustavo, Gutierrez, *On Job: God-Talk and the Suffering of the Innocent*, Orbis Books, Maryknoll, NY, 1987.

Hallendy, Norman, *Inuksuit: Silent Messengers of the Artic*, with photographs by the author, Douglas & McIntyre, Vancouver/Toronto, 2000.

Harjo, Joy, *A Map to the Next World: Poems and Tales*, WW Norton Co, NY, 2000. (See also: *She had some Horses, Secrets from the Center of the World, The Woman Who Fell from the Sky, Re-Inventing the Enemy's Language* [co-ed.]).

Hawking, Stephen with Mlodinow, Leonard, *A Briefer History of Time*, Bantam Press, 2006.

Hawley, Susan (ed.), *Proclaim Liberty: Reflections on Theology and Debt*, Christian Aid, London, 1998.

Hendrickx, Herman, *Social Justice in the Bible*, Claretian Pub., Quezon City, Philippines, 1985.

Henriot, Peter, SJ, *Opting for the Poor: A Challenge for North Americans*, Center of Concern, Washington DC, 1990.

Henriot, Peter, SJ, *Opting for the Poor: The Challenge for the Twenty-First Century*, Center of Concern, Washington DC, 2004.

Henry, Jeannette and Costo, Rupert, *A Thousand Years of American Indian Storytelling: A Weewish Tree Reader*, The Indian Historian Press, San Francisco, CA, 1988.

Heschel, Abraham J., *The Prophets*, Vols 1 & 2, Harper Torchbooks, NY, 1962.

Himes, Kenneth R., OFM, *Responses to 101 Questions on Catholic Social Teaching*, Paulist Press, NJ, 2001.

Hogan, Linda, Metzger, Deena and Peterson, Brenda, *Intimate Nature: The Bond Between Women and Animals*, Fawcett Columbine, Ballatine, NY, 1998.

Hogan, Linda, *Human Rights: Christian Perspectives on Development Issues*, Trocaire, Veritas, CAFOD, Ireland/UK, 1998.

Hogan, Linda, Power, WW Norton Co, NY, 1998. (Other titles: *The Book of Medicines; Dwellings: A Spirituality History of the Living World; Savings; Red Clay; The Story we Hold Secret; Mean Spirit* – anything she writes.)

Holland, Joe and Henriot, Peter, *Social Analysis: Linking Faith and Justice*, Orbis Books in collaboration with Center of Concern, 1980.

Hug, James and Scherschel, Rose Marie, *Social Revelation: Profound Challenge for Christian Spirituality*, Center of Concern, Washington DC, 1987.

Hughes, Langston, *Let America Be America Again*, and other poems, Vintage Books, Random House, NY, 2004.

Hughes, Ted, *Tales of the Early World*, Farrar, Straus & Giroux, NY, 1991.

International Commission on JPIC, *Manual for Promoters of Justice, Peace and Integrity of Creation*, Claretian Pub., Quezon City, Philippines, 1998.

Jesuit Centre for Faith and Justice, *Windows on Social Spirituality*, Columba Press, Dublin, 2003.

John Paul II, *On Social Concern* (Sollicitudeo Rei Socialis), 30 December 1987, USCC, Pub. No. 205–5, Washington DC.

Jones, Shirley (ed.), *Simply Living: The Spirit of the Indigenous Peoples*, New World Library, Novato, CA, 1999.

Kane, Sean, *Wisdom of the Mythtellers*, Broadview Press, Ontario, Canada, 1994.

King, Thomas, SJ, *Teilhard's Mass: Approaches to 'The Mass on the World'*, Paulist Press, NJ, 2005.

King, Ursula, *Pierre Teilhard de Chardin: Writings Selected*, Orbis, Maryknoll, NY, 1999.

Kittredge, William, *The Nature of Generosity*, Vintage, Random House, NY, 2000.

Klagsburn, Francine, *Voices of Wisdom: Jewish Ideals and Ethics for Everyday Living*, David R. Godine Publisher, 1980.

Knitter, Paul F. and Muzaffar, Chandra (eds), *Subverting Greed: Religious Perspectives on the Global Economy*, Orbis, Maryknoll, NY, 2002.

Kolbert, Elizabeth, *Field Notes from a Catastrophe: Man, Nature, and Climate Change*, Bloomsbury Publishing, NY, 2006.

Kugel, James L., *Traditions of the Bible*, Harvard University Press, Cambridge, MA, 1998.

Kunst, Judith M., *The Burning Word: A Christian Encounter with Jewish Midrash*, Paraclete Press, Brewster, MA, 2006.

Lane, Belden C., *The Solace of Fierce Landscapes: Exploring Desert and Mountain Spirituality*, Oxford University Press, NY, 1998.

LaPena, Frank, Bates, Craig D. and Medley, Steven (compilers), *Legends of the Yosemite Miwok*, Yosemite National Park, CA, 1981.

Lesau, Charlotte and Wolf, *African Folktales*, Peter Pauper Press, 1963.

Lopez de Mariscal, Blanca, *The Harvest Birds/Los Pajaros de la Cosecha*, Children's Book Press, Emeryville, CA, 1995.

Lopez, Barry, *About this Life: Journeys on the Threshold of Memory*, Alfred Knopf, NY, 1998.

Lopez, Barry, *Crossing Open Ground*, Charles Scribner & Sons, NY, 1978. (Any book by him: *Desert Notes: Reflections in the Eye of a Raven, Of Wolves and Men; River Notes: The Dance of Herons; Winter Count; Artic Dreams; Giving Birth to Thunder, Sleeping With his Daughter; Coyote Builds North America*, etc.)

Maas, Weigert Kathleen and Kelley, Alexia K. (eds), *Living the Catholic Social Tradition: Cases and Commentary*, Sheed and Ward/Rowman and Littlefield, Lanham, MD, 2005.

Maguire, Daniel C., *Sacred Energies: When the World's Religions Sit Down to Talk about the Future of Human Life and the Plight of this Planet*, Fortress Press, Minneapolis, MN, 2000.

Malchow, Bruce V., *Social Justice in the Hebrew Bible*, Liturgical Press, Collegeville, MN, 1996.

Mayo, Gretchen Will, *Earthmaker's Tales: North American Indian Stories About Earth Happenings*, Walker and Co, NY, 1989.

McDonagh, Sean, *Passion for the Earth: The Christian Vocation to Promote Justice, Peace and the Integrity of Creation*, Orbis, Maryknoll, NY, 1994.

McDonagh, Sean, *Why Are we Deaf to the Cry of the Earth?* Veritas, Dublin, 2001.

McDonagh, Sean, *The Death of Life: The Horror of Extinction*, Columba Press, Dublin, 2004.

McFague, Sallie, *The Body of God*, Fortress Press, Minneapolis, MN, 1993.

McFague, Sallie, *Life Abundant: Rethinking Theology and Economy for a Planet in Peril*, Fortress Press, Minneapolis, MN, 2001.

McKenna, Kevin E., *A Concise Guide to Catholic Social Teaching*, Ave Maria Press, Notre Dame, Ind., 2002.

McLaughlin, Nellie, *Out of Wonder: The Evolving Story of the Universe*, Veritas, Dublin, 2004.

McNamee, Gregory (ed.), *The Sierra Club Desert Reader: A Literary Companion,* Sierra Club Books, San Francisco, CA, 1995.

Merton, Thomas, *When The Trees Say Nothing: Writings on Nature*, Kathleen Deignan (ed.), Sorin Books, Notre Dame Press, Notre Dame, Ind., 2003.

Metz, Johann Baptist and Schillebeeckx, Edward, *No Heaven Without Earth*, Concilium 1991/4 SCM Press/London and Orbis, Maryknoll, NY.

Miller, Gordon, *Wisdom of the Earth: Visions of an Ecological Faith*, Vol. 1, Ancient Christianity, Green Rock Press, Seattle, WA, 1997.

Milne, Courtney (photographs), *The Sacred Earth*, foreword The Dalai Lama, Penguin Books, Toronto, Canada, 1991.

Moe-Lobeda, Cynthia D., *Healing a Broken World: Globalization and God*, Fortress Press, Minneapolis, MN, 2002.

Mowry, Elizabeth, *The Poetic Landscape: A Contemporary Visual and Psychological Exploration*, Watson-Guptill Pub., NY, 2001.

Moyers, Bill, *Talking about Genesis: A Resource Guide*, Doubleday, NY, 1996.

No-Nonsense Guides, New Internationalist and Verso, Toronto, Ontario or see www.newint.org. There are guides to *Water, Globalization, Climate Change, International Migration, Arms Trade, International Development, Indigenous Peoples, World Poverty, Women's Rights, Fair Trade* among others.

Northcott, Michael, *Life after Debt: Christianity and Global Justice*, SPCK, London, 1999 (CAFOD).

O'Halloran, James, SDB, *Saving the Fish from Drowning: Reflections from the Barrio*, Columba Press, Dublin, 2006.

O'Murchu, Diarmuid, MSC, *Our World in Transition: Making Sense of a Changing World*, Claretian Pub., Quezon City, Philippines, 2003.

O'Reilley, Mary Rose, *The Love of Impermanent Things: A Threshold Ecology*, Milkweed Editions, Minneapolis, MN, 2006.

Ochoa, George, Hoffman, Jennifer and Tin, Tina, *Climate: The Force That Shapes Our World and the Future of Life on Earth*, Rodale Institute, London, 2005.

Olsen, Dennis L., *Shared Spirits: Wildlife And Native Americans*, North Wood Press, Inc, Minocqua, WI, 1995.

Paulines, *Stone Soup: Reflections on Economic Justice*, Canadian Religious Conference, Jesuit Center for Justice and Peace, Toronto, Canada, 1998.

Paulines/Development and Peace, *From Charity to Justice: Seven Parables for a Changing World*, Monteal, Canada, 1999.

Pearce, Fred, *When the Rivers Run Dry: Journeys into the Heart of the World's Water Crisis*, Ken Porter Books, Toronto, 2006.

Penn, W.S. (ed.), *The Telling of the World: Native American Stories and Art*, Stewart, Tabori & Chang, NY, 1996.

Pilch, John J., *The Cultural World of Jesus: Sunday by Sunday, Cycle C*, Liturgical Press, Collegeville, MN, 1997.

Pope Paul VI, *On the Development of Peoples (Populorum Progressio)* March 26, 1967, USCC, Pub. No. VI-60, Washington DC.

Power, Susan, *The Grass Dancer*, Berkley Books, NY, 1994.

Premnath, D.N., *Eighth-Century Prophets: A Social Analysis*, Chalice Press, St Louis, MO, 2003.

Raffelt, Albert (ed.), 'Easter: A Faith that Loves the Earth', in *The Great Church Year*, Crossroads, NY, 1993.

Reagan, Michael (ed.), *Inside the Mind of God: Images and Words of Inner Space*, Templeton Foundation Press, Philadelphia, PA, 2002.

Reed, A.W., *Aboriginal Legends – Animal Tales*, Reed New Holland, Australia 1998.

Regan, David, *Why Are they Poor?* Helder Camara in Pastoral Perspective, Theologie und Praxis, LIT VERLAG, Munster/London, and Transaction Pub. Rutgers University, NJ, 2000.

Rhoades, Robert, 'The World's Food Supply at Risk', National Geographic, April 1991.

Riffkin, Ira, *Spiritual Perspectives on Globalization: Making Sense of Economic and Cultural Upheaval*, Skylight Paths Pub., Woodstock, Vermont, 2004.

Rothenbert, David and Ulvaeus, Marta (eds), *Writing on Water*, Terra Nova Book, MIT Press, Cambridge, MA, 2001.

Roy, Arundhati, *Power Politics* (new updated edition), South End Press, Cambridge, MA, 2001.

Russell Sanders, Scott, *The Force of Spirit*, Beacon Press, Boston, MA, 2000.

Ryan, Maura and Whitmore, Todd David, *The Challenge of Global Stewardship: Roman Catholic Responses*, University of Notre Dame Press, Notre Dame, Ind., 1997.

Savage, Candace, *Prairie: A Natural History*, Greystone Books, David Suzuki Foundation, Douglas & McIntyre Pub Group, Berkeley, 2004.

Schachter-Shalomi, Rabbi Zalman, with Segel, Joel, *Jewish with Feeling: A Guide to Meaningful Jewish Practice*, Riverhead Books, NY, 2005.

Shapiro, Rabbi Rami, *The Hebrew Prophets: Selections Annotated and Explained*, Skylight Illuminations, Woodstock, Vermont, 2004.

Sobel, Dava, *The Planets*, Viking, Penguin, NY, 2005 (also of interest *Longitude* and *Galileo's Daughter*).

Sobrino, Jon and Pico, Juan Hermandez, *Theology of Christian Solidarity*, Orbis, Maryknoll, NY, 1985.

Sobrino, Jon, *500 Years – Structural Sin/Structural Grace: Reflections for Europe on Latin America*, 1992 Pope Paul VI Memorial Lecture, *The Tablet*, London, England.

Sobrino, Jon, *The Principle of Mercy: Taking the Crucified People from the Cross*, Orbis, Maryknoll, NY, 1994.

Sorbino, John, *Where Is God? Earthquake, Terrorism, Barbarity, and Hope*, Orbis, Mayknoll, NY, 2004.

Soelle, Dorothee *On Earth as in Heaven: A Liberation Spirituality of Sharing*, Westminster/John Knox Press, Louisville, KY, 1993.

Solnit, Rebecca, *A Field Guide to Getting Lost*, Penguin Books, NY, 2005.

Suzuki, David, *David Suzuki Reader: A Lifetime of Ideas from Leading Activist and Thinker*, Greystone Books, Douglas & McIntyre, Berkeley, CA, 2003.

Swift, Carolyn, *World Myths and Tales*, Childrens' Poolbeg, Dublin, Ireland, 1993.

Swimme, Brian, *The Hidden Heart of the Cosmos*, Orbis, Maryknoll, NY, 1999.

Tal, Alon (ed.), *Speaking of Earth: Environmental Speeches that Moved the World*, Rutgers University Press, New Brunswick, NJ, 2006.

Tamez, Elsa, *Bible of the Oppressed*, Orbis, Maryknoll, NY, 1982.

Tamez, Elsa, *The Scandalous Message of James: Faith Without Works is Dead*, Crossroads, NY, 1990.

Tanner, Kathryn, *Economy of Grace*, Fortress Press, Philadelphia, PA, 2005.

Thayer, Cynthia, *Strong for Potatoes*, St Martin's Griffin, NY, 1998.

The Book of Job: From the Holy Bible, preface: Ozick, Cynthia, Vintage Spiritual Classics, Random House, NY, 1998.

Toolan, David, SJ, *At Home in the Cosmos*, Orbis, Maryknoll, NY, 2001.

Van de Weyer, Robert and Saunders, Pat (compilers), *The Creation Spirit: An Anthology*, Darton, Longman and Todd, London, 1990.

Vinck, Jose de, *Religion and Science*, Allendale, NY, 2005.

Wallis, Velma, *Two Old Women: An Alaskan Legend of Betrayal, Courage and Survival*, Epicenter Press, Fairbanks/Seattle, 1993.

Weatherford, Jack, *Indian Givers: How the Indians of the Americas Transformed the World*, Crown Pub. Inc, NY, 1988.

Weldon, Johnson James, *God's Trombones: Seven Negro Sermons in Verse, esp. 'Creation'*, Penguin Poets, NY, 1927.

Wessels, Cletus, *Jesus in the New Universe Story*, Orbis, Maryknoll, NY, 1970.

Wessesl, Cletus, *The Holy Web: Church and the New Universe*, Orbis, Maryknoll, NY, 2000.

Williams, Terry Tempest, *Red: Passion and Patience in the Desert*, Pantheon Books, 2001. (Other titles: *Pieces of White Shell; Coyote's Canyon; Refuge; Earthly Messengers; An Unspoken Hunger*, etc.)

Williams, Terry Tempest, *The Open Space of Democracy*, the Orion Society, Barrington, MA, 2204.

Williams, Terry Tempest, with Lopez, Barry and Nelson, Richard, *Patriotism and the American Land*, the Orion Society, Barrington, MA, 2003.

Wirzba, Norman, 'Noah and the Ark: Becoming Creation', in *The Living Pulpit*, April-June 2000.

Woods, Richard J., OP, *Christian Spirituality: God's Presence through the Ages*, (expanded edition) Orbis, Maryknoll, NY, 2006.

Worldwatch Institute, *Vital Signs 2006–2007: The Trends that are Shaping our Future*, Norton Worldwatch Books, NY, 2006.

Zornberg, Avivah Gottlieb, *The Beginning of Desire: Reflections on Genesis*, Image, Doubleday, NY, 1995.

MAGAZINES AND PERIODICALS

Amnesty International and Amnesty Partners at www.amnestyusa.com.

Audubon, National Audubon Society, Membership Data Center, PO Box 51003, Boulder, Co 80323-1003 or www.audubon.org.

Earth Island Journal: News of the World Environment, www.earthisland.org.

Inquiring Mind, 'Semiannual Journal of the Vipassana Community', Vol. 22, No. 1, Fall 2005 "Earth Dharma" Berkeley, CA.

In these Times, www.inthesetimes.com.

Mother Jones (Mary Harris "Mother Jones" Jones (1837–1930) Orator, Union Organizer, Hell-raiser, www.motherjones.com.

The Nation at wwwthenation.com.

National Wildlife: Journal of the National Wildlife Federation at www.NWF.ORG.

New Internationalist: The people, the ideas, the action in the fight for global justice at www.newint.org.

PA Political Affairs: A Marxist Monthly at www.politicalaffairs.net.

ODE for Intelligent Optimists at www.odemagazine.com.

Orion, the Orion Society at www.oriononline.org (along with AUDOBAN the best nature/sustainability/geography magazines).

The *Progressive* at www.progressive.org.

Yes: A Journal of Positive Futures at www.YesMagazine.org.

World Watch: Vision for a Sustainable World (Institute) at www.worldwatch.org.

Z Magazine, Institute for Social and Cultural Communications, Cambridge, MA at Z Magazine Online www.zmag.org.

DVD/Programmes

Crossan, John Dominic, *Victory and Peace or Justice and Peace? Living the Questions* (with study guide) 2005 at www.livingthequestions.com.

The Elegant Universe: Superstrings, Hidden Dimensions, and the Quest for the Ultimate Theory, NOVA, seen on PBS at WGBH Boston Video at www.shop.wgbh.org.

Poverty and Prayer, Gerard Thomas Straub 2004. The San Damiano Foundation PO Box 1794, Burbank, Ca 91507; 'Putting the power of film at the service of the poor' on line at www.sandamianofoundation.org (these films are good for both content and reflection).

Endless Exodus: The Sorrowful Flight of the Migrants, Gerard Thomas Straub 2004, San Damiano Foundation.

Swimme, Brian, *Canticle to the Cosmos: The Classic Course on the Story of the Universe, Earth, Life and Human, Center for the Story of the Universe*, 134 Coleen St, Livermore, CA, 94550 or www.brianswimme.org.

Swimme, Brian, *The Powers of the Universe: An Exploration of the Powers Coursing through the Universe and Each of Us* (as above and www.brianswimme.org).

REFERENCE VOLUMES

The Oxford American Desk Dictionary and Thesaurus, 2nd edition, Berkley Books, NY, 2001.

The Jewish Study Bible: Tanakh Translation, Torah, Nevi'im, Kethuvim (Tanakh Translation), Jewish Publication Society, Oxford University Press, NY, 2004.